GW00418662

HANDBOOK ON PLANNING, MONITORING AND EVALUATING FOR DEVELOPMENT RESULTS

United Nations Development Programme

HANDBOOK ON PLANNING, MONITORING AND EVALUATING FOR DEVELOPMENT RESULTS

Copyright © UNDP 2009, all rights reserved.
Manufactured in the United States of America. Printed on recycled paper.

United Nations Development Programme
One United Nations Plaza
New York, NY 10017, USA
Handbook Web site: http://www.undp.org/eo/handbook

Design: Suazion, Inc. (NY, suazion.com)
Production: A.K. Office Supplies (NY)

FOREWORD

Supporting national capacity development for poverty reduction and the attainment of the Millennium Development Goals lies at the very heart of UNDP's mandate. That means that we must work with programme countries to assist in the formulation of those strategies, policies, structures, and processes, which will have system-wide developmental impact.

Active in 166 countries around the world, UNDP must be relevant to the emerging needs of programme countries. We must have a clear vision of the direction in which we need go and the outcomes we want to help achieve. We must be able to respond quickly and appropriately to challenges and opportunities.

Results-based management provides a set of principles, approaches, and tools which can help us achieve these goals. By always trying to answer the "so what difference does our intervention make?" question, we will keep our focus on how we can support real and sustainable improvements being made in the lives of those we serve.

This, in turn, requires us to embrace a culture of evaluation. The tremendous store of knowledge which UNDP has, and has access to, including the lessons learned from evaluations, should more fully inform our programming and our decision making.

I hope that the publication of this handbook will help us and our partners to be even clearer about the higher-level results we want to achieve; to develop and act on strategies to achieve those results; to use systematically lessons drawn from evaluations to make decisions; and, ultimately, to improve our contribution to the advancement of human development.

Helen Clark
Administrator

PREFACE

This 2009 version of the 'Handbook on Planning, Monitoring and Evaluating for Development Results' aims to support UNDP in becoming more results-oriented and to improve its focus on development changes and real improvements in people's lives. It replaces and updates the previous Handbook from 2002. It was a breakthrough in driving the effective application of the results-based management approach in programming and performance management.

The Handbook recognizes that planning, monitoring and evaluation require a focus on nationally owned development priorities and results, and should reflect the guiding principles of national ownership, capacity development and human development. Globally, there has been a significant shift away from the project approach in favour of programme and national approaches. All partners and members of the Executive Board expect UNDP to demonstrate tangible results in development cooperation. UNDP also faces intensified calls for accountability to citizens for how resources are used, what results are achieved, and how effective these results are in bringing about progress in human development.

In June 2006, a UNDP Evaluation Policy was approved by the Executive Board. In 2007, an independent evaluation of the adoption and use of results-based management in UNDP found that UNDP continued to demonstrate a weak results culture despite notable progress on some fronts. The evaluation recommended that UNDP improve its capacities to manage for outcome-level change. This Handbook, therefore, complements the programme and operations policies and procedures by providing practical guidance on how to plan, monitor and evaluate for development results. The Handbook cannot, on its own, foster a culture of results in UNDP or among its partners. However, together with other initiatives, we hope it will make a significant difference.

This updated Handbook marks a departure from the previous publication. First, recognizing that results planning is a prerequisite for effective programme design, monitoring and evaluation, the revised Handbook integrates planning, monitoring and evaluation in a single guide. Second, the Handbook reflects the requirements and guiding principles of the evaluation policy, including national ownership, which is now mainstreamed throughout the cycle of planning, monitoring and evaluation. Third, the revised Handbook includes a comprehensive chapter on evaluation design for quality assurance to guide UNDP staff and evaluators in ensuring professional standards of quality in evaluation. There will be online training and regional workshops to support the application of the Handbook across the organization at all levels.

While the primary audience for the Handbook is UNDP staff, we hope that it will contribute to the efforts of all our partners who, like UNDP, strive towards greater development effectiveness. To facilitate wider dissemination of the publication, in addition to the printed version of this Handbook, the document is available on the UNDP website at www.undp.org/eo/handbook.

This Handbook is a joint product of the Bureau for Development Policy, Evaluation Office and Operation Support Group. We would like to thank colleagues in these units who helped conceive, draft and refine the Handbook over a number of iterations. Special thanks go to the core authors of the Handbook: Asoka Kasturiarachchi and Thomas Eriksson of the Bureau for Development Policy, Stephen Rodriques of the Operation Support Group, and Azusa Kubota of the Evaluation Office, who also marshaled the process as the Task Manager for the Handbook. Nurul Alam of the Evaluation Office provided overall quality assurance and guidance throughout the process.

The revision of the Handbook benefited from the commitment of many individuals, who provided substantive and technical inputs to the various drafts. In December 2008, a review workshop was held in New York where a number of UNDP country office senior managers, programme officers, monitoring and evaluation specialists and representatives from the Headquarters units and regional bureaux helped refine the draft. Heather Bryant, Monitoring and Evaluation Officer from the UNDP Nepal country office, deserves special mention. Thanks also go to Enid Marshall for support on evaluation methodology and Jessica Murray for substantive editorial support. Comments and feedback solicited from UNDP colleagues through the knowledge network discussions were also extremely helpful, and we are grateful to the many contributors and to Florencia Tateossian, the EvalNet facilitator.

Last, but not least, we would like to acknowledge the invaluable contributions and administrative assistance of the Evaluation Office staff, Anish Pradhan and Concepcion Cole, the copy editing of Margo Alderton, and the design and format of the Handbook by Julia Dudnik Stern.

Saraswathi Menon
Director
Evaluation Office

Judith Karl
Director
Operations Support Unit

Kanni Wignaraja
Director, Capacity
Development Group
Bureau for Development Policy

CONTENTS

Figures

Tables

ACRONYMS AND ABBREVIATIONS

ADR	Assessment of Development Results
APR	Annual Project Report
AWP	Annual Work Plan
BCPR	Bureau for Crisis Prevention and Recovery
BDP	Bureau for Development Policy
CCA	Common Country Assessment
CPD	Country Programme Document
CPAP	Country Programme Action Plan
DAC	Development Assistance Committee
ERBM	Enhanced Results-based Management
ERC	Evaluation Resource Centre
M&E	Monitoring and Evaluation
MDGs	Millennium Development Goals
MfDR	Managing for Development Results
NGO	Non-governmental Organization
OECD	Organisation for Economic Co-operation and Development
POPP	Programme and Operations Policies and Procedures (of the UNDP)
RBM	Results-based Management
SMART	Specific, Measurable, Achievable, Relevant and Time-bound
ToR	Terms of Reference
UNCT	United Nations Country Team
UNCDF	United Nations Capital Development Fund

UNDAF	United Nations Development Assistance Framework
UNDP	United Nations Development Programme
UNDG	United Nations Development Group
UNEG	United Nations Evaluation Group
UNESCO	United Nations Educational, Scientific and Cultural Organization
UNIFEM	United Nations Development Fund for Women
UNV	United Nations Volunteers

INTRODUCTION

This 'Handbook on Planning, Monitoring and Evaluating for Development Results' is an updated edition of the 2002 edition of 'Handbook on Monitoring and Evaluating for Results'.[1] It seeks to address new directions in planning, monitoring and evaluation in the context of the United Nations Development Programme (UNDP) corporate strategic plan, the requirements of the UNDP evaluation policy approved by the Executive Board in 2006 and the United Nations Evaluation Group (UNEG) 'Standards for Evaluation in the UN System'.[2] The updated Handbook also incorporates information recommended by key users of the Handbook during various workshops held by UNDP units.

The guiding framework of UNDP for planning, monitoring and evaluation is provided in the 'Programme and Operations Policies and Procedures' (POPP)[3], the evaluation policy[4], and the UNEG 'Standards for Evaluation in the UN System'. The POPP and evaluation policy aim to provide guidance to UNDP management and staff on key functions and mechanisms through which the results and principles enshrined in the overarching programmatic documents of UNDP, including the strategic plan, are to be achieved. They reflect the intentions of the Executive Board and also inform UNDP stakeholders of how UNDP conducts its work.

These documents provide the prescriptive content on what needs to be done, by whom and by when. This Handbook complements this content by providing UNDP

---

1 UNDP, 'Handbook on Monitoring and Evaluating for Results', Evaluation Office, New York, NY, 2002.
2 UNEG, 'Standards for Evaluation in the UN System', 2005. Available at: http://www.uneval.org/papersandpubs/documentdetail.jsp?doc_id=22.
3 UNDP, 'Programme and Operations Policies and Procedures', 2008. Available at: http://content.undp.org/go/userguide.
4 UNDP, 'The Evaluation Policy of UNDP', Executive Board Document DP/2005/28, May 2006. Available at: http://www.undp.org/eo/documents/Evaluation-Policy.pdf.

programme units with guidance on 'how to' and practical tools to strengthen results-oriented planning, monitoring and evaluation in UNDP.

WHAT DOES THE HANDBOOK DO?

The **objectives** of this Handbook include the following:

- To provide the reader with:
  - A basic understanding of the purposes, processes, norms, standards and guiding principles for planning, monitoring and evaluation within the UNDP development context
  - Knowledge of the essential elements of the planning and monitoring processes in UNDP: developing a robust results framework for projects and programmes, with clear indicators, baselines, and targets; and setting up an effective monitoring system
  - Knowledge of the essential elements of the evaluation process in UNDP: developing an evaluation plan; managing, designing and conducting quality evaluations; and using evaluation for managing for development results, learning and accountability
- To enhance the results-based culture within UNDP and improve the quality of planning, monitoring and evaluation

WHO IS THE HANDBOOK FOR?

The Handbook has multiple and diverse **audiences**:

- **UNDP staff** in country offices, regional bureaux, regional centres, Bureau for Development Policy (BDP), Bureau for Crisis Prevention and Recovery (BCPR), Partnership Bureau, and other units that manage programmes[5], such as:
  - Planning and monitoring global, regional and country programmes and other projects and activities
  - Managing the commissioning process of evaluations
- **UNDP managers** who oversee and assure the quality of planning, monitoring and evaluation processes and products, and use monitoring and evaluation for decision making
- **Stakeholders and partners,** such as governments, United Nations and development partners, and beneficiaries, who are involved in UNDP planning, monitoring and evaluation processes
- The **UNDP Executive Board,** which oversees and supports the activities of UNDP, ensuring that the organization remains responsive to the evolving needs of programme countries

---

5 This includes country offices, regional bureaux, regional centres, Bureau for Development Policy (BDP), Bureau for Crisis Prevention and Recovery (BCPR), Partnership Bureau, and others that have programmatic responsibilities for development initiatives (programmes, projects and activities).

- **Independent evaluators** who need to understand guiding principles, standards and processes for evaluation within the UNDP context

- **Members of the national, regional and global development and evaluation community**

The reader of the Handbook will understand:

- The importance of good programme and project design for effective implementation, monitoring and evaluation

- The critical role of monitoring in demonstrating the performance of programmes and projects, and in steering the implementation process towards the intended results

- How monitoring lays the groundwork for evaluation

- Different types of evaluations in UNDP and their contributions to learning and accountability

- The role of monitoring and evaluation in strengthening UNDP development effectiveness and managing for development results

- Principles, norms, standards, policy, processes and responsibilities governing planning, monitoring and evaluation in UNDP

- Where to look for references and materials for additional information and guidance

HOW IS THE HANDBOOK ORGANIZED?

Chapter 1 of the Handbook provides an overview of the integrated nature of planning, monitoring and evaluation, and describes the critical role they play in managing for development results. Underlying the entire Handbook is the principle that planning, monitoring and evaluation must at all times be considered in relation to, and build upon, one another. Chapter 2 provides an overview of the conceptual foundations of planning and specific guidance on planning techniques and the preparation of results frameworks that guide monitoring and evaluation. Chapter 3 provides guidance on how to plan for monitoring and evaluation before implementing a plan. Chapter 4 focuses on issues related to monitoring, reporting and review. Chapters 5 through 7 provide an overview of the UNDP evaluation function and the policy framework, introduce key elements of evaluation design and tools and describe practical steps in managing the evaluation process. Chapter 8 presents practical steps and examples in using knowledge from monitoring and evaluation in managing for development results.

HOW SHOULD THE HANDBOOK BE USED?

This Handbook is not designed to be read cover-to-cover. It is intended to be used as a reference throughout the programme cycle.

The Handbook is about planning, monitoring and evaluating **results.** It is not a Handbook on programme or project management. Some of the topics that would normally be covered in a programme and project management manual will therefore not be addressed in this Handbook, such as cost-benefit analyses, environmental impact assessments, technical appraisals and so forth. For these topics, the POPP should be consulted.

In addition, the following compendiums should accompany this Handbook to enhance understanding of pertinent topics:

■ Planning, monitoring and evaluation in conflict prevention and recovery settings, developed by BCPR

■ Guidelines on Outcome Evaluations (under development)

The compendiums are available on the Evaluation Office website at www.undp.org/eo/handbook.

The development of this Handbook was led jointly by the BDP, Evaluation Office and Operations Support Group, and was supported by valuable input from UNDP colleagues in Headquarters, regional bureaux and country offices.

PLANNING, MONITORING AND EVALUATION FOR DEVELOPMENT RESULTS

Good planning, monitoring and evaluation enhance the contribution of UNDP by establishing clear links between past, present and future initiatives and development results. Monitoring and evaluation can help an organization extract relevant information from past and ongoing activities that can be used as the basis for programmatic fine-tuning, reorientation and future planning. Without effective planning, monitoring and evaluation, it would be impossible to judge if work is going in the right direction, whether progress and success can be claimed, and how future efforts might be improved.

This chapter describes the purposes of planning, monitoring and evaluation in the context of results-based management (RBM) and managing for development results (MfDR) and explains how these functions are important to an organization such as UNDP. It also provides key definitions and principles that are integral to planning, monitoring and evaluation. This chapter is intended for UNDP managers, staff, key partners and stakeholders who are involved in the design and implementation of development initiatives and decision making. The culture of results orientation and the principles of RBM and MfDR must be embraced by all in order for UNDP to effectively contribute to human development.

1.1 INTRODUCTION

The opening paragraph of the UNDP 2008-2011 Strategic Plan states that all UNDP work—policy advice, technical support, advocacy, and contributions to strengthening coherence in global development—is aimed at one end result: "real improvements in people's lives and in the choices and opportunities open to them."[6] Improvements in

---

6   UNDP, 'UNDP Strategic Plan, 2008-2011: Accelerating Global Progress on Human Development', Executive Board Document DP/2007/43, (pursuant DP/2007/32), reissued January 2008.

people's lives are a common goal shared by many governments and development partners across the countries in which UNDP works. This is also the reason many agencies now use the term 'managing for development results' or MfDR, as opposed to 'results-based management' or RBM in their policy documents, guidelines and statements. Traditionally, RBM approaches have focused more on internal results and performance of agencies than on changes in the development conditions of people. MfDR applies the same basic concepts of RBM—good planning, monitoring, evaluation, learning and feeding back into planning—but seeks to keep the focus on development assistance demonstrating real and meaningful results.

MfDR is also an effort to respond to the growing demands for public accountability to citizens in both the developed and developing world on how assistance is used, what results are achieved, and how appropriate these results are in bringing about desired changes in human development. This approach encourages development agencies to focus on building partnerships and collaboration and ensure greater coherence. Similarly, it promotes stronger focus on sustainability through measures that enhance national ownership and capacity development.

MfDR is RBM in action, but it is oriented more towards the external environment and results that are important to programme countries and less towards an agency's internal performance.

Achieving development results, as most realize, is often much more difficult than imagined. To achieve development results and changes in the quality of people's lives, governments, UNDP and other partners will often develop a number of different plans, strategies, programmes and projects. These typically include:

- A National Development Plan or Poverty Reduction Strategy
- Sector-based development plans
- A United Nations Development Assistance Framework (UNDAF)
- A corporate strategic plan (such as the UNDP 2008-2011 Strategic Plan)
- Global, regional and country programme documents (CPDs) and country programme action plans (CPAPs)
- Monitoring and evaluation (M&E) frameworks and evaluation plans
- Development and management work plans
- Office and unit specific plans
- Project documents and annual work plans

However, good intentions, large programmes and projects, and lots of financial resources are not enough to ensure that development results will be achieved. The quality of those plans, programmes and projects, and how well resources are used, are also critical factors for success.

To improve the chances of success, attention needs to be placed on some of the common areas of weakness in programmes and projects. Four main areas for focus are identified consistently:

1. Planning and programme and project definition—Projects and programmes have a greater chance of success when the objectives and scope of the programmes or projects are properly defined and clarified. This reduces the likelihood of experiencing major challenges in implementation.

2. Stakeholder involvement—High levels of engagement of users, clients and stakeholders in programmes and projects are critical to success.

3. Communication—Good communication results in strong stakeholder buy-in and mobilization. Additionally, communication improves clarity on expectations, roles and responsibilities, as well as information on progress and performance. This clarity helps to ensure optimum use of resources.

4. Monitoring and evaluation—Programmes and projects with strong monitoring and evaluation components tend to stay on track. Additionally, problems are often detected earlier, which reduces the likelihood of having major cost overruns or time delays later.

Good planning, combined with effective monitoring and evaluation, can play a major role in enhancing the effectiveness of development programmes and projects. Good planning helps us focus on the results that matter, while monitoring and evaluation help us learn from past successes and challenges and inform decision making so that current and future initiatives are better able to improve people's lives and expand their choices.

Box 1. Understanding inter-linkages and dependencies between planning, monitoring and evaluation

- Without proper planning and clear articulation of intended results, it is not clear what should be monitored and how; hence monitoring cannot be done well.

- Without effective planning (clear results frameworks), the basis for evaluation is weak; hence evaluation cannot be done well.

- Without careful monitoring, the necessary data is not collected; hence evaluation cannot be done well.

- Monitoring is necessary, but not sufficient, for evaluation.

- Monitoring facilitates evaluation, but evaluation uses additional new data collection and different frameworks for analysis.

- Monitoring and evaluation of a programme will often lead to changes in programme plans. This may mean further changing or modifying data collection for monitoring purposes.

Source: Adapted from UNEG, 'UNEG Training—What a UN Evaluator Needs to Know?', Module 1, 2008.

Planning can be defined as the process of setting goals, developing strategies, outlining the implementation arrangements and allocating resources to achieve those goals. It is important to note that planning involves looking at a number of different processes:

- Identifying the vision, goals or objectives to be achieved

- Formulating the strategies needed to achieve the vision and goals

- Determining and allocating the resources (financial and other) required to achieve the vision and goals

- Outlining implementation arrangements, which include the arrangements for monitoring and evaluating progress towards achieving the vision and goals

There is an expression that "failing to plan is planning to fail." While it is not always true that those who fail to plan will eventually fail in their endeavours, there is strong evidence to suggest that having a plan leads to greater effectiveness and efficiency. Not having a plan—whether for an office, programme or project—is in some ways similar to attempting to build a house without a blueprint, that is, it is very difficult to know what the house will look like, how much it will cost, how long it will take to build, what resources will be required, and whether the finished product will satisfy the owner's needs. In short, planning helps us define what an organization, programme or project aims to achieve and how it will go about it.

Monitoring can be defined as the ongoing process by which stakeholders obtain regular feedback on the progress being made towards achieving their goals and objectives. Contrary to many definitions that treat monitoring as merely reviewing progress made in **implementing** actions or activities, the definition used in this Handbook focuses on reviewing progress against **achieving** goals. In other words, monitoring in this Handbook is not only concerned with asking "Are we taking the actions we said we would take?" but also "Are we making progress on achieving the results that we said we wanted to achieve?" The difference between these two approaches is extremely important. In the more limited approach, monitoring may focus on tracking projects and the use of the agency's resources. In the broader approach, monitoring also involves tracking strategies and actions being taken by partners and non-partners, and figuring out what new strategies and actions need to be taken to ensure progress towards the most important results.

Evaluation is a rigorous and independent assessment of either completed or ongoing activities to determine the extent to which they are achieving stated objectives and contributing to decision making. Evaluations, like monitoring, can apply to many things, including an **activity, project, programme, strategy, policy, topic, theme, sector** or **organization**. The key distinction between the two is that evaluations are done independently to provide managers and staff with an objective assessment of whether or not they are on track. They are also more rigorous in their procedures, design and methodology, and generally involve more extensive analysis. However, the aims of both monitoring and evaluation are very similar: to provide information that can help inform decisions, improve performance and achieve planned results.

In assessing development effectiveness, monitoring and evaluation efforts aim to assess the following:

- Relevance of UNDP assistance and initiatives (strategies, policies, programmes and projects designed to combat poverty and support desirable changes) to national development goals within a given national, regional or global context

Box 2. The distinction between monitoring and evaluation and other oversight activities

Like monitoring and evaluation, **inspection, audit, review** and **research** functions are oversight activities, but they each have a distinct focus and role and should not be confused with monitoring and evaluation.

Inspection is a general examination of an organizational unit, issue or practice to ascertain the extent it adheres to normative standards, good practices or other criteria and to make recommendations for improvement or corrective action. It is often performed when there is a perceived risk of non-compliance.

Audit is an assessment of the adequacy of management controls to ensure the economical and efficient use of resources; the safeguarding of assets; the reliability of financial and other information; the compliance with regulations, rules and established policies; the effectiveness of risk management; and the adequacy of organizational structures, systems and processes. Evaluation is more closely linked to MfDR and learning, while audit focuses on compliance.

Reviews, such as rapid assessments and peer reviews, are distinct from evaluation and more closely associated with monitoring. They are periodic or *ad hoc*, often light assessments of the performance of an initiative and do not apply the due process of evaluation or rigor in methodology. Reviews tend to emphasize operational issues. Unlike evaluations conducted by independent evaluators, reviews are often conducted by those internal to the subject or the commissioning organization.

Research is a systematic examination completed to develop or contribute to knowledge of a particular topic. Research can often feed information into evaluations and other assessments but does not normally inform decision making on its own.

Source: UNEG, 'Norms for Evaluation in the UN System', 2005. Available at: http://www.unevaluation.org/unegnorms.

- Effectiveness of development assistance initiatives, including partnership strategies

- Contribution and worth of this assistance to national development outcomes and priorities, including the material conditions of programme countries, and how this assistance visibly improves the prospects of people and their communities

- Key drivers or factors enabling successful, sustained and scaled-up development initiatives, alternative options and comparative advantages of UNDP

- Efficiency of development assistance, partnerships and coordination to limit transaction costs

- Risk factors and risk management strategies to ensure success and effective partnership

- Level of national ownership and measures to enhance national capacity for sustainability of results

While monitoring provides real-time information required by management, evaluation provides more in-depth assessment. The monitoring process can generate questions to be answered by evaluation. Also, evaluation draws heavily on data generated through monitoring during the programme and project cycle, including, for example, baseline data, information on the programme or project implementation process and measurements of results.

Figure 1. The RBM life-cycle approach

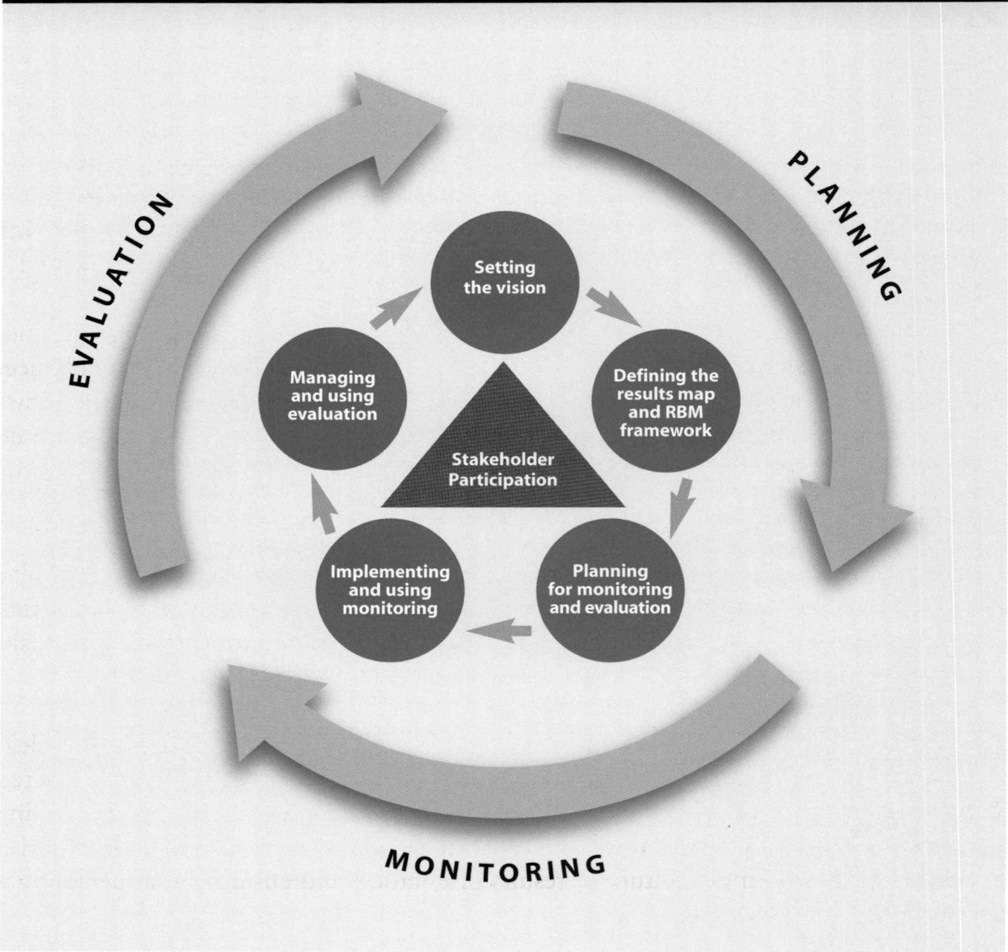

Note: Planning, monitoring and evaluation should not necessarily be approached in a sequential manner. The conduct of an evaluation does not always take place at the end of the cycle. Evaluations can take place at any point in time during the programming cycle. This figure aims to illustrate the inter-connected nature of planning, monitoring and evaluation to support MfDR. Planning for monitoring and evaluation must take place at the planning stage (see Chapter 3).

1.2 PUTTING PLANNING, MONITORING AND EVALUATION TOGETHER: RESULTS-BASED MANAGEMENT

Planning, monitoring and evaluation come together as RBM. RBM is defined as "a broad management strategy aimed at achieving improved performance and demonstrable results,"[7] and has been adopted by many multilateral development organizations, bilateral development agencies and public administrations throughout the world (as noted earlier, some of these organizations now refer to RBM as MfDR to place the emphasis on development rather than organizational results).

---

7   UNEG, 'The Role of Evaluation in Results-based Management', 21 August 2007. Available at: http://www.unevaluation.org/papersandpubs/documentdetail.jsp?doc_id=87.

Good RBM is an ongoing process. This means that there is constant feedback, learning and improving. Existing plans are regularly modified based on the lessons learned through monitoring and evaluation, and future plans are developed based on these lessons.

Monitoring is also an ongoing process. The lessons from monitoring are discussed periodically and used to inform actions and decisions. Evaluations should be done for programmatic improvements while the programme is still ongoing and also inform the planning of new programmes. This ongoing process of **doing, learning and improving** is what is referred to as the RBM life-cycle approach, which is depicted in Figure 1.

RBM is concerned with learning, risk management and accountability. Learning not only helps improve results from existing programmes and projects, but also enhances the capacity of the organization and individuals to make better decisions in the future and improves the formulation of future programmes and projects. Since there are no perfect plans, it is essential that managers, staff and stakeholders learn from the successes and failures of each programme or project.

There are many risks and opportunities involved in pursuing development results. RBM systems and tools should help promote awareness of these risks and opportunities, and provide managers, staff, stakeholders and partners with the tools to mitigate risks or pursue opportunities.

RBM practices and systems are most effective when they are accompanied by clear accountability arrangements and appropriate incentives that promote desired behaviour. In other words, RBM should not be seen simply in terms of developing systems and tools to plan, monitor and evaluate results. It must also include effective measures for promoting a culture of results orientation and ensuring that persons are accountable for both the results achieved and their actions and behaviour.

The main objectives of good planning, monitoring and evaluation—that is, RBM—are to:

- Support substantive accountability to governments, beneficiaries, donors, other partners and stakeholders, and the UNDP Executive Board

- Prompt corrective action

- Ensure informed decision making

Figure 2. RBM helps managers and staff to...

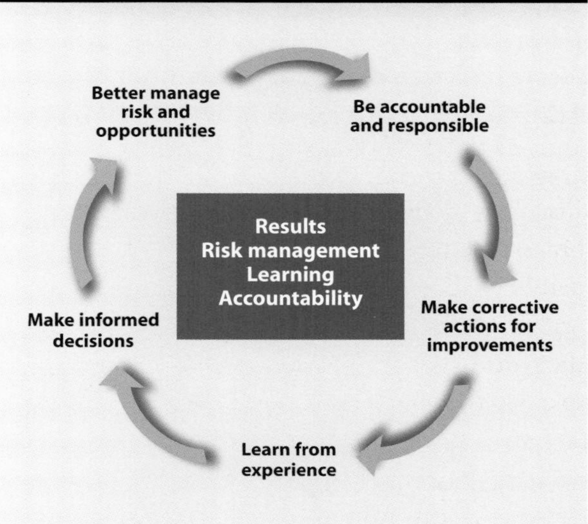

Better manage risk and opportunities

Be accountable and responsible

Make corrective actions for improvements

Learn from experience

Make informed decisions

Results
Risk management
Learning
Accountability

- Promote risk management

- Enhance organizational and individual learning

These objectives are linked together in a continuous process, as shown in Figure 2.

1.3 PRINCIPLES OF PLANNING, MONITORING AND EVALUATING FOR DEVELOPMENT RESULTS

This section addresses some of the principles that readers should have in mind throughout the entire process of planning, monitoring and evaluation.

OWNERSHIP

Ownership is fundamental in formulating and implementing programmes and projects to achieve development results. There are two major aspects of ownership to be considered:

- The depth, or level, of ownership of plans and processes

- The breadth of ownership

Depth of ownership: Many times, units or organizations go through the planning process to fulfil requirements of their governing or supervisory bodies, such as a Board of Directors or Headquarters. When this is the case, plans, programmes or projects tend to be neatly prepared for submission, but agencies and individuals return to business as usual once the requirements are met. When these plans are formulated to meet a requirement and are not used to guide ongoing management actions, organizations have greater risk of not achieving the objectives set out in the plans. Ownership is also critical for effectively carrying out planned monitoring and evaluation activities and linking the information generated from monitoring and evaluation to future programme improvements and learning.

In later sections, this Handbook will address techniques to promote ownership. The process is not about compliance and meeting requirements. In some ways it is similar to the difference between having **RBM systems** and having a **culture of results-orientation**—while it is important to have the systems, it is more important that people understand and appreciate why they are doing the things they are doing and adopt a results-oriented approach in their general behaviour and work.

Breadth of ownership: There are two questions to address with respect to breadth of ownership: Who does the development programme or project benefit or impact, and do a sufficient number of these agencies and persons feel ownership of the programme or project?

Programme countries are ultimately responsible for achieving development results, which is why all development plans, programmes and projects should be owned by national stakeholders. Ownership by programme countries does not mean that UNDP is not accountable for the results. UNDP accountability generally applies to the **contributions** UNDP makes to country results and the use of financial resources. (Details are outlined in the Accountability Framework and Standard Basic

Agreement.)[8] The goals and objectives relating to the changes in development conditions that programmes and projects aim to achieve, however, should be owned by the national stakeholders and beneficiaries.

A key aim of managing for results is to ensure that ownership goes beyond a few select persons to include as many stakeholders as possible. For this reason, monitoring and evaluation activities and the findings, recommendations and lessons from ongoing and periodic monitoring and evaluation should be fully owned by those responsible for results and those who can make use of them.

ENGAGEMENT OF STAKEHOLDERS

Throughout all stages of planning, monitoring, evaluating, learning and improving, it is vital to engage stakeholders, promote buy-in and commitment, and motivate action.

A strong results-management process aims to engage stakeholders in thinking as **openly and creatively** as possible about what they want to achieve and encourage them to organize themselves to achieve what they have agreed on, including putting in place a process to monitor and evaluate progress and use the information to improve performance.

FOCUS ON RESULTS

Planning, monitoring and evaluation processes should be geared towards **ensuring that results are achieved**—not towards ensuring that all activities and outputs get produced as planned.

It is not often clear what development partners such as UNDP are accountable for and what they should therefore focus on. It is sometimes suggested that since development agencies' initiatives are generally small, have limited impact and are not accountable for development changes or high-level results, they should focus on outputs.

This Handbook argues that what really matters are the development changes that occur in countries and lead to improvements in people's lives. This means that while individual agency outputs and activities are very important, they must always be seen as being in support of national development efforts. Agency outputs should, wherever possible, derive from national planning documents and be coordinated with and remain centred on supporting national objectives.

This argument is in line with the global approach to development being encouraged through international agreements such as the Paris Declaration and the Accra Agenda for Action. These agreements urge planners to think in terms of how they should work together to support national partners in achieving **national priorities**, rather than maintaining the traditional emphasis on agency initiatives or the requirements of their corporate Headquarters.

---

8   UNDP, 'Accountability Framework'. Available at: http://content.undp.org/go/userguide/results-management---accountability/?lang=en#top

Since national outcomes (which require the collective efforts of two or more stakeholders) are most important, planning, monitoring and evaluation processes should focus more on the partnerships, joint programmes, joint monitoring and evaluation and collaborative efforts needed to achieve these higher level results, than on UNDP or agency outputs. This is the approach that is promoted throughout this Handbook.

FOCUS ON DEVELOPMENT EFFECTIVENESS

Results management also means focusing on achieving **development effectiveness**. Meaningful and sustainable development results require more than just a generic plan of outcomes, outputs and activities. **How we do** development is often equally if not more important than **what we do** in development work. For this reason, many development agencies attempt to incorporate various themes into their planning, monitoring and evaluation processes to improve the overall effectiveness of their efforts. For example, planning, monitoring and evaluation must focus on sustainability. This conclusion was reached after years of experience with projects and programmes that had short-term impact but failed to alter the development conditions of countries or communities in any meaningful manner.

Similarly, there is now a focus on gender in planning, monitoring and evaluation. Many projects and programmes often failed to achieve their objectives because there was little or no analysis of, and attention to, the differences between the roles and needs of men and women in society. Inequalities, discriminatory practices and unjust power relations between groups in society are often at the heart of development problems.

The same applies to the concept of national or community ownership of development programmes. There is greater pride and satisfaction, greater willingness to protect and maintain assets, and greater involvement in social and community affairs when people have a vested interest in something—that is, when they feel 'ownership'.

Applying these principles to planning, monitoring and evaluation in a concrete manner means that these processes should be designed in such a way that they do the following:

- Ensure or promote national ownership—Ensure that, as appropriate, processes are led or co-led by the government and/or other national or community partners and that all plans, programmes, projects, and monitoring and evaluation efforts are aimed primarily at supporting national efforts, rather than agency objectives. Important questions to ask in MfDR include: "Are the people for whom the plan, programme or project is being developed involved in the planning, monitoring and evaluation process?"; "Do they feel that they are a part of the process?"; and "Do they feel ownership of the processes and the plan or programme?"

- Promote national capacity development—Ask throughout the processes: "Will this be sustainable?"; "Can national systems and processes be used or augmented?"; "What are the existing national capacity assets in this area?"; "Are we looking at the enabling environment, the organization or institution, as well as the individual capacities?"; and "Can we engage in monitoring and evaluation activities so that we help to strengthen national M&E systems in the process?"

- Promote inclusiveness, gender mainstreaming and women's empowerment—Ensure that men, women and traditionally marginalized groups are involved in the planning, monitoring and evaluation processes. For example, ask questions such as: "Does this problem or result as we have stated it reflect the interests, rights and concerns of men, women and marginalized groups?"; "Have we analysed this from the point of view of men, women and marginalized groups in terms of their roles, rights, needs and concerns?"; and "Do we have sufficiently disaggregated data for monitoring and evaluation?"

POPP[9] should be consulted for more information about the UNDP approach to these principles and how they should be applied in the various stages of programme and project design and implementation. Additionally, there are many tools that can be used for capacity diagnostics and gender analysis. These can also be found in the additional resources sections of the POPP and other guides.

Throughout this Handbook, reference will be made to the principles, with examples of the types of questions that could be asked or addressed at the different stages of the planning, monitoring and evaluation processes.

Box 3. Planning, monitoring and evaluation in crisis settings

Crisis settings (both relating to conflicts and disasters) are 'not normal'. This has ramifications on all aspects of programming including planning, monitoring and evaluation. In general, 'normal' planning, monitoring and evaluation methods and mechanisms presented in this Handbook are transferable to crisis settings, with several important caveats:

- Crisis situations are dynamic and UNDP programming should quickly respond to radical changes that often take place in such circumstances. Therefore, the situation should continually be analysed and monitored to ensure that programming remains relevant. Changes should be documented so that monitoring and evaluating of the relevance and appropriateness of development initiatives takes into consideration the fluid situations in which they were conceived and implemented. This will involve continuous situational and conflict analysis.

- At the same time, crisis situations are characteristically ones of raised (or potentially raised) tension between different parties. Thus crisis and conflict-sensitivity should be exercised in all aspects of programming—including planning, monitoring and evaluation—to ensure that both the substance and process of programming is conducted in a way to reduce, or at the least not heighten, tensions between different parties. Security of programme staff, beneficiaries, and M&E staff can be a constant concern, and risk analysis for all those involved should be constantly monitored and factored into M&E activities.

- It is important to keep a 'big picture' perspective: The connectivity of projects and programmes to the wider peace process is critical, particularly for conflict prevention and peace-building programming. Planning, monitoring and evaluation should always include this aspect to avoid a situation where a project is 'successful' in terms of meeting the desired results, but either doesn't have an impact on the wider peace or negatively impacts it.

Additional guidance on how to apply methods and mechanism in crisis settings is presented throughout the Handbook, when relevant. The 'Compendium #1: Planning, Monitoring and Evaluation in Conflict Prevention and Recovery Settings' provides further guidance.

---

9 UNDP, 'Programme and Operations Policies and Procedures', 2008. Available at: http://content.undp.org/go/userguide.

1.4 OVERVIEW OF KEY ROLES AND RESPONSIBILITIES

All UNDP programme units have important roles in planning, monitoring and evaluating for development results. Table 1 provides a brief overview of some of key deliverables in this area.

In addition to programme units, the following units have key responsibilities in supporting planning, monitoring and evaluation in UNDP:

- The **Operations Support Group** provides corporate guidance as well as quality support and assurance on issues related to planning and corporate monitoring.

- The **BDP** provides the policy framework for programming, including monitoring, and provides advice and support to UNDP units in this regard.

- The **Evaluation Office** conducts independent evaluations and provides standards, guidance on procedures and quality assurance for 'decentralized' evaluations, that is, evaluations conducted by UNDP programme units.

- Monitoring and evaluation advisers and specialists in **UNDP bureaux** provide relevant programme units with direct advisory support in monitoring and evaluation (for example, regional evaluation advisers supporting relevant country offices).

- **Regional bureaux** provide direct oversight regarding evaluations carried out by country offices. They monitor the quality and implementation of planning, monitoring and evaluation.

- **UNDP management** plays a key role in fostering an RBM culture. It leads the programme planning process and ensures that monitoring takes place and the

Table 1. Key deliverables of programme units in planning, monitoring and evaluation

Programme unit	Planning	Monitoring	Evaluation
Country offices	■ UNDAF, including M&E framework ■ CPD and CPAP, including M&E framework[10] ■ Project documents and annual work plans, including M&E framework	■ Programme monitoring reports ■ Project monitoring reports	■ Evaluations as planned in the evaluation plan ■ Management responses to evaluations
Regional and policy bureaux	■ Regional and global programme documents, including M&E framework ■ Project documents, including M&E framework	■ Programme monitoring reports ■ Project monitoring reports	■ Evaluations as planned in the evaluation plan ■ Management responses to evaluations

10 Drawing from the UNDAF M&E plan, programme units are required to submit an evaluation plan highlighting planned evaluations for the programming cycle, along with the country, regional and global programmes to the Executive Board.

resulting information is used to strengthen programme implementation. Management also ensures that decentralized evaluations are conducted and lessons learned from both decentralized and independent evaluations are taken into account in future planning.

- The **UNDP Executive Board** plays an overarching role in shaping and approving the broader programmatic framework of UNDP. It also reviews regular monitoring reports on the programme's performance, as provided by UNDP management, and evaluation reports on different aspects of UNDP programmes, as conducted by the Evaluation Office. Based on regular corporate reporting and evaluation findings and recommendations, it provides guidance and makes decisions on subsequent strategic programme planning.

PLANNING FOR RESULTS: PRACTICAL APPLICATIONS

> "The true measure of success for the United Nations is not how much we promise but how much we deliver for those who need us most."
>
> UN Secretary General, Ban Ki-moon

This chapter provides step-by-step guidance on how to undertake planning for results. It focuses on the tasks involved in planning for desired results and includes consider-ations for operationalizing results. As noted in Box 1, monitoring and evaluation are closely related to planning. Therefore in planning it is essential to bear in mind not only intended results, but also how results, and the process of achieving them, will be monitored and evaluated. In particular, planning needs to ensure that planned initia-tives are evaluation-ready.

Planning can be done in many different ways. This chapter is designed to make the persons involved in planning more comfortable with the main steps involved in preparing a plan that can be implemented, monitored and evaluated. **The steps and approaches recommended apply generally to all planning processes, whether for a global, regional or country programme; a project; or a unit work plan.** This chapter is not intended to provide detailed instructions on preparing specific plans but rather to present the core approaches and steps generally involved in planning. At points, it will provide guidance for planning programmes and projects within the context of UNDP. However, for specific instructions on what is required for each UNDP planning document, the user should consult POPP.[11]

This chapter is divided into five main sections as shown in Figure 3. Planning to monitor and evaluate, which is also a critical part of the planning phase, is dealt with in Chapter 3.

---

11 UNDP, 'Programme and Operations Policies and Procedures', 2008. Available at: http://content. undp.org/go/userguide.

Figure 3. Organization of the chapter

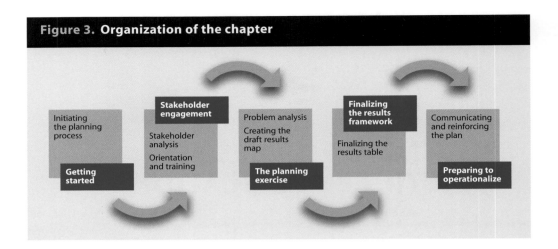

Development organizations often use a variety of tools throughout the planning cycle. Similarly, different organizations may require stakeholders to produce different sets of 'deliverables' as they go through the planning process. This Handbook will draw on some of the most commonly used tools. It will also walk the user through preparing eight deliverables that are normally used to develop and finalize programme and project results frameworks. Where relevant, the Handbook will show the relationship of the tools and deliverables mentioned with either United Nations Development Group (UNDG) or UNDP tools and deliverables. However, the Handbook is not intended to elaborate on UNDG and UNDP instruments. Instead, it is intended to be a how-to guide for doing planning, monitoring and evaluation based on good practices.

The eight main deliverables that will be covered are shown in Box 4.

Box 4. Main deliverables to be produced in the planning for results process

1. The initial **issues note** and draft **work plan** for the planning process (outline of activities and schedule and cost)

2. Stakeholder **influence and importance matrix**

3. List of **key problems identified**

4. **Prioritized list of problems**

5. Cause-effect diagram or **problem tree** analysis for each prioritized problems

6. **Vision statement** for each prioritized problem

7. **Results map** for each prioritized problem

8. **Results framework** for the programme or project document

Note: Deliverables 1 through 4 are normally part of the United Nations Country Team's plan of engagement or work plan (see http://www.undg.org/toolkit/toolkit.cfm?sub_section_id=301&topid2=on&topid=2 for additional information). Similarly, the Common Country Assessment (CCA) done by UN organizations, would normally include deliverables 3,4 and 5. Guidance on the CCA preparation can be found at: http://www.undg.org/toolkit/toolkit.cfm?sub_section_id=267&topid2=on&topid=2. At the project level, deliverables 1 to 6 can used in the 'justifying a project phase' of the UNDP project development cycle. All the deliverables would be used for the 'defining a programme' and 'defining a project' steps as these require results, roles, accountabilities and risks to be defined.

THE BENEFITS OF PLANNING

There are four main benefits that make planning worthwhile:

- Planning enables us to know what should be done when—Without proper planning, projects or programmes may be implemented at the wrong time or in the wrong manner and result in poor outcomes. A classic example is that of a development agency that offered to help improve the conditions of rural roads. The planning process was controlled by the agency with little consultation. Road repair began during the rainy season and much of the material used for construction was unsuitable for the region. The project suffered lengthy delays and cost overruns. One community member commented during the evaluation that the community wanted the project, but if there had been proper planning and consultation with them, the donors would have known the best time to start the project and the type of material to use.

- Planning helps mitigate and manage crises and ensure smoother implementation— There will always be unexpected situations in programmes and projects. However, a proper planning exercise helps reduce the likelihood of these and prepares the team for dealing with them when they occur. The planning process should also involve assessing risks and assumptions and thinking through possible unintended consequences of the activities being planned. The results of these exercises can be very helpful in anticipating and dealing with problems. (Some planning exercises also include scenario planning that looks at 'what ifs' for different situations that may arise.)

- Planning improves focus on priorities and leads to more efficient use of time, money and other resources—Having a clear plan or roadmap helps focus limited resources on priority activities, that is, the ones most likely to bring about the desired change. Without a plan, people often get distracted by many competing demands. Similarly, projects and programmes will often go off track and become ineffective and inefficient.

- Planning helps determine what success will look like—A proper plan helps individuals and units to know whether the results achieved are those that were intended and to assess any discrepancies. Of course, this requires effective monitoring and evaluation of what was planned. For this reason, good planning includes a clear strategy for monitoring and evaluation and use of the information from these processes.

2.1 GETTING STARTED

At the beginning of the process, the core planning team—usually from the government and UNDP or the United Nations Country Team (UNCT)—should discuss the planning exercise and how it will be approached. For global, regional and country programmes, projects and UNDAFs, UNDP or UNCT staff should consult their internal policies and procedures for information on the timelines, roles and responsibilities involved in these processes as well as the internal quality assurance and approval arrangements.

Prior to the first planning meeting, information should be collected on the major global, regional, country or community challenges that need to be addressed in the programmes or projects to be developed. This could be collected by either the government, UNDP or UNCT. Possible sources of information include national development plans, poverty reduction strategies, Millennium Development Goal (MDG) reports, national human development reports, gender equality documents, independent evaluations and reviews, country risk assessments, and so forth.

The information collected should be examined in relation to the comparative advantages of either UNDP or UNCT. The purpose of this is for the government and UNDP or UNCT to begin with fairly clear ideas on what the critical issues are **and in which areas UNDP or UNCT would be best prepared to provide support.** This will help manage expectations and ensure focus during the early stages of planning.

At this stage, attention should be focused on selecting broad areas rather than specific solutions. For example, in the initial discussions around a new country programme, attention should be focused on sectors and broad challenges such as governance, security, environment and climate change. At the project level, initial attention should be focused on the type or nature of the challenges faced (such as inner city unemployment, gender inequalities, national planning and monitoring capacity) rather than solutions (such as microfinance lending and gender awareness programmes). The aim is to ensure that the areas of work identified are broadly aligned with UNDP or UNCT mandates and capacities while avoiding the risk of predetermining the solutions. Section 2.3 addresses the more detailed process of problem identification and prioritization.

ISSUES NOTE AND DRAFT WORK PLAN (FIRST DELIVERABLE)

In the initiation phase, the team should put together a brief **issues note** and **draft work plan**. This can be refined as the planning process proceeds. The note should capture whatever information is available on the critical challenges that need to be addressed. This is the **first deliverable** in the planning process. The note may reflect key priorities in national, regional or global policy and strategy documents; concerns expressed by senior public and private officials or community members; as well as the findings of various analyses, such as a national or regional human development report, an MDG report, a community needs assessment, or an agency capacity assessment. The note should have at least three sections:

Section 1: Background and purpose of note

In this section, the core team should outline the rationale for preparing the note. This would generally include:

- Background to the note (why the team got together to initiate a planning process)
- The nature of the planning process that is being embarked on (preparing for a Poverty Reduction Strategy Paper, UNDAF, CPD, new project, etc.)

- Which stakeholders will be involved in the exercise (Section 2.2 of the Handbook can be used to prepare the initial list of stakeholders. The process should be fluid enough to involve additional stakeholders as more information becomes available during the problem analysis phase. Once the problems are better defined during the problem analysis process, it may be helpful to conduct a second stakeholder analysis to determine which additional persons should be involved.)

Section 2: Overview of priority issues

- Major development challenges identified
- Groups most adversely affected
- Critical areas of capacity constraints

The overview should, where possible, highlight the different impacts that the problems are having on men, women and marginalized populations.

Section 3: Work plan for completing the planning exercise

The core team should prepare a simple outline of the activities, schedules and resources for the overall planning process at this stage to ensure that the main issues are considered before additional stakeholders are engaged. The work plan should address a number of issues that the team should consider before actual commencement of the planning exercise. Specifically, the team should ask itself:

- What is the overall time frame we have for planning the programme or project?
- What are the key milestones in the process that we must meet to ensure that we produce the plan within the expected time frame?
- At what stage will we finalize the monitoring and evaluation plan? (It is usually better to do this as part of the process of preparing the plan so that the same stakeholders can be involved in the process.)
- How participatory should the process be given the context within which stakeholders are operating? (See Section 2.2 to help make the decision on how participatory the process should be.)
- What resources will be needed for the planning exercises? (For example, facilitators, venues, resource persons, important speakers, etc.)
- Who will be responsible for the different elements of the planning process? (For example, organizing workshops, inviting participants, contracting facilitators, etc.)
- How much will it all cost?

Table 2 provides a sample format for the work plan. An initial draft work plan can be prepared and subsequently finalized with greater details for specific activities.

Table 2. Sample draft work plan for the planning process (with illustrative examples)

Major Steps	Who Is Responsible for Organizing?	When Will It Take Place?	Notes
Recruitment of consultant for data gathering	UNICEF	10 May 2010	Terms of Reference to be prepared by UNICEF and shared with national planning agency
Initial brainstorming exercise	Resident Coordinator	15 May 2010	Resident Coordinator's office will convene initial meeting with key counterparts to prepare analysis
Stakeholder analysis	Resident Coordinator	15 May 2010	Will be done as part of brainstorming
Invitation to stakeholders	Minister of Planning & Resident Coordinator	30 May 2010	Resident Coordinator's office will send out invitations and make follow-up calls
Planning workshop(s): 1. Orientation and training session for stakeholders	National planning agency	20 June 2010	Resident Coordinator's office will provide logistics support to the national planning agency
2. Problem analysis workshop	National planning agency	27-28 June 2010	As above, the session will include a presentation on planning with monitoring and evaluation in mind
3. Additional data gathering on identified problems	National planning agency and consultant	July 2010	(This could be part of a CCA process)
4. Workshop to complete problem analysis and finalize the results framework	National planning agency	14-15 August 2010	As above
5. Meeting to finalize arrangements for monitoring and evaluation	National planning agency	23 August 2010	As above
Review of draft results framework: 1. Review by stakeholders (or by peers)	National planning agency	31 August 2010	
2. Review by Headquarters	Resident Coordinator	15 September 2010	
Preparation of plan for communication of results framework	Sub-team on communications	22 September 2010	UNFPA communications office to lead

Resources	Funding	Cost	Notes
Venues	UNICEF	15,000	Possible venues – Niagra Hotel and Tunoko Hotel as they are convenient for rural stakeholders
Facilitators	National planning agency	6,000	Need facilitators well trained in participatory techniques
Communications	UNFPA	10,000	Will need communication strategy targeting different types of stakeholders and the general public
Resource persons (e.g. M&E specialist, gender adviser, poverty specialist)	UNCT	10,000	Local experts from government and NGO sector to be involved; UN organizations to explore bringing in experts from respective Headquarters
Consultants (e.g. for data collection)	Resident Coordinator	10,000	
Equipment and material	Resident Coordinator	5,000	
Other	Resident Coordinator	2,000	
Total		**58,000**	

It is generally useful for the core team to think in terms of a series of meetings or workshops rather than one planning workshop. This approach is particularly relevant for programme planning but can be useful for large or complex projects as well. In either case, a clear work plan with a schedule and budget is highly recommended.

> **NOTE** The issues note and work plan can be used as key elements in preparing the UNCT plan of engagement at the programme or project level and used in the 'justifying a project stage' for UNDP. Sample plans of engagement and work plans for the UNDAF preparation process can be found on the UNDG website at: http://www.undg.org/toolkit/toolkit.cfm?sub_section_id=301&topid2=on&topid=2.

2.2 STAKEHOLDER ENGAGEMENT

Inadequate stakeholder involvement is one of the most common reasons programmes and projects fail. Therefore, every effort should be made to encourage broad and active stakeholder engagement in the planning, monitoring and evaluation processes. This is particularly relevant to crisis situations where people's sense of security and vulnerability may be heightened and where tensions and factions may exist. In these situations, the planning process should aim to ensure that as many stakeholders as possible are involved (especially those who may be least able to promote their own interests), and that opportunities are created for the various parties to hear each other's perspectives in an open and balanced manner. In crisis situations this is not just good practice but is fundamental to ensuring that programming 'does no harm' at the least and, hopefully, reduces inherent or active tensions. Perceptions of UNDP neutrality, and at times the success of the programme or project, depend on representatives of the different main stakeholder groups (including those relating to different parties of the tension) being equally consulted. In some situations, a planning fora that brings stakeholders together so that they can hear each other's views may itself be a mechanism for reducing tensions.

STEP 1: STAKEHOLDER ANALYSIS

Any given programme, project or development plan is likely to have a number of important stakeholders. Effective planning is done with the participation of these stakeholders. Stakeholders are the people who will benefit from the development activity or whose interests may be affected by that activity. Therefore, a simple stakeholder analysis is generally recommended for all planning processes. A stakeholder analysis can help identify:

- Potential risks, conflicts and constraints that could affect the programmes, projects or activities being planned
- Opportunities and partnerships that could be explored and developed
- Vulnerable or marginalized groups that are normally left out of planning processes

Various stakeholder analysis tools can be used to identify stakeholders and determine the type of involvement that they should have at different stages of the process (planning, implementation, monitoring, reporting, evaluation, etc.) These range from basic consultations and focus group discussions for simple programmes and projects to more elaborate workshops for large or complex programmes. The planning or management team should use their judgement to determine what is most appropriate, bearing in mind that the main objective is to properly identify key stakeholders who may have a strong interest in or ability to influence what is being planned. Generally, for UNDP programmes and projects, at least one UNDP officer and one government official would be part of the stakeholder group involved in planning.

> **TIP** There is a tendency for core planning teams not to involve certain stakeholders in planning. This typically occurs with complex programmes and projects and work that involves developing policy. Marginalized groups, poor rural community members, minorities and others are often left out because planners assume that these groups are not well informed or educated enough to contribute to the planning process. This assumption often turns out to be very costly. A good planner should always ask: **"Whose voice is normally not heard on this issue?"** Planners are often pleasantly surprised at the insights that previously unheard stakeholders have to offer.

Tables 3 and 4 and Figure 4 are examples of three simple tools often used to conduct a stakeholder analysis. (For purposes of illustration, the tables contain some examples of the type of information that could be entered in the various columns for challenges related to public participation in an election support programme.) Table 3 seeks to identify the stakeholders, who may have an interest in the programme or project being planned, and determine the nature of that interest. Table 4 assesses the importance and influence of those stakeholders in the programme or project. Here, importance relates to who the programme or project is **intended for**, which may be different from the level of **influence** they may have.

Figure 4. Stakeholder importance and influence matrix

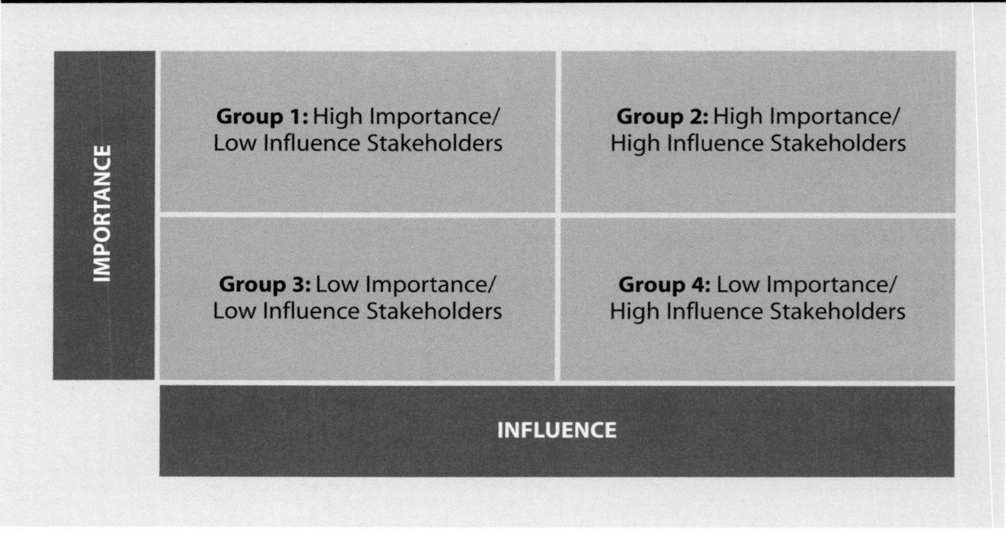

IMPORTANCE	
Group 1: High Importance/ Low Influence Stakeholders	**Group 2:** High Importance/ High Influence Stakeholders
Group 3: Low Importance/ Low Influence Stakeholders	**Group 4:** Low Importance/ High Influence Stakeholders
INFLUENCE	

Table 3. Identification of key stakeholders and their interests

Stakeholders (examples)	Interest in Activity	Nature of Interest (+ve or –ve)*
Office of the Prime Minister	Greater citizen participation	+
Universities	Political culture and civic behaviour	+
Main political parties	Free and fair elections, opportunities for greater influence?	+ +/-
Religious umbrella organizations	Ethics in politics, fairness	+
NGO groups (e.g. a watchdog NGO)	Fairness, greater influence	+
Private sector organizations	Opportunities for influence, fairness	+/-
Minority group representatives	Opportunities to participate	+
Youth umbrella organizations	Opportunities to participate	+
Electoral administrative body	Maintain own neutrality	+
International observer group	Fairness	+
Citizens' organizations	Rights of citizens, fairness	+
Women's organizations	Rights of women, fairness	+
Informal political leaders	Threats to their power	-

Note: NGO indicates non-governmental organization.

* Positive or negative interest has to do with whether a stakeholder or stakeholder group would be supportive or disruptive of the programme or project being planned or in terms of whether their interest could help or impede what is being planned. In some cases, a stakeholder group may have both a negative and a positive interest, as would be the case, for example, if some umbrella private sector groups were supportive of a programme that others opposed.

Table 4. Importance and influence of stakeholders

Stakeholders (examples)	Importance (Scale of 1 to 5, 5 = highest)	Influence (Scale of 1 to 5, 5 = highest)
Office of the Prime Minister	5	5
Universities	3	2
Main political parties	5	4
Religious umbrella organization	3	2
NGO groups (e.g. a watchdog NGO)	3	3
Private sector organizations	3	4
Minority group representatives	5	1
Youth umbrella organizations	5	1
Electoral administrative body	4	3
International observer group	1	3
Citizens' organizations	5	2
Women's organizations	5	2
Informal political leaders	2	4

Note: NGO indicates non-governmental organization.

The tables and matrix can be helpful in communicating about the stakeholders and their role in the programme or activities that are being planned.

Stakeholder importance and influence matrix (deliverable two)

The stakeholder importance and influence matrix, which is the **second deliverable** in the planning process, becomes the main tool used to determine who should be involved in the planning session and how other stakeholders should be engaged in the overall process.

Group 1 stakeholders are very important to the success of the activity but may have little influence on the process. For example, the success of an electoral project will often depend on how well women and minorities are able to participate in the elections, but these groups may not have much influence on the design and implementation of the project or the conduct of the elections. In this case, they are highly important but not very influential. They may require special emphasis to ensure that their interests are protected and that their voices are heard.

Group 2 stakeholders are central to the planning process as they are both important and influential. These should be key stakeholders for partnership building. For example, political parties involved in a national elections programme may be both very important (as mobilizers of citizens) and influential (without their support the programme may not be possible).

Group 3 stakeholders are not the central stakeholders for an initiative and have little influence on its success or failure. They are unlikely to play a major role in the overall process. One example could be an international observer group that has little influence on elections. Similarly, they are not the intended beneficiaries of, and will not be impacted by, those elections.

Group 4 stakeholders are not very important to the activity but may exercise significant influence. For example, an informal political leader may not be an important stakeholder for an elections initiative aimed at increasing voter participation, but she or he could have major influence on the process due to informal relations with power brokers and the ability to mobilize people or influence public opinion. These stakeholders can sometimes create constraints to programme implementation or may be able to stop all activities. Even if they are not involved in the planning process, there may need to be a strategy for communicating with these stakeholders and gaining their support.

> **TIP** The planning team should devote time to discussing the issue of how to effectively involve stakeholders. There are many examples of how to do this. For example, some teams have budgeted resources to assist certain stakeholders with travel and accommodation expenses. Others have rearranged meeting times to be more suitable to specific stakeholders. In most cases, official letters of invitation are sent to stakeholders by senior government or UN officials. This can be helpful in conveying the importance attached to stakeholder participation. The team should discuss the most suitable arrangements given the local context.

Based on the stakeholder analysis, and on what is practical given cost and location of various stakeholders, the identified stakeholders should be brought together in a planning workshop or meeting. This may be the first meeting to plan the UNDAF or a UNDP country programme or project.

> **NOTE** The stakeholder analysis can be used to outline who the stakeholders will be in the UNCT plan of engagement or, at the project level, to outline the stakeholders in the draft proposal prepared by UNDP in the 'justifying a project' stage of project development.

STEP 2: ORIENTATION AND TRAINING OF STAKEHOLDERS

Orientation on the planning process

Stakeholders should be made aware of what the planning process will involve. Whether planning a national strategy, a UNDAF, or a global, regional or country programme, the process will often require a series of workshops and meetings over several months to analyse the problems, commission studies, undertake research, discuss and come to conclusions on priorities and approaches, formulate a results framework, and put together a monitoring and evaluation plan. Project-level planning may also involve a series of meetings and include one or more workshops based on the size and complexity of the project.

The planning team should provide the stakeholders with a copy of the draft issue note and work plan at the initial meeting. The work plan should include sufficient time for preparing the results framework and the monitoring and evaluation plan. It should

---

Box 5. Preparing a timeline for UN programme documents

The UNDAF is the main planning document for the UN team in a given country. The UNDAF is prepared with the government and other national stakeholders. In preparing the UNDAF, all the main steps discussed in this Handbook would be undertaken between June and December of the year preceding the completion of the five-year UNDAF cycle.

For UNDP country programmes, it is normal for the steps leading to the preparation of a draft country programme and results framework to be completed in parallel with the UNDAF process (between June and December) with greater elaboration of the UNDP components of the UNDAF between September and February of the following year. In March, the completed country programme is submitted with an evaluation plan to the UNDP Executive Board.

Many units use the CPAP process between March and September to refine their results frameworks (outcomes, outputs and indicators), develop monitoring plans, and refine their evaluation plans. This approach is often taken given that between March and September national partners would have begun engaging with UNDP on the specific projects to be developed and would therefore have more information on the relevant outputs, indicators and targets. However, in many other planning processes, the full results framework along with the M&E plan are developed and finalized at the same time that the plan is prepared.

Projects are planned at various points during the programme cycle, and there is no prescribed time-frame for when these should be done.

also allow for potential challenges in conducting stakeholder meetings in crisis settings when meetings between different parties can be sensitive and time consuming.

If appropriate, the stakeholders involved in the planning process should be provided with orientation or training on issues such as gender analysis, rights-based approaches to development, conflict-sensitivity and analysis, and capacity development. (When planning UNDAFs, it is also usually helpful to include a deliverable on the UN reform process and aid effectiveness to increase awareness of the direction in which the United Nations is moving globally and at the national level.) This initial session is intended to raise awareness of these issues and enable participants to adopt a more rigorous and analytical approach to the planning process. Some of the ways in which this can be done include:

- Having a gender expert provide an overview to participants on the importance of gender and how to look at development programming through a gender lens. This session would include an introduction to the gender analysis methodology

- Including a gender expert as a stakeholder in the workshop as an additional means of ensuring that gender and women's empowerment issues receive attention

- Having a presenter address the group on capacity development methodology as a tool to enhance programme effectiveness and promote more sustainable development[12]

- Having a presenter address the group on promoting inclusiveness and a rights-based approach to development[13]

Expert support in organizing and presenting these cross-cutting thematic issues can be obtained by contacting the relevant units in BDP, BCPR and the UN Staff College.

Considerations at the project level

This type of briefing for stakeholders applies equally to programmes and projects. However, most small projects are unlikely to have enough resources to provide expert trainers on some of the themes. In these situations, the planning team should consider cost-effective options for increasing stakeholder awareness. This may include preparing short presentations or briefing guides and circulating them to stakeholders ahead of the meetings. Also, it may be useful to invite persons with training in the particular areas to be stakeholders in the process. For example, a representative from a human rights, women's or gender NGO could be invited to be a project stakeholder. Similarly, gender or human rights analysts in national planning agencies or from other partner development agencies could be involved as stakeholders. This can be an effective way of ensuring ongoing focus on the issues, as opposed to only at the beginning of the planning exercise.

---

12 Refer to the UNDP policy note on capacity development: UNDP, 'Supporting Capacity Development: The UNDP Approach'. Available at: http://www.capacity.undp.org/indexAction.cfm?module=Library&action=GetFile&DocumentAttachmentID=2141.

13 Guidance can be found in the common learning package on UNDG website: UNDG, 'Human Rights Based Approach to Development'. Available at: http://www.undg.org/index.cfm?P=74.

Orientation on approaches to dialogue

At the start of the planning process, it is important that all stakeholders start at the same point. They should all understand:

- Why it is important for them to work together

- Why they have been selected for the planning exercise

- The rules of the planning exercise and how stakeholders should dialogue, especially in crisis settings, where these fora could be the first time different parties have heard each others' perspectives and goals for development

It is important to bring stakeholders together not only for the resources they have but also because each has a unique perspective on the causes of the problems and what may be required to solve them. A government minister, a community member, a social worker, an economist, a business person, a woman, a man and UNDP staff may all be involved in designing a plan—and may all have different views on what they are confronting and what changes they would like to see occur. It is common in the early stages of planning for persons to use anecdotes to get stakeholders to see how easy it is to look at the same issue and yet see it differently.

The core planning team should find ways to encourage stakeholders to:

- Suspend judgement—Stakeholders should not start the process with any pre-set ideas and should not rush to conclusions. They should be prepared to hear different points of view before coming to conclusions.

- Be open to all points of view—In the planning exercise, all points of view are equally valid, not just those of persons considered important. The planning exercise should be conducted in such a way that everyone (men, women, margin-alized individuals) feels free to express their views. The views expressed by stakeholders are neither 'right' nor 'wrong.'

- Be creative—Stakeholders should understand that long-standing challenges are unlikely to be solved by traditional approaches, many of which may have been tried before. They should therefore be open to fresh ideas, especially those that may, at first, seem unworkable or unrealistic.

The same approach to explaining these basic guidelines to stakeholders can be applied in both programme-level and project-level planning.

Once the orientation is completed, the stakeholders can proceed to the actual planning exercise.

NOTE It is useful to remind stakeholders that the planning process is not about developing a UNDP or UNCT plan but about developing a plan that addresses the needs and priorities of the country or community, which UNDP or UNCT will support as one partner in the process.

2.3 THE PLANNING EXERCISE

The planning process should help stakeholders design programmes or projects that address the right problems and the right causes of those problems. For this reason, stakeholders should undertake a thorough problem and situation analysis before developing goals and objectives or planning programmes or projects. A problem analysis, which is sometimes referred to as a cause-effect analysis, is a requirement for all UN and UNDP programming. For global, regional and country programmes, problem definition and analysis is useful to analyse what is happening in certain sectors and major global, regional and macro-policy issues. At the project level, the analysis may help in understanding specific challenges or issues within a sector, region or community.

A thorough problem analysis at the programme level may reduce the need for one at the project level. Once the problem is properly analysed in the national strategy, UNDAF, CPAP or other documents, projects can be developed at different times and by different agencies to address the specific causes without undergoing another problem analysis. However, in some situations, only a limited set of stakeholders would have been involved in the programme-level analysis. In other cases, the process may not have been based on a thorough analysis. In these situations, it should not be assumed that all the critical issues at the project or output level have been well identified. A project-level problem analysis involving additional stakeholders, particularly those most affected by the problem, will often help to ensure a better understanding of the challenges, constraints and possible solutions.

In general, the problem analysis plays a crucial role in:

- Developing a clear understanding of not only the surface problems, but also their **underlying causes** and constraints

Box 6. The Common Country Assessment

The Common Country Assessment (CCA) commissioned by UN development organizations can be a useful tool to aid in identifying and analysing problems. The CCA is most useful when the government, other national partners and the UNCT are involved in the assessment. The problem analysis described in this Handbook is very similar to the process normally used in preparing the analytical sections of the CCA.

The CCA is generally undertaken when there is inadequate data or analysis in place or when additional analysis is needed to better understand the issues. A rigorous CCA provides a strategic analysis of the major problems of the country and their root causes and effects on the population, particularly on excluded groups such as women, minorities, indigenous peoples, migrants and displaced persons. It also addresses the opportunities for (and obstacles to) free, active and meaningful participation by stakeholders in national governance and development processes and outcomes.

A well prepared CCA should provide enough information to inform the preparation of a UNDAF. However, additional analysis may be needed for the preparation of agency-specific programmes and projects.

Additional information on the CCA, including examples and tools, can be found on the UNDG website, at: http://www.undg.org/index.cfm?P=227.

- Determining the real size and complexity of the problem and the **relationships** between different contributing factors

- Determining how the problem affects groups (women, men, marginalized populations) or may be caused by the **unequal treatment** of different groups in society

- Determining short-, medium- and long-term interventions that may be necessary for a **sustainable** solution

- Identifying the **partnerships** that may be necessary to effectively address the problem

- Assessing the **roles** that different stakeholders may need to play in solving the problem

- Estimating the **resources** that may be required to deal with the problem and its causes

Additionally, the **analysis plays an important role in building stakeholder consensus**. It is very difficult to develop a common vision and strategy if there is no shared understanding of the problems and their causes.

Considerations at the programme level

For large programmes or in situations where there are insufficient macro-level analysis and data, a series of workshops is recommended for the problem analysis. The analysis will often take several weeks while information is gathered. Partners may need to review existing studies or commission new studies. In some cases, a macro-level capacity assessment may be commissioned to assess key areas of strength and weakness in national capacity that may need to be addressed in the programme.

Considerations at the project level

For smaller projects, focus group discussions and consultations with various stakeholders may suffice to conduct the problem analysis. **However, it is generally recommended to bring different stakeholders together in one place so that the whole group may benefit from discussing different points of view.** Large or complex projects may require a series of workshops similar to a programme. Even in smaller projects, it should not be assumed that all the issues will be identified and clearly understood by the stakeholders based on only an initial discussion, which may also only involve a few persons. Stakeholders often underestimate the time required to study a problem. This can lead to numerous unexpected issues arising in implementation. Therefore, enough time should be set aside for proper consultation and research.

STEP 1: IDENTIFYING MAIN PROBLEMS

Once the stakeholders are gathered together, they should begin looking at the problems to be addressed. (This could be done as part of a CCA workshop, where initial analysis is presented then stakeholders identify priority problems that need further research.) At this stage, the aim is not to define a solution to the problem in the form of a programme or project but to correctly identify what needs to be addressed.

- Stakeholders should seek to identify the problems facing the region, country or community—not problems for UNDP or a particular stakeholder to solve. (This Handbook will later address how to prioritize and select challenges for UNDP or UNCT programming.)

- Stakeholders should refer to the original concept note that was prepared.

- They should be guided by a few key questions:
  - Are the initial problems identified the most critical problems to be addressed?
  - Are we adequately capturing the problems facing both **men** and **women**?
  - Are we capturing the problems affecting **marginalized groups and the rights of various groups**?
  - Are we addressing problems that relate to key issues of **national capacity**?

- A key part of the process should focus on discussing **what** is happening and to **whom**. This should involve discussing whether particular groups are affected more than others by a denial of their rights.

- Stakeholders should reflect on these questions as they start identifying the main problems.

- All stakeholders should brainstorm the major problems as they see them, though it may be necessary to limit the exercise to a certain sector or issue that is within the scope of the stakeholders to address.[14]

- Problems should be stated in terms of negative conditions or realities, and not in terms of specific things being unavailable. This is important, as very often the way the problem is stated influences what stakeholders consider to be the solution. For example, consider the difference between stating a problem as (a) **"minorities and marginalized groups do not have the right to vote"** versus (b) **"minorities and other marginalized groups do not participate in elections"** or (c) **"low levels of participation by minorities in elections."** The first case (a) is an example of formulating the problem in terms of what is missing—in this case, the right to vote. The danger with this approach is that it may lead stakeholders to think that updating laws to extend the right to vote to these groups is a solution. This may then lead to a project being created to update those laws. If the aim, however, was to actually increase voting by minorities and other marginalized groups, then changing the laws may only be one component of the solution. In fact, changing the laws may not result in minorities and other marginalized groups actually voting if there are cultural, economic and other factors that constrain them. The second and third examples (b) and (c) would be better ways of stating the problem as they could lead stakeholders to analyse all the factors causing these groups not to participate or vote. In summary, the problem should be stated in a manner that facilitates thorough analysis and does not bias attention to one particular issue.

- Similarly, stakeholders should focus on the present and not the future. Problems should not be stated as "if we do not address X, then Y may happen", or "in the future, X is likely to happen." In the problem analysis process, which will be

---

14 This is a practical point that has to be managed during workshops: while it may be necessary to identify critical problems and not problems for UNDP to solve, at the same, it is necessary to guide the discussions so that the group doesn't end up preparing a complete analysis of, for example, the education sector problem, which UNDP would not address in its programme (although UNICEF or another agency might).

discussed later, stakeholders will have the opportunity to review the existing and potential consequences and effects of the problem. At this stage, the focus is on having everyone agree on what the problem itself is. Combining both too early in the discussion can often create confusion over what is to be addressed.

◾ Stakeholders should examine all the problems identified against the main questions noted above: Do they adequately capture concerns faced by men and women as well as marginalized groups, and do they address core concerns of national capacity?

Examples of problems that may have been identified in the process include the following:

◾ Lack of involvement of women, indigenous and marginalized populations in electoral processes

◾ Weak e-governance capacity in key state institutions to engage with the public

◾ Electoral laws, systems and processes disenfranchise voters, particularly women, indigenous and other marginalized populations

◾ Low levels of engagement of civil society organizations in the oversight of elections

◾ Weak capacity of national electoral management authority to administer elections in a free and fair manner

These are only examples of problems relating to governance and particularly elections. Other problems may also be identified in various sectors or themes, such as problems with the environment, climate change, education, economic development and culture.

The **list of problems** identified is the **third deliverable** in the planning process. While UNDP or the UNCT may not provide support to national partners on all the identified problems, it is important to have a record of them for analytical purposes and as a possible basis for advocating for action by other agencies or individuals.

> **NOTE** The list of problems can be used as part of the UNCT's plan of engagement and the CCA. Different problems would be selected by different UN organizations to include in their specific country programmes as applicable. At the project level, one or more of these problems would be used in preparing the initial UNDP project proposal during the 'justifying a project' stage.

STEP 2: ORGANIZING AND PRIORITIZING MAIN PROBLEMS

Several major problems are likely to be identified during the problem identification process. Some of the problems may appear to be closely related, and some may appear to be causes or consequences of another problem. For example, one person may have identified "low levels of participation in elections by minorities" as a problem, while another person may have identified the problem as "minorities do not have the right to vote." When this happens, there should be further discussion on which of the statements best reflects the central problem that the group wants to address. In doing this, it helps to examine if some of the problems are actually part of other problems or consequences of those problems. If this is the case, then these should be noted for later discussion.

Once there is agreement on the major problems, stakeholders should prioritize them. The aim of prioritization is first to ensure that the problems are considered critical by the global, regional, national or community stakeholders, and second to determine what challenges UNCT or UNDP will support in the UNDAF or global, regional or country programme or project.

Many public and non-profit organizations use a simple model to determine the priority of problems and which problems to address. The model involves looking at the identified problems through three lenses: value, support, and capacity and comparative advantage. (This is the same model used in UNDG guidance for preparing CCAs and UNDAFs.) Using the earlier examples, the planning team would write down the main problems and ask the stakeholders to consider these using the model described in Figure 5.

The area where all three circles overlap—area 1—is often referred to as the 'Just Do It' zone, as it represents a challenge that is a major priority, and for which UNDP or UNCT would have partner support, internal capacity and comparative advantage. Problems classified in this area should be a high priority for UNDP.

Area 2 is often a good area for advocacy—working on these issues could bring tremendous value to stakeholders, and UNDP or UNCT has capacity and comparative advantage. But efforts may be needed to mobilize support and build partnerships and further awareness.

UNDP and UNCT should generally avoid challenges in areas 3 and 4. With respect to area 3, other public, private or non-profit agencies with greater capacity or comparative advantage should provide support. For example, a UN organization engaged in discussions with national partners may not have sufficient capacity or mandate to engage on e-governance or education issues and may be better positioned to address mobilization of women and marginalized groups. Another partner may need to address the e-governance challenges.

Area 4 relates to challenges that may be within the mandate and existing capacity of UNDP—and therefore tempting for UNDP to take up—but may not be national priorities, have sufficient ownership by key stakeholders, or bring value to the community, country or region.

NOTE The prioritized problems would be the main ones elaborated in the UNDAF and the CPD. They would also provide the starting point for developing project proposals in the 'justifying a project' phase of the UNDP project development cycle.

Figure 5. Stakeholder importance and influence matrix

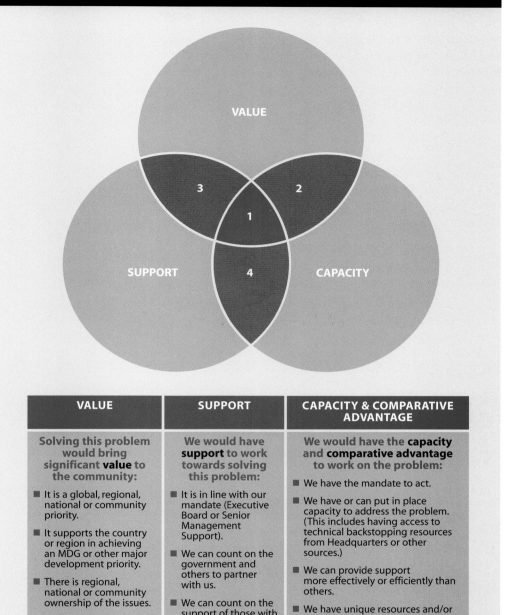

VALUE	SUPPORT	CAPACITY & COMPARATIVE ADVANTAGE
Solving this problem would bring significant **value** to the community:	We would have **support** to work towards solving this problem:	We would have the **capacity** and **comparative advantage** to work on the problem:
■ It is a global, regional, national or community priority.	■ It is in line with our mandate (Executive Board or Senior Management Support).	■ We have the mandate to act.
■ It supports the country or region in achieving an MDG or other major development priority.	■ We can count on the government and others to partner with us.	■ We have or can put in place capacity to address the problem. (This includes having access to technical backstopping resources from Headquarters or other sources.)
■ There is regional, national or community ownership of the issues.	■ We can count on the support of those with decision-making power and resources.	■ We can provide support more effectively or efficiently than others.
		■ We have unique resources and/or attributes (e.g., neutrality, legitimacy, reputation, convening role).

Once the priority problems for UNDP or UNCT support have been identified, stakeholders should put in place a process to gather more information on the problems to feed into the next steps. The **prioritized problems** are the **fourth deliverable** in the planning process.

STEP 3: THE PROBLEM ANALYSIS

For each priority problem selected, stakeholders should undertake a problem (cause-effect) analysis. This generally requires additional data. These may include summaries of analyses done on the problems or issues; data or statistics on the problem (**the data should be disaggregated by age, gender, socio-economic group and other variables if possible**); and results of macro-level capacity assessments, agency or community assessments and so forth. In preparing a UNDAF or country programme, the CCA should provide most of the problem analysis needed. However in some cases, this may not be available or sufficient. Also, additional analysis with specific stakeholders may be needed at the project level.

If research and data already exist, the stakeholders should rely on these. Otherwise, it may be necessary to commission new research to gain a better understanding of the specific issues. Stakeholders should review the findings from any studies prior to embarking on the problem analysis. This will help inform the quality of the group's analysis of the problems. In many planning exercises, this process takes place a few weeks after the initial problem identification meeting or workshop, in order to allow time for research and data collection.

There are many different types of problem analysis models, including the problem tree that is used in this Handbook.[15] The models apply equally to programme and project-

---

Box 7. One difference between a 'project' and a 'results-based' approach to development

In some situations, the problem may have been previously identified and presented with an analysis and proposal for the government, UNDP or other funding partner to consider. A common problem in these situations is that many project proposals are presented to the funding agency with a fixed solution. Quite often, the solution presented only relates to part of a bigger problem. This is often because the agency presenting the proposal tends to be concerned with obtaining financing for the component(s) for which it has a strong interest. For example, an NGO may submit a proposal for assistance to strengthen its capacity to participate in monitoring national elections. While this may be an important project, it is likely that it would only address part of a bigger problem.

Good results-oriented programming requires that all project-level proposals be subject to a problem analysis to determine whether the stated problem is part of a bigger problem and whether the proposed solution will be adequate to address the challenges. The answers to these questions can sometimes be found, particularly in situations where the projects proposed are within the context of an already designed national programme (such as a Poverty Reduction Strategy Paper, UNDAF or country programme). However, in many cases, there will need to be deeper discussions of what the larger problem is and what other actions are needed by different partners to solve that problem. The aim in asking these questions is not to slow down the process of project review and approval but to ensure that problems are analysed properly and appropriate solutions are found. These solutions may involve actions beyond the scope of the specific project. This is one of the differences between a project approach and a results focused approach to development.

---

15 Development practitioners have come up with a range of other problem analysis models for use with different groups. Where there are major language barriers or differences in education levels, simpler methods may be better suited and equally effective. These generally include using pictures or images, allowing persons to draw, or using simple focus group discussions.

level problem analysis. The main purpose of these models is to study the root **causes** and major **effects** of problems in order to better design solutions. A well constructed cause-effect problem analysis diagram will make the process of developing a results map, covered in step 4, much easier.[16]

Using the **problem tree model** to undertake the **problem analysis (deliverable five)**, stakeholders will generally:

- Begin with a major issue or problem that was identified and write it down on the trunk of the problem tree (see Figure 6). For example, one problem identified may

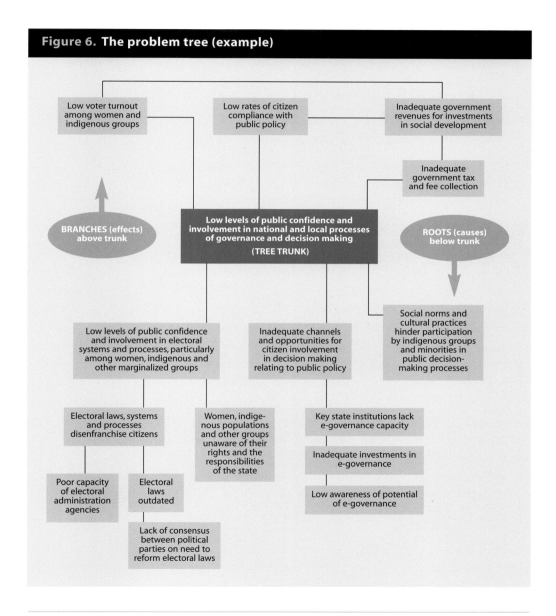

Figure 6. The problem tree (example)

---

16 The results map is what is sometimes referred to as an 'outcome model', 'logic model', 'results chain', 'logical framework', 'programme model', etc. At this stage, it is not important which terms are used, as long as the core concepts are properly understood and communicated in the planning process.

be "low levels of public confidence and involvement in national and local processes of governance and decision making."

- Brainstorm on the major **causes** of the problem. It is often helpful to think in terms of categories of causes, such as policy constraints, institutional constraints, capacity weaknesses, or social or cultural norms.

- Brainstorm the possible causes of the problem by asking "What is causing this to happen?" Stakeholders should try to analyse the issues at a deeper level. They should explore the extent to which the problem has underlying root causes that may be based on exclusion, discrimination and inequality.

- Attach the answers to roots of the tree (see Figure 6).

- For each answer, drill down further by asking "Why has this happened?" Stakeholders should not stop at the first level of a reason or cause, but ask whether there is something else behind that cause.

- Repeat this exercise for each cause identified. Stakeholders should stop when they run out of additional reasons or ideas on what is causing the problem.

- Once the roots of the problem tree are complete, the group should look to see if it provides a good understanding of what has caused the problem. See if there are subcauses that are repeated on different roots. These are likely to be priority concerns to be addressed in the results framework.

In the example in Figure 6, the core problem illustrated on the trunk of the tree in the shaded box, "low levels of public confidence and involvement in national and local processes of governance and decision making," could be considered a programme-level problem that could be taken up at the UNDAF and UNCT level. Below the trunk, a narrower problem has been identified, "local levels of public confidence and involvement in electoral systems and processes, particularly among women, indigenous and other marginalized groups." UNDP and partners might address this challenge in the country programme and projects. For illustrative purposes, another lower-level problem has also been identified in the shaded box "social norms and cultural practices hinder participation by minorities in public decision-making processes." In this case, United Nations Educational, Scientific and Cultural Organization (UNESCO) or another agency could take up this challenge in their country programme and projects. The choice of which level and type of problem to work on depends on the partners involved, their capacities and comparative advantages, and the resources available. The same steps in the problem analysis apply at all levels.

Stakeholders often find it helpful to also show and discuss the **effects** of the problem. In this case, branches can be created on the problem tree to illustrate how the problem affects the region, country or community. The process involves:

- Identifying the most direct effects of the problem—They can be classified using the same categories as were used for the analysis of the causes, such as policy constraints, institutional constraints, capacity weaknesses, or social or cultural norms.

- Identifying the main indirect effects of the problem—For example, because of the low levels of public confidence in processes of governance, few people pay their taxes, a direct consequence or effect, which could lead to other indirect problems.

- Discussing whether the problem affects men and women differently—Both men and women should have an opportunity to comment during the discussions.

- Discussing whether particular groups, such as marginalized populations (persons with disabilities, indigenous groups, etc.) are affected—Asking whether their rights and interests are affected.

In the project tree example, the effects of the higher level problem are captured in the boxes above the trunk. For a lower level (such as project level) tree, the effects would begin with the immediate boxes above the shaded boxes. In both cases, one of the shared effects would be the low voter turn-out among marginalized groups.

The main difference in a problem tree diagram for a programme, as opposed to a project, is that the programme-level diagram would normally have a wider range of root causes than the project-level diagram. In other words, the higher the level of the problem identified, the more causes there are likely to be. For example, in the programme-level tree in Figure 6, the problem is stated as low levels of public confidence and involvement in both governance and decision making. As such, the causes involve problems with not only the electoral processes and systems, but also the capacity of the government to engage citizens through other means. Hence, at this level, there will need to be an analysis of both sets of problems, whereas the project-level analysis would focus on the causes and effects of only the problem related to the electoral process.

Box 8. Note on problem trees

While programme-level problems generally have a wider set of root causes and a more elaborate problem tree, many large or complex projects may also have elaborate problem trees with a wide range of root causes. Even in the cases where a project or lower level problem is the starting point, the analysis should nonetheless lead to the identification of higher level effects of the problem.

Through this process of **looking up** at the problem tree, stakeholders are likely to identify other causes of the effects of the problem and may conclude that the immediate solution to the project-level problem identified may not be adequate to address some of these other causes of the higher level effects. For example, assuming a situation where a project identified weaknesses in the electoral process and systems as a major problem, an identified effect would be the low levels of public confidence in the electoral process. In examining this effect, stakeholders should assess what other factors may be contributing to it. In doing so, they may decide to either undertake a bigger project, or they may seek to influence other partners and non-partners to take other actions to solve the higher level effects.

NOTE The completed problem analysis would provide critical data for the CCA, UNDAF, CPD and CPAP. At the project level, this problem analysis would be done at the beginning of the 'defining a project' stage of the UNDP project cycle.

QUICK CHECKLIST FOR REVIEWING A PROBLEM TREE	YES	NO
✓ We have identified problems and causes that relate to the policy and legislative environment		
✓ We have identified problems and causes that relate to gaps in institutional capacities		
✓ We have identified problems and causes that relate to cultural and social norms		
✓ We have identified problems that affect men, women and marginalized populations, and the rights of different groups		
✓ We can see many layers of causes of the problems we have identified		
✓ We have defined the problems in the broadest terms, looking beyond the issues that individual agencies or stakeholders are concerned with		
✓ We have defined the problems and their causes without initially focusing only on the dimensions that one or more agencies have capacity to address through projects		

STEP 4: CREATING THE VISION OF THE FUTURE (DELIVERABLE SIX— THE VISION STATEMENT)

Based on the problem analysis, stakeholders should engage in a process of formulating solutions. This exercise may simply involve rewording the problems and their causes into positive statements or objectives. However, stakeholders should first engage in a visioning process before rewording the problems. The aim of this process is to visualize what the future would look like if the problems were resolved. The benefits of doing a visioning process before rewording the problems include the following:

■ Visioning brings energy to the group. Rather than immediately beginning another detailed process of working on each problem, groups can be energized by thinking positively about what the future would look like if these problems were solved. This exercise encourages creativity and helps ensure that the process is not too analytical and methodical.

TIP It is not necessary for all stakeholders who are involved in a problem analysis and visioning process to have prior knowledge or understanding of the results chain or logical framework model. In fact, **in the initial stages of the process, it can be very useful not to introduce any of the results matrix or logical framework terminologies** (such as outcomes and outputs), as this could result in extensive discussions about the meaning of terms and detract from the main aim of the exercise. In many project settings, especially where there are language barriers or differences in education or skills between members of the group, it may not be necessary to introduce the results matrix and logical framework model. Instead, the process could be approached in a less formal manner to obtain the same information and present it in different forms, including maps, diagrams and pictures.

- The vision of the future may identify additional ideas that would not have emerged if the process was confined to simply rewording problems into positive results.

- Visioning is a good way to engage members of the group who are not relating well to the more structured processes of problem analysis.

- Coming to a shared vision of the future can be a powerful launching pad for collective action.

Vision as the changes we want to see

The objective of the visioning exercise is for stakeholders to come up with a clear, realistic and agreed upon vision of how things will have positively changed in a period of time (normally 5 to 10 years). They should think in terms of how the region, society, community or affected people's lives will have improved within the time period. Good questions to ask are: "If we were successful in dealing with this problem, what would this region/country/community be like in five years?"; "What would have changed?"; "What would we see happening on the ground?"

Stakeholders should re-examine their problem analysis and reflect on what they have come up with. After initial reflections, group members should discuss the situation as it now is, assessing the extent to which the problem analysis represents a true picture of the current reality. After reviewing the current reality, stakeholders should visualize and describe what a better future (development change) would look like.

Once the visioning is complete, stakeholders should articulate their visions in one or more statements or use drawings and images. The vision should be a clear and realistic statement of the future, positive situation. Using the example from the problem tree, the group may develop a vision of a "vibrant democratic society in which all persons, including men, women, youth and minorities, have equal rights and actively

---

Box 9. Guides to use in visioning

- Do not focus on how the situation will be improved, or what needs to be done to change the current situation.

- Focus instead on what the future would look like: What is different in the community? How have people's lives changed? How have things improved for men? For women? For marginalized groups?

- Looking at this problem (for example, low public confidence and involvement in governance), what should the country be like in five years?
  - In what ways would the lives of women, indigenous and marginalized groups be different?
  - In what ways would government officials and regular citizens behave differently?
  - How have the capacities of people and institutions been strengthened and are they working more effectively?
  - In what ways are men and women relating to each other differently?
  - What else has changed as a result of an improvement in the problem of poor public confidence and involvement in governance?

participate in the political process and in shaping decisions that affect their lives." The vision can become an important tool for communicating the goals and objectives of the programme or project.

A **vision statement** can be created for each major problem that was identified and analysed. These statements become the **sixth deliverable** in the planning process. Once the broad vision statement is in place, stakeholders should be ready to embark on the next step.

> **NOTE** The vision statement can help in formulating the statements of regional and national goals and priorities in UNDAFs, CPDs, CPAPs, regional programme documents and project documents.

STEP 5: CREATING THE DRAFT RESULTS MAP (DELIVERABLE SEVEN)

This step provides guidance on how to create a draft results map using what is commonly referred to as a 'results mapping technique'. At the end of the section, the Handbook will illustrate how to convert the map into the specific tabular format used by UNDP.

Developing the draft results map can be time-consuming but is extremely worthwhile. The fundamental question that stakeholders in the planning session should answer is "What must be in place for us to achieve the vision and objectives that we have developed in the particular problem area?"

Creating a set of positive results

A good starting point in creating a results map is to take each major problem identified on the trunk of the problem tree and reword it as the immediate positive result with longer-term positive results or effects. For example, if the problem were stated as "low public confidence and involvement in governance" the immediate positive result could be "greater public confidence and involvement in governance." This could **lead to** longer term positive results such as "wider citizen participation in elections, particularly by women, indigenous and marginalized populations" and "greater compliance with public policies, particularly taxation policies."

Likewise, a challenge of "low levels of public confidence and involvement in electoral systems and processes, particularly among women, indigenous and other marginalized groups" could be translated into a positive result such as "greater public confidence and involvement in the electoral process, particularly by women, indigenous and other marginalized groups" **leading to** "higher levels of citizen participation in elections, particularly by women, indigenous and marginalized populations."

Results should be stated as clearly and concretely as possible. The group should refer back to its vision statement and see if there are additional long-term effects that are desired. These longer term effects should look like a positive rewording of the 'effects' identified on the problem tree. They should also be similar to, or form part of, the broader vision statement already developed.

Note that the **first or immediate positive result,** that is, the result derived from restating the major problem identified on the trunk of the problem tree, is the main result that the stakeholders will focus on. (Other stakeholders may focus on some of the higher level results, possibly in a UNDAF or National Development Strategy.)

With this immediate positive result, stakeholders should be able to prepare the map of results. A **results map (sometimes referred to as a results tree)** is essentially the reverse of the problem tree. In some planning exercises, stakeholders create this results map by continuing to reword each problem, cause and effect on the problem tree as a positive result. While this approach works, a more recommended approach involves asking the stakeholders "What must be in place for us to achieve the positive result we have identified?" When groups start with this approach, the process is often more enriching and brings new ideas to the table.

A key principle for developing the results map is working **backwards from the positive result.** Stakeholders should begin with the positive result identified in the step before. This is the statement that sets out what the situation should be once the main problem on the trunk of the tree is solved. The aim is then to map the complete set of lower level results (or conditions or prerequisites) that must be in place before this result can be realized. These are the main tasks for this exercise:

1. Stakeholders should write down both the immediate positive result and all the longer term results of effects that they are trying to achieve. Going back to our example, this positive result could be "greater public confidence and involvement in governance."

2. Stakeholders should then work backwards and document the major prerequisites and changes needed for this result. For example, using the result above, stakeholders might indicate that in order to achieve this, the country may need to have "greater public confidence in the electoral process and in government," "increased awareness among the population, and particularly by women and indigenous populations, of their democratic rights and of the responsibilities of the state," "improved capacity of the state electoral machinery to administer elections in a free and fair manner," "changes to government policy to make it easier for women and indigenous groups to exercise their democratic rights," "greater acceptance, tolerance and respect for minorities and indigenous populations," and so forth. **Stakeholders should compare these conditions and prerequisites with the set of underlying causes identified on the problem tree. The conditions should read like a solution to those causes or should be closely related to them. Note that while they should be closely related, they may not always be the same.**

3. Next, stakeholders should document other lower level prerequisites that are needed for the first set of changes and conditions to be in place. For example, in order to have "improved capacity of the state electoral machinery to administer elections" there may need to be "bi-partisan consensus between the major political

parties to improve electoral laws and the administration of the electoral system." These lower level results should be closely related to the lower level causes identified on the problem tree.

4. Stakeholders should note that these prerequisites are not actions that UNDP or any one group of stakeholders need to take, but rather the set of key things that must be in place. The question should be phrased as "If the country were successful in achieving this positive result we have identified, what would we see happening in the country or on the ground?", not "What should be done by UNDP or the government?"

5. Once the various prerequisite intermediate changes have been identified, stakeholders should then identify the interventions that are necessary to achieve them. At this point, only general interventions are necessary, not their implementation details. For example, "bi-partisan consensus on the need for reform of electoral laws and systems" may require "training and awareness programme for key parliamentarians on global practices and trends in electoral reform and administration" or "major advocacy programme aimed at fostering bi-partisan consensus." Likewise, a result relating to increased awareness of women, indigenous populations and other marginalized groups may require a mass-media communication programme, an advocacy initiative targeted at specific stakeholders, and so forth.

6. Throughout the process, stakeholders should think critically about specific interventions that may be needed to address the different needs of men, women and marginalized groups.

Stakeholders should be aware that the results map may need more thought and narrative documentation over time. In addition, the results map may change as stakeholders gain new information or more understanding about how the programme works or as they begin the implementation process. Therefore, the group should be open to revisiting and revising the map.

These maps initially avoid the traditional input-to-output-to-outcome linear tables, which tend to confine discussion to an agency's specific outputs. In this model, the process focuses on all the things that need to be in place, irrespective of who needs to produce them. Returning to our example, a basic results map may look like Figure 7.

In this example, stakeholders have begun to identify additional 'things' that must be in place (oval-shaped boxes), some of which could be developed as projects.

> **TIP** While lower level conditions or interventions are often referred to as outputs, every effort should be made not to label them as such at this stage of the exercise. If labeled as outputs or projects, the tendency will be to concentrate discussions on which agency or partner can produce the outputs, rather than on what needs to be in place, irrespective of whether there is existing capacity to produce it.

Figure 7. Basic results map (example)

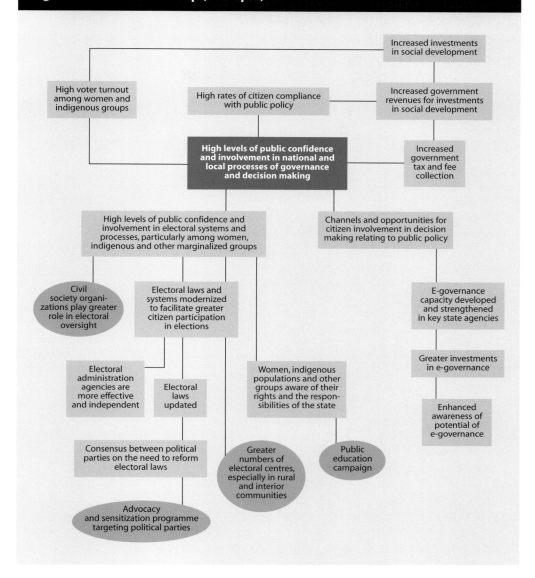

Box 10. Results map tips

■ Developing a results map is a team sport. The temptation is for one person to do it so that time is saved, but this can be ineffective in the long run.

■ Time needs to be taken to develop the map. The more care taken during this phase, the easier the job of monitoring and evaluation becomes later on.

■ In developing the map, focus should be on thinking through what needs to be on the ground in order to impact the lives of people. The exercise is not intended to be an academic exercise but rather one grounded in real changes that can improve people's lives—including men, women and marginalized groups.

In developing these models, stakeholders should consider not only the contributions (interventions, programmes and outputs) of UNDP, but also those of its partners and **non-partners**. This type of model can be extremely useful at the monitoring and evaluation stages, as it helps to capture some of the assumptions that went into designing the programmes. The draft results map is the **seventh deliverable** in the process.

> **NOTE** The completed results map would provide critical data for the UNDP 'defining a programme or project' phase of the programme and project cycle.

QUICK CHECKLIST FOR REVIEWING A RESULTS MAP	YES	NO
✓ We have identified results that relate to addressing policy and legislative constraints		
✓ We have identified results that relate to addressing gaps in institutional capacities		
✓ We have identified results that relate to addressing relevant cultural and social norms		
✓ We have identified results to improve the condition of men, women and marginalized groups		
✓ We have identified results that address the rights of different groups in society		
✓ We can see many layers of results		
✓ We have defined the results in broad terms, looking beyond the specific contribution of individual agencies or stakeholders		
✓ The results map provides us with a picture of the broad range of actions that will be needed (including advocacy and soft support) and does not only focus on projects or tangible outputs		
✓ The results map shows us where action will be needed by both partners and non-partners in our effort		

Identify unintended outcomes or effects and risks and assumptions

While elaborating the results map, stakeholders should note that sometimes well intentioned actions may lead to negative results. Additionally, there may be risks that could prevent the planned results from being achieved. Therefore, it is necessary to devote time to thinking through the various assumptions, risks and possible unintended effects or outcomes.

Assumptions are normally defined as "the necessary and positive conditions that allow for a successful cause-and-effect relationship between different levels of results." This means that when stakeholders think about the positive changes they would like to see and map the prerequisites for these changes, they are assuming that **once those things are in place the results will be achieved.** When a results map is being developed, there will always be these assumptions. The question to ask is: "If we say that having X in place should lead to Y, what are we assuming?" For example, if stakeholders say that having "high levels of public confidence and involvement in governance and decision making" should lead to "higher levels of voter turnout in elections particularly among marginalized and indigenous groups," then stakeholders should ask, "What are we assuming?" or "Under what conditions should this happen?" Often the assumptions relate to the context within which stakeholders will work towards the desired results. In many situations, interventions are designed assuming the government will take action or allocate resources to support achievement of results. There is often a general assumption of continued social, economic and political stability within the programme's environment.

Stating assumptions enrich programme design by identifying additional results or inputs that should be included. They also help identify risks. Assumptions may be internal or external to UNDP and the particular programme. When an assumption fails to hold, results may be compromised (see Figure 8).

The assumptions that are made at the lowest levels of the results map can be expected to come true in most cases. For example, if stakeholders had stated that having "a good mass-media communication programme" and "an advocacy initiative targeted at specific stakeholders" should result in "increased awareness of women, indigenous populations, and other marginalized groups," they may have assumed that sufficient resources would be mobilized by the partners to implement communication and awareness programmes.

A different example is a situation where the result of "high levels of public confidence and involvement in governance and decision making" was expected to lead to "higher voter turnout." The stakeholders in this situation may have assumed that sufficient budgetary resources would be allocated to constructing voting centres and improving roads used by rural marginalized populations to get to voting centres.

It could be argued that the assumption in the first example of being able to mobilize resources for the communication and advocacy campaigns is more probable than the assumption in the second example relating to the higher level result. This is because stakeholders usually have a higher level of influence on the lower level results and assumptions.

Additional examples of assumptions include the following:

- Priorities will remain unchanged over the planning period
- The political roundtable agreement for bi-partisan consensus will be adopted as expected

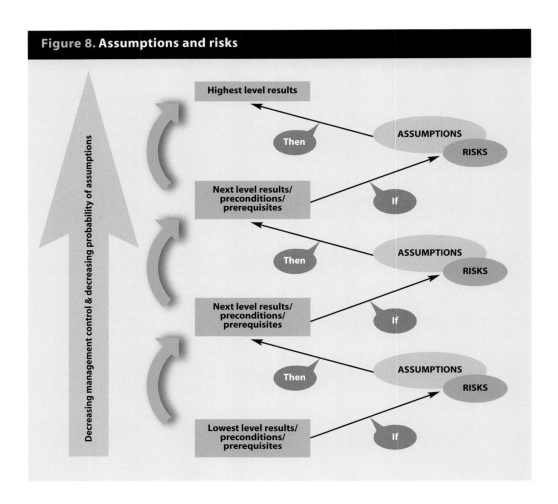

Figure 8. Assumptions and risks

- Political, economic and social stability in the country or region
- Planned budget allocations to support the electoral process are actually made
- Resource mobilization targets for interventions are achieved

At this stage, stakeholders should review their results map and, for each level result, ask: "What are we assuming will happen for this result to lead to the next higher result?" The list of assumptions generated should be written on the results map.

TIP Though stakeholders will focus most of their effort on achieving the positive result that they have developed, they must remain aware of the longer term vision and changes that they want to see. The assumptions stage is generally a good time to ask: "If we achieve the positive result we have identified, will we in fact see the longer term benefits or effects that we want?" and "What are we assuming?" In this process of thinking through the assumptions being made about the context, environment and actions that partners and non-partners should take, useful ideas may emerge that could inform advocacy and other efforts aimed at encouraging action by others.

Risks are potential events or occurrences beyond the control of the programme that could adversely affect the achievement of results. While risks are outside the direct control of the government or UNDP, steps can be taken to mitigate their effects. Risks should be assessed in terms of probability (likelihood to occur) and potential impact. Should they occur, risks may trigger the reconsideration of the overall programme and its direction. Risks are similar to assumptions in that the question stakeholders ask is: "What might happen to prevent us from achieving the results?" However, risks are not simply the negative side of an assumption. The assumption relates to a condition that should be in place for the programme to go ahead, and the probability of this condition occurring should be high. For example, in one country there could be an assumption that there will be no decrease in government spending for the programme. This should be the assumption if the stakeholders believe that the probability that there will not be a decrease is high. Risks, however, relate to the possibility of external negative events occurring that could jeopardize the success of the programme. There should be a moderate to high probability that the risks identified will occur. For example, in another country stakeholders could identify a risk of government spending being cut due to a drought, which may affect government revenue. The probability of the spending cut occurring should be moderate to high based on what is known.

Risk examples include the following:

- Ethnic tensions rise, leading to hostilities particularly against minorities
- Result of local government elections leads to withdrawal of political support for the electoral reform agenda
- Planned merger of the Department of the Interior and Office of the Prime Minister leads to deterioration of support for gender equality strategies and programmes
- Project manager leaves, leading to significant delays in project implementation (this type of risk could come during the project implementation stage)

Stakeholders should therefore again review their results map and try to identify any important risks that could affect the achievement of results. These risks should be noted beside the assumptions for each level of result.

The checklist on the following page can assist in reviewing risks and assumptions.

Unintended outcomes

Programmes and projects can lead to unintended results or consequences. These are another form of risk. They are not risks that a programme's or project's activities will not happen, but are risks that they will happen and may lead to undesirable results.

Once the results, assumptions and risks are in place, stakeholders should discuss and document any possible unintended results or consequences. The discussion should

QUICK CHECKLIST FOR VALIDATING ASSUMPTIONS AND RISKS	YES	NO
✓ The assumed condition is outside the control of the programme or project		
✓ The assumed condition is necessary for programme success.		
✓ The assumed condition is **not** a result that could be included in the results framework		
✓ There is a **high probability** that the assumption will hold true		
✓ The assumption is specific and verifiable—its status can be checked by calling partners or donors		
✓ The assumption is stated as if it is actually the case		
✓ The risk is clearly beyond the control of the programme		
✓ The risk is NOT simply the negative restating of an assumption		
✓ The consequences of the risk are sufficiently grave as to pose a serious threat to overall programme success		
✓ There is a **moderate to high probability** that the risk may occur		

centre around the actions that may be necessary to ensure that those unintended results do not occur. This may require other small adjustments to the results map—such as the addition of other conditions, prerequisites or interventions. It is not necessary to put the unintended results on the map itself.

Box 11. An unintended result: "Our husbands weren't ready for these changes"

In one country, an evaluation was conducted on a programme designed to train and provide capital to women micro-entrepreneurs. The programme was part of a broader strategy aimed at fostering women's empowerment through increased income and livelihood opportunities. The evaluation found that the intended results were achieved: The training and micro-enterprise programme were successful and women who participated in the programme saw an increase in self-employment and income. Moreover, the women felt more empowered to make decisions for themselves and within their households.

However, the evaluation also found that many of the women were unhappy at the end of the programme, as there had been an increase in marital and partner problems and a few relationships had ended as a result of the changes in the women's empowerment. Some of the women reported that their partners were not prepared for these changes and did not know how to relate to them. They suggested that maybe these problems could have been less had there been some counseling provided to their partners at the beginning and during the programme to better prepare them for the coming changes.

2.4 FINALIZING THE RESULTS FRAMEWORK (DELIVERABLE EIGHT)

At this stage of the process, stakeholders should be ready to begin converting the results map into a results framework. In many situations, a smaller group of stakeholders are engaged in this undertaking. However, the wider group can participate in preparing a rough draft of the framework, using simple techniques and without going into the details and mechanics of RBM terminologies.

CREATING THE DRAFT RESULTS FRAMEWORK

Table 5 provides a starting point for converting the results map into a draft framework for UNCT and UNDP programme and project documents. It shows how to translate some of the general terms and questions used in the planning session into the common programming language used by UNCTs and UNDP. The table can be used to produce an **initial draft** of the results framework with all or most stakeholders. It can be particularly helpful at the project level or in situations involving a diverse group of stakeholders.

Table 5. Rough guide for creating an initial draft of the results framework	
Questions and General Terminologies	**Equivalent UNDP RBM Terminology**
Terms such as: vision, goal, objective, longer term outcome, long-term results **Questions such as:** What are we trying to achieve? Why are we working on this problem? What is our overall goal?	**Impact**
Terms such as: first, positive result or immediate result, prerequisites, short- and medium-term results **Questions such as:** Where do we want to be in five years? What are the most immediate things we are trying to change? What are the things that must be in place first before we can achieve our goals and have an impact?	**Outcome**
Terms such as: interventions, programmes **Questions such as:** What are the things that need to be produced or provided through projects or programmes for us to achieve our short- to medium-term results? What are the things that different stakeholders must provide?	**Outputs**
Terms such as: actions **Questions such as:** What needs to be done to produce these outputs?	**Activities**
Terms such as: measure, performance measurement, performance standard **Questions such as:** How will we know if we are on track to achieve what we have planned?	**Indicators**[17]
Terms such as: data sources, evidence **Questions such as:** What precise information do we need to measure our performance? How will we obtain this information? How much will it cost? Can the information be monitored?	**Means of verification**[17]

---

17 Because of the relative complexity, we have not introduced indicators and means of verification up to this point, so it would not be necessary to have the sections for indicators and means of verification filled in for the draft results framework.

FORMULATING STRONG RESULTS AND INDICATORS

Having a smaller group of persons with greater familiarity with RBM terminologies usually helps when undertaking this task. This is because it may be difficult to make progress with a large group given the technicalities involved in articulating the results framework. However, when using a smaller group, the information should be shared with the wider group for review and validation. In doing this, exercise stakeholders should:

- Use a version of Table 6.

- Refer to the guidance below on formulating the various components of the framework.

- Complete a table for each major result. Each major result (outcome) may have one or more related impacts. The expected impacts should be filled in for each major result (outcome). Likewise each outcome will have one or more outputs and so forth.

Good quality results—that is, well formulated impacts, outcomes, outputs, activities and indicators of progress—are crucial for proper monitoring and evaluation. If results are unclear and indicators are absent or poorly formulated, monitoring and evaluating progress will be challenging, making it difficult for staff and managers to know how well plans are progressing and when to take corrective actions.

The RBM terms used in this section are the harmonized terms of the UNDG, and are in line with the Organisation for Economic Co-operation and Development-Development Assistance Committee (OECD-DAC) definitions.

Table 6. The results framework					
Results	**Indicators**	**Baseline**	**Target**	**Means of Verification**	**Risks & Assumptions**
Impact statement (*Ultimate benefits for target population*)	Measure of progress against impact				Assumptions made from outcome to impact. Risks that impact will not be achieved.
Outcome statement (*Short- to medium-term change in development situation*)	Measure of progress against outcome				Assumptions made from outputs to outcome. Risks that outcome will not be achieved.
Outputs (*Products and services—tangible and intangible—delivered or provided*)	Measure of progress against output				Assumptions made from activities to outputs. Risks that outputs may not be produced.
Activities (*Tasks undertaken in order to produce research outputs*)	Milestones or key targets for production of outputs				Preconditions for implementation of activities.

RESULTS AND RESULTS CHAIN

The planning exercise up to this point should have led to the creation of many results and an overall results map. These results and the results map can be converted into a results chain and results framework using the standard RBM approach and terminologies.

First, a 'result' is a defined as a describable or measurable development change resulting from a cause-and-effect relationship. Different levels of results seek to capture different development changes. The planning exercise (see Section 2.3) led to the creation of various results that were labeled as visions, effects, results, preconditions, prerequisites, interventions and so on. In the traditional RBM approach, these results are linked together into what is commonly referred to as a results chain. The results chain essentially tells us what stakeholders want to achieve, why they want to achieve it and how they will go about it. This is not very different from the results map. Now we will convert those results into more specific RBM language and begin to add performance measures to them.

As shown in the draft results framework (Table 5), the vision and longer term goals developed in the results mapping exercise are the impacts that will appear in the results framework, the immediate positive results and some of their preconditions and prerequisites will appear as outcomes, lower-level prerequisites will appear as outputs, and so on. These can be shown in the format of a results chain where the lowest level prerequisites are labeled as inputs and the highest as impacts, as illustrated in Figure 9.

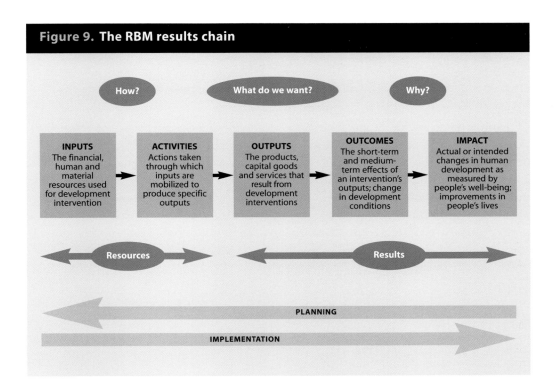

Figure 9. The RBM results chain

FORMULATING THE IMPACT STATEMENT

Impacts are actual or intended changes in human development as measured by people's well-being. Impacts generally capture changes in people's lives.

The completion of activities tells us little about changes in development conditions or in the lives of people. It is the results of these activities that are significant. Impact refers to the 'big picture' changes being sought and represents the **underlying goal** of development work. In the process of planning, it is important to frame planned interventions or outputs within a context of their desired impact. Without a clear vision of what the programme or project hopes to achieve, it is difficult to clearly define results. An impact statement explains why the work is important and can inspire people to work toward a future to which their activities contribute.

Similar to outcomes, an impact statement should ideally use a verb expressed in the past tense, such as 'improved', 'strengthened', 'increased', 'reversed' or 'reduced'. They are used in relation to the global, regional, national or local **social, economic and political conditions** in which people live. Impacts are normally formulated to communicate substantial and direct changes in these conditions over the long term—such as reduction in poverty and improvements in people's health and welfare, environmental conditions or governance. The MDG and other international, regional and national indicators are generally used to track progress at the impact level.

Using the example from the results map (Section 2.3, step 5), some of the longer term impacts could be "increased public participation in national and local elections, particularly by women, indigenous populations and other traditionally marginalized groups" and "strengthened democratic processes and enhanced participation by all citizens in decisions that affect their lives." These impacts would be part of the broader vision of a more vibrant and democratic society.

FORMULATING THE OUTCOME STATEMENT

Outcomes are actual or intended changes in development conditions that interventions are seeking to support.

Outcomes describe the intended changes in development conditions that result from the interventions of governments and other stakeholders, including international development agencies such as UNDP. They are medium-term development results created through the delivery of outputs and the contributions of various partners and non-partners. Outcomes provide a clear vision of what has changed or will change globally or in a particular region, country or community within a period of time. They normally relate to **changes in institutional performance or behaviour** among individuals or groups. Outcomes cannot normally be achieved by only one agency and are not under the direct control of a project manager.

Since outcomes occupy the middle ground between outputs and impact, it is possible to define outcomes with differing levels of ambition. For this reason, some documents may refer to immediate, intermediate and longer term outcomes, or short-, medium- and long-term outcomes. The United Nations uses two linked outcome level results that reflect different levels of ambition:

- UNDAF outcomes

- Agency or country programme outcomes

UNDAF outcomes are the strategic, high-level results expected from UN system cooperation with government and civil society. They are highly ambitious, nearing impact-level change. UNDAF outcomes are produced by the combined effects of the lower-level, country programme outcomes. They usually require contribution by two or more agencies working closely together with their government and civil society partners.

Country programme outcomes are usually the result of programmes of cooperation or larger projects of individual agencies and their national partners. The achievement of country programme outcomes depends on the commitment and action of partners.

When formulating an outcome statement to be included in a UNDP programme document, managers and staff are encouraged to specify these outcomes at a level where UNDP and its partners (and non-partners) can have a reasonable degree of influence. In other words, if the national goals reflect changes at a national level, and the UNDAF outcomes exist as higher level and strategic development changes, then the outcomes in UNDP programme documents should reflect the comparative advantage of and be stated at a level where it is possible to show that the UNDP contribution can reasonably help influence the achievement of the outcome. For example, in a situation where UNDP is supporting the government and other stakeholders in improving the capacity of the electoral administration agency to better manage elections, outcomes should not be stated as "improved national capacities" to perform the stated functions, but rather "improved capacities of the electoral adminis-tration bodies" to do those functions. "Improved national capacity" may imply that all related government ministries and agencies have improved capacity and may even imply that this capacity is also improved within non-government bodies. If this was indeed the intention, then "improved national capacities" could be an accurate outcome. However, the general rule is that government and UNDP programme outcomes should be fairly specific in terms of what UNDP is contributing, while being broad enough to capture the efforts of other partners and non-partners working towards that specific change.

An outcome statement should ideally use a verb expressed in the past tense, such as 'improved', 'strengthened' or 'increased', in relation to a global, regional, national or local process or institution. An outcome should not be stated as "UNDP support provided to Y" or "technical advice provided in support of Z," but should specify the result of UNDP efforts and that of other stakeholders for the people of that country.

- An outcome statement should avoid phrases such as "to assist/support/develop/ monitor/identify/follow up/prepare X or Y."

- Similarly, an outcome should not describe how it will be achieved and should avoid phrases such as "improved through" or "supported by means of."

	Figure 10. SMART outcomes and impacts
S	**Specific:** Impacts and outcomes and outputs must use change language—they must describe a specific future condition
M	**Measurable:** Results, whether quantitative or qualitative, must have measurable indicators, making it possible to assess whether they were achieved or not
A	**Achievable:** Results must be within the capacity of the partners to achieve
R	**Relevant:** Results must make a contribution to selected priorities of the national development framework
T	**Time-bound:** Results are never open-ended—there is an expected date of accomplishment

- An outcome should be measurable using indicators. It is important that the formulation of the outcome statement takes into account the need to measure progress in relation to the outcome and to verify when it has been achieved. The outcome should therefore be specific, measurable, achievable, relevant and time-bound (SMART).

- An outcome statement should ideally communicate a change in institutional or individual behaviour or quality of life for people—however modest that change may be.

The following illustrate different levels of outcomes:

- Policy, legal and regulatory framework reformed to substantially expand connectivity to information and communication technologies (short to medium term)

- Increased access of the poor to financial products and services in rural communities (medium to long term)

- Reduction in the level of domestic violence against women in five provinces by 2014 (medium to long term)

- Increased volume of regional and subregional trade by 2015 (medium to long term)

Using the previous elections example, the outcome at the country programme level may be "enhanced electoral management systems and processes to support free and fair elections" or "electoral administrative policies and systems reformed to ensure freer and fairer elections and to facilitate participation by marginalized groups."

FORMULATING THE OUTPUT STATEMENT

Outputs are short-term development results produced by project and non-project activities. They must be achieved with the resources provided and within the time-frame specified (usually less than five years).

Since outputs are the most immediate results of programme or project activities, they are usually within the greatest control of the government, UNDP or the project manager. It is important to define outputs that are likely to make a significant contribution to achievement of the outcomes.

In formulating outputs, the following questions should be addressed:

- What kind of policies, guidelines, agreements, products and services do we need in order to achieve a given outcome?

- Are they attainable and within our direct control?

- Do these outputs reflect an appropriate strategy for attaining the outcome? Is there a proper cause and effect relationship?

- Do we need any additional outputs to mitigate potential risks that may prevent us from reaching the outcome?

- Is the output SMART—specific, measurable, achievable, relevant and time-bound?

It is important to bear in mind:

- Outputs must be deliverable within the respective programming cycle.

- Typically, more than one output is needed to obtain an outcome.

- If the result is mostly beyond the control or influence of the programme or project, it cannot be an output.

Outputs generally include a **noun** that is qualified by a *verb* describing positive change. For example:

- **Study of environment-poverty linkages** *completed*

- **Police forces and judiciary** *trained* in understanding gender violence

- **National, participatory forum** *convened* to discuss draft national anti-poverty strategy

- **National human development report** *produced* and *disseminated*

Returning to our example, there could be a number of outputs related to the outcome "electoral management policies and systems reformed to ensure freer and fairer elections and to facilitate participation by marginalized groups." Outputs could include:

- **Advocacy campaign** aimed at building consensus on need for electoral law and system reform *developed* and *implemented*

- Systems and procedures *implemented* and competencies *developed* in the **national electoral management agency** to administer free and fair elections

- **Training programme** on use of new electoral management technology *designed* and *implemented* for staff of electoral management authority

- **Revised draft legislation on rights of women and indigenous populations to participate in elections** *prepared*

- **Electoral dispute resolution mechanism** *established*

FORMULATING THE ACTIVITIES

Activities describe the actions that are needed to obtain the stated outputs. They are the coordination, technical assistance and training tasks organized and executed by project personnel.

In an RBM context, carrying out or completing a programme or project activity does not constitute a development result. Activities relate to the processes involved in generating tangible goods and services or outputs, which in turn contribute to outcomes and impacts.

In formulating activities the following questions should be addressed:

- What actions are needed in order to obtain the output?
- Will the combined number of actions ensure that the output is produced?
- What resources (inputs) are necessary to undertake these activities?

It is important to bear in mind:

- Activities usually provide quantitative information and they may indicate periodicity of the action.
- Typically, more than one activity is needed to achieve an output.

Activities generally start with a *verb* and describe an activity or action. Using our example, activities could include:

- *Provide* technical assistance by experts in the area of electoral law reform
- *Develop* and deliver training and professional development programmes for staff
- *Organize* workshops and seminars on electoral awareness
- *Publish* newsletters and pamphlets on electoral rights of women and minorities
- *Procure* equipment and supplies for Electoral Management Authority
- *Engage* consultants to draft revised electoral laws

FORMULATING INPUTS

Inputs are essentially the things that must be put in or invested in order for activities to take place.

Though not dealt with in detail in this manual, inputs are also part of the results chain. Inputs include the time of staff, stakeholders and volunteers; money; consultants; equipment; technology; and materials. The general tendency is to use money as the main input, as it covers the cost of consultants, staff, materials, and so forth. However, in the early stages of planning, effort should be spent on identifying the various resources needed before converting them into monetary terms.

The guidance above should help to prepare the first column ('results') in the results framework.

Table 7. The 'results' sections of the results framework

Results
Impact statement *Ultimate benefits for target population*
Outcome statement *Short to medium-term change in development situation* Normally more than one outcome will be needed to attain the impact
Outputs *Products and services (tangible/intangible) delivered or provided* Normally more than one output will be needed to achieve the outcome
Activities *Tasks undertaken in order to produce research outputs* Each output normally has a number of activities

Box 12. Note on results framework

The results framework can be completed with all the outcomes, outputs, activities and inputs that the stakeholders have identified. However, in many cases, a more limited framework showing only the specific outcomes and outputs related to a particular agency (such as UNDP) and its partners will be needed to satisfy internal requirements. In these cases where a more focused results framework is created, every effort should be made to show information on the broader agenda of actions being pursued and the partners and non-partners working towards achieving the overall outcomes and impacts in the narrative of the wider strategy document (such as the UNDAF; the global, regional or country programme action plan; or the project document). The strategy document should not be confined to only what the agency will produce. It should instead show how the efforts of different stakeholders will contribute to the achievement of the common overall vision and intended impacts. This will also aid the monitoring and evaluation processes.

FORMULATING PERFORMANCE INDICATORS

Indicators are signposts of change along the path to development. They describe the way to track intended results and are critical for monitoring and evaluation.

Good performance indicators are a critical part of the results framework. In particular, indicators can help to:

- Inform decision making for ongoing programme or project management

- Measure progress and achievements, as understood by the different stakeholders

- Clarify consistency between activities, outputs, outcomes and impacts

- Ensure legitimacy and accountability to all stakeholders by demonstrating progress

- Assess project and staff performance[18]

18 UNDP, 'RBM in UNDP: Selecting Indicators', 2002, p 3.

Indicators may be used at any point along the results chain of activities, outputs, outcomes and impacts, but must always directly relate to the result being measured. Some important points include the following:

- **Who** sets indicators is fundamental, not only to ownership and transparency but also to the effectiveness of the indicators. Setting objectives and indicators should be a participatory process.

- A **variety** of indicator types is more likely to be effective. The demand for objective verification may mean that focus is given to the quantitative or simplistic at the expense of indicators that are harder to verify but may better capture the essence of the change taking place.

- The fewer the indicators the better. Measuring change is costly so use as few indicators as possible. However, there must be indicators in sufficient number to measure the breadth of changes happening and to provide cross-checking.

Box 13. Note on performance indicators

A frequent weakness seen in formulating indicators is the tendency to use general and purely quantitative indicators that measure number or percentage of something, for example, "number of new policies passed." These are often weak indicators as they merely communicate that something has happened but not whether what has happened is an important measure of the objective. For example, take a situation where an audit report finds 10 weaknesses in a business unit, 3 of which are considered serious and the other 7 routine. If the 7 routine issues were dealt with, an indicator that measures performance as "number or percentage of recommendations acted on" may capture the fact that some action has been taken but not convey a sense of whether these are the important actions.

In general, indicators should direct focus to **what is critical.** For example, there could be different ways of measuring whether an outcome relating to greater **commitment** by government partners to HIV/AIDS concerns is being realized.

Examine the following indicator: **"Number of government ministries that have an HIV/AIDS sector strategy."**

Now compare it with another quantitative indicator such as: **"Number of government ministries that have an HIV/AIDS sector strategy developed in consultation with non-governmental stakeholders."**

And further compare it with a possible **qualitative** indicator: **"Number of government ministries that have a strong HIV/AIDS sector strategy."**

Measured by:

- Strategy was developed in **consultation** with non-government stakeholders (X points)
- Ministry's **senior officials** involved in strategy development and implementation processes (X points)
- Ministry has in place a **budget** to finance implementation of strategy (X points)

In the first case, a strategy could have been designed with no stakeholder involvement, no senior management engagement and no budget. Simply counting the number of ministries that have done this would not be a measure of real progress against the outcome that deals with the real commitment of the government partners.

Box 14. SMART indicators

Specific: Is the indicator specific enough to measure progress towards the results?

Measurable: Is the indicator a reliable and clear measure of results?

Attainable: Are the results in which the indicator seeks to chart progress realistic?

Relevant: Is the indicator relevant to the intended outputs and outcomes?

Time-bound: Are data available at reasonable cost and effort?

The process of formulating indicators should begin with the following questions:

- How can we measure that the expected results are being achieved?
- What type of information can demonstrate a positive change?
- What can be feasibly monitored with given resource and capacity constraints?
- Will timely information be available for the different monitoring exercises?
- What will the system of data collection be and who will be responsible?
- Can national systems be used or augmented?
- Can government indicators be used?[19]

Quantitative and qualitative indicators

Indicators can either be quantitative or qualitative. Quantitative indicators are statistical measures that measure results in terms of:

- Number
- Percentage
- Rate (example: birth rate—births per 1,000 population)
- Ratio (example: sex ratio—number of males per number of females)

Qualitative indicators reflect people's judgements, opinions, perceptions and attitudes towards a given situation or subject. They can include changes in sensitivity, satisfaction, influence, awareness, understanding, attitudes, quality, perception, dialogue or sense of well-being.

Qualitative indicators measure results in terms of:

- Compliance with…
- Quality of…
- Extent of…
- Level of …

Note that in the example used in Box 13 on the commitment of government partners, subindicators are being used to assess the **quality** of the strategy, "Did it benefit from

---

19 OCHA, 'Guidelines: Results-Oriented Planning & Monitoring', 2007, p. 11.

the involvement of other stakeholders?"; **the extent** of senior management engagement; and the **level of** commitment, "Is there also a budget in place?"

As far as possible, indicators should be disaggregated. Averages tend to hide disparities, and recognizing disparities is essential for programming to address the special needs of groups such as women, indigenous groups and marginalized populations. Indicators can be disaggregated by sex, age, geographic area and ethnicity, among other things.

The key to good indicators is credibility—not volume of data or precision in measurement. Large volumes of data can confuse rather than bring focus and a quantitative observation is no more inherently objective than a qualitative observation. An indicator's suitability depends on how it relates to the result it intends to describe.

Proxy indicators

In some instances, data will not be available for the most suitable indicators of a particular result. In these situations, stakeholders should use proxy indicators. Proxy indicators are a less direct way of measuring progress against a result.

For example, take the outcome: "improved capacity of local government authorities to deliver solid waste management services in an effective and efficient manner." Some possible **direct** indicators could include:

- Hours of down time (out-of-service time) of solid waste vehicle fleet due to maintenance and other problems
- Percentage change in number of households serviced weekly
- Percentage change in number of commercial properties serviced weekly
- Percentage of on-time pick-ups of solid waste matter in [specify] region within last six-month period

Assuming no system is in place to track these indicators, a possible **proxy or indirect indicator** could be:

- A survey question capturing the percentage of clients satisfied with the quality and timeliness of services provided by the solid waste management service. (The agency may find it easier to undertake a survey than to introduce the systems to capture data for the more direct indicators.)

The assumption is that if client surveys show increased satisfaction, then it may be reasonable to assume some improvements in services. However, this may not be the case, which is why the indicator is seen as a proxy, rather than a direct measure of the improvement.

Similarly, in the absence of reliable data on corruption in countries, many development agencies use the information from surveys that capture the perception of corruption by many national and international actors as a proxy indicator.

In the Human Development Index, UNDP and other UN organizations use 'life expectancy' as a proxy indicator for health care and living conditions. The assumption is that if people live longer, then it is reasonable to assume that health care and living conditions have improved. Real gross domestic product/capita (purchasing power parity) is also used in the same indicator as a proxy indicator for disposable income.

Levels of indicators

Different types of indicators are required to assess progress towards results. Within the RBM framework, UNDP uses three types of indicators:

- Impact indicators
- Outcome indicators
- Output indicators

Impact indicators describe the changes in people's lives and development conditions at global, regional and national levels. In the case of community-level initiatives, impact indicators can describe such changes at the subnational and community levels. They provide a broad picture of whether the development changes that matter to people and UNDP are actually occurring. In the context of country-level planning (CPD), impact indicators are often at the UNDAF and MDG levels, and often appear in the UNDAF results framework. Impact indicators are most relevant to global, regional and national stakeholders and senior members of the UNCT for use in monitoring. Table 8 includes some examples of impact indicators.

Table 8. Impact indicators	
Sample Impacts	**Sample Indicators (i.e., "What can we see to know if change is happening?")**
■ Increased public participation in national and local elections, particularly by women, indigenous populations and other traditionally marginalized groups	■ Overall proportion of eligible voters who vote in the national (or local) elections ■ Percentage of eligible women who vote in the elections ■ Percentage of eligible indigenous people who vote in elections
■ Improved educational performance of students in region of the country	■ Percentage of students completing primary schooling ■ Pass rates in standardized student tests
■ Reduction in poverty and hunger	■ Poverty rate ■ Gini coefficient ■ Percentage of population living in extreme poverty ■ Level of infant malnutrition
■ People are healthier and live longer	■ Longevity ■ Infant mortality ■ HIV/AIDS prevalence rate

NOTE Outcome indicators are not intended to only measure what an agency (such as UNDP) does or its contribution. They are indicators of change in development conditions and are therefore expected to be at a higher level than the indicators of the agency's outputs.

Table 9. Outcome indicators

Sample Outcomes	Sample Indicators (i.e., "What can we see to know if change is happening?")
■ Electoral administrative policies and systems reformed to ensure freer and fairer elections and to facilitate participation by marginalized groups	■ Percentage of citizens surveyed that believe that the electoral management process is free and fair. (This is a proxy indicator. Instead of a general survey of citizens, a more limited survey could be done of a selected group of persons as well.) ■ Percentage of women and minorities surveyed that are aware of their rights under the new electoral administration laws. ■ Annual percentage increase in number of women registered to vote. (This is an intermediate indicator of progress, getting to the point when the impact indicator of how many of these groups actually vote can be measured.) ■ Annual percentage increase in number of indigenous people registered to vote. ■ Ratio of voter registration centres per population in rural areas.
■ Policy, legal and regulatory framework reformed to substantially expand connectivity to information and communication technologies	■ Number and proportion of the population with access to the Internet, disaggregated by gender. (This could be occurring without the changes to the framework. It is useful to track an indicator of this nature because it goes beyond the immediate result and looks at the impacts that partners are concerned with.) ■ Number of key national policies on information technology that are revised and promulgated. (For example, this could be used where it is known that there are a few specific legislations that need to be reformed.)
■ Improved e-governance capacity of key central government ministries and agencies by 2015	■ Extent to which key central government bodies have strong online facilities for citizen engagement. This is measured by composite indicator totaling a selected number of points: ● Key central government ministries have websites established (10 points) ● Websites contain functional contact information (10 points) ● Websites provide functional access to major government policy documents and publications (10 points) ● Websites facilitate access to persons with disabilities (or is available in second language) (10 points) ● Websites provide links to other major government departments (10 points) ● Websites facilitate online payment for important government services (taxes, motor vehicle registration, etc.) (10 points) ■ Percentage of property tax revenue collected through online payment systems.
■ Reduced levels of corruption in the public sector by 2016	■ Corruption perception index. (This is usually measured by a composite survey indicator of the perceptions of national and international experts and the general population about corruption in the country.) ■ Overall conclusion or rating of government performance in addressing corruption in the Independent Audit Office Annual Report.
■ Reduction in level of violence against women by 2013	■ Number of reported cases of domestic abuse against women.[20] ■ Percentage of women who feel that violence against women has reduced within the last five years (based on survey). ■ Proportion of men who believe that wife beating is justified for at least one reason (based on survey).

---

20 Care has to be taken in using indicators of this nature. In some cases, particularly where awareness programmes are implemented, reported cases may spike as more persons become aware and feel empowered to report cases. Over time, however, there should be a gradual reduction in the number of reported cases. A complementary indicator could track number of reported cases of violence against women at medical facilities. This might remove some of the element of awareness and examine cases where persons are being hurt to the extent that they need treatment.

Outcome indicators assess progress against specified outcomes. They help verify that the intended positive change in the development situation has actually taken place. Outcome indicators are designed within the results framework of global, regional and country programmes. Outcome indicators are most often useful to the UN organization and its partners working on the specific outcome. Table 9 gives a few examples.

In the second example in Table 9, an indicator on whether policies are being changed is used together with one on number of people with access to the Internet to give a broad and complementary view of overall progress against the outcome. It is often necessary to use a set of complementary indicators to measure changes attributable to reasons other than the intervention in question. Also, composite indicators can be used to provide more qualitative measures of progress. Stakeholders can agree on their own composite indicators in areas where no good composite indicator already exists.

Output indicators assess progress against specified outputs. Since outputs are tangible and deliverable, their indicators may be easier to identify. In fact, the output itself may be measurable and serve as its own indication of whether or not it has been produced. Table 10 includes some examples.

Table 10. Output indicators	
Sample Outputs	**Sample Indicators (i.e., "What can we see to know if change is happening?")**
■ Draft new policy on electoral reform formulated and submitted to Cabinet	■ Level of progress made in drafting new policy (see Box 15)
■ National electoral management agency has systems, procedures and competencies to administer free and fair elections	■ Percentage of electoral centres using multiple forms of voter identification measures ■ Number of centres that are headed by trained professional staff ■ Percentage of electoral management office staff and volunteers trained in techniques to reduce voter fraud ■ Percentage of electoral management office staff who believe that their agency is more professional and better run than one year ago
■ District school teachers trained	■ Number of teachers trained by end of 2010 ■ Percentage of teachers trained that were rated as more effective in doing their jobs one year later*
■ National human development report produced and disseminated	■ Number of copies of National Human Development Report distributed ■ Percentage of parliamentarians who receive copy ■ Extent to which National Human Development Report findings and recommendations were used to inform high-level policy discussions (can be composite indicator that looks at whether there was a discussion in Parliament, Cabinet, Meeting of Social Policy Ministers, etc. to discuss findings) *
■ Civil society and community organiza-tions in region have resources and skills to contribute to monitor-ing of local poverty reduction strategies	■ Number of NGO staff completing training courses in poverty analysis by end of 2009 ■ Percentage of trained NGO staff who feel that they are more effective at doing their jobs one year later* ■ Percentage of districts with Monitoring Committees ■ Percentage of districts with Citizen Community Boards

*These indicators represent **result** type indicators. It is useful to have at least two indicators for an output: one **process** indicator that gives an idea as to whether the product or service was completed or delivered, and one **result** indicator that addresses whether the completed output is bringing about intended changes. In this way, programme and project managers can discuss not only the progress of planned outputs and activities, but the quality and impact of those outputs and activities.

Box 15. Using 'level of progress made' as an output indicator

In many situations, people struggle with what type of indicator to use for certain outcomes, particularly where counting numbers of things produced may not be meaningful. In this Handbook, we suggest that for certain complex outputs or those outputs, where the quality and not the number of what is produced is most critical, one indicator could be 'level of progress made'. Targets would be set for the level of progress to be made each year. These level-of-progress indicators can be complemented by client satisfaction indicators assessing the extent to which persons were satisfied with what was produced.

QUICK CHECKLIST FOR REVIEWING OUTCOMES AND OUTCOME INDICATORS	YES	NO
✔ The outcomes and their indicators are specific, measurable, achievable, realistic and time-bound (SMART).		
✔ The outcomes clearly outline an area of work where the agency and its partners can have significant influence.		
✔ The outcomes are worded in such a way that they communicate what has changed, for whom (if relevant) and by when. (Outcomes should generally be achievable within five years.)		
✔ The outcomes clearly address the interests and concerns of men, women and marginalized groups (if relevant).		
✔ The outcomes address changes in institutional capacities and behaviour that should lead to sustainable development of the country or region.		
✔ The outcomes speak to changes in conditions and capacities and not delivery of products and services.		
✔ The outcomes have indicators that signal how the desired change will be measured.		
✔ The outcome indicators are measures of change that go beyond what one agency will produce or deliver. They are measures of change in the country or region and not measures of what projects will produce.		
✔ The outcome and its indicators provide a very clear and precise image or picture of what the future should look like, and is not so general that it could cover almost anything.		

QUICK CHECKLIST FOR REVIEWING OUTPUTS AND OUTPUT INDICATORS	YES	NO
✓ The outputs and their indicators are specific, measurable, achievable, realistic and time-bound (SMART).		
✓ The outputs are defined as products or services made possible by the resources provided in a project.		
✓ The language used to describe the outputs includes the noun or thing to be produced, as well as the verb describing what happens on completion of the output.		
✓ The outputs are defined as things over which one or more agencies have control and can be held accountable for delivering.		
✓ The outputs defined are necessary ingredients for achieving the outcomes.		
✓ There are indicators that measure both the process of producing the outputs (e.g. how many of something was done), as well as the quality and/or effect of what was produced (e.g. level of usage or user satisfaction with what was produced).		

Baselines and targets

Once the indicators are identified, the stakeholders should establish baselines and targets for the level of change they would like to see. It is often better to have a small group undertake the effort of researching the baseline separately, as stakeholders may not have all the data at the time. The baseline and target should be clearly aligned with the indicator, using the same unit of measurement. (For practical reasons, some indicators may need to be adjusted to align with existing measures, such as national surveys or censuses.)

Baseline data establishes a foundation from which to measure change. Without baseline data, it is very difficult to measure change over time or to monitor and evaluate. With baseline data, progress can be measured against the situation that prevailed before an intervention.[21]

---

21 Ideally, the baseline should be gathered and agreed upon by stakeholders when a programme is being formulated. However for some ongoing activities, baseline data may not have been established at that time. In this case, it may be possible to approximate the situation when the programme started by using data included in past annual review exercises. If this data does not exist, it still may be possible to obtain a measure of change over time. For example, to establish a baseline pertaining to local governance, one might conduct a survey and ask: "Compared to three years ago, do you feel more or less involved in local decision making?" When it is impossible to retroactively establish any sense of change, establish a measure of what the situation is now. This will at least allow for the assessment of change in the future. In some situations, a new indicator may be created, and this may not have a baseline from a previous year. In this situation and other situations, the team can agree to develop the baseline as they move forward with implementing the programme.

Once the baseline is established, a target should be set. The target will normally depend on the programme period and the duration of the interventions and activities. For example, within the context of a UNDAF, targets are normally set as five-year targets so as to correspond with the duration of the UNDAF. Likewise, global, regional and country programmes will normally have four- to five-year targets. While some development change can take a long time to occur, often 10 years or more, the inclusion of a target for the programme or project cycle is intended to enable stakeholders to look for 'signs' of overall change. If targets cannot be set for a four- to five-year period, then the indicator used was probably too high a level, and the team will need to find other indicators of progress within the short to medium term.

At the output level, targets can be set for a much shorter period, such as one year, six months and so forth. Relating this to our indicator examples above, Table 11 gives examples of baselines and targets.

It may not always be possible to have a strong or high output indicator target for the first year of implementation. For example, consider the indicator in Table 10: "percentage of electoral management office staff and volunteers trained in techniques to reduce voter fraud." A number of actions may need to be taken in the first year before training begins in the second year. The target for this indicator could therefore be 0 percent in 2009. This does not mean that the indicator is weak. In situations such as this, a 'comments' field could be used to explain the target. This is another reason why having two or more indicators to capture different dimensions of the output is recommended (the same applies to the outcome). In this case, another indicator on "level of progress made" in putting in place basic systems, training materials and so forth could be used in addition to the numeric indicator. This would allow for qualitative targets to be set for each year and could address the things that are to be put in place to form the platform for activities that will occur in future years.

Means of verification

Results statements and indicators should be SMART. The 'M' in SMART stands for 'measurable', which implies that data should be readily available in order to ascertain the progress made in achieving results. In defining results and corresponding indicators, it is thus important to consider how data will be obtained through monitoring and evaluation processes.

Means of verification play a key role in grounding an initiative in the realities of a particular setting. Plans that are too ambitious or developed too hastily often fail to recognize the difficulties in obtaining evidence that will allow programme managers to demonstrate the success of an initiative. Without clearly defining the kind of evidence that will be required to ascertain the achievement of results, without fully considering the implications of obtaining such evidence in terms of effort and cost, planners put the integrity of the programme at risk. If results and indicators are not based on measurable, independently verifiable data, the extent to which an initiative is realistic or achievable is questionable.

Table 11. Indicators, baselines and targets

Indicator	Baseline	Target
IMPACT: Increased public participation in national and local elections, particularly by women, indigenous populations and other traditionally marginalized groups		
Overall proportion of eligible voters who vote in the national (or local) elections	2006: 42% of eligible voters voted in national elections	2010: 70% of eligible voters vote in national elections
Percentage of eligible women who vote in the elections	2006: 0% voted (women were not allowed to vote)	2010: 50% of eligible women vote in national elections
Percentage of eligible indigenous people who vote in elections	2006: 15% voted (no efforts were made to encourage or support voting by indigenous people living in the interior)	2010: 45% of eligible indigenous persons vote in national elections
OUTCOME: Electoral administrative policies and systems reformed to ensure freer and fairer elections and to facilitate participation by marginalized groups		
Percentage of public that believe that the electoral management process is free and fair	2006: 30% (based on last survey conducted)	2010: 80%
Percentage of women and minorities aware of their rights under the new electoral administration laws	2007: 20% of minorities said they were aware of their rights (survey done by [specify] agency; note: women were not allowed to vote)	2010: 70% of women and minorities aware of their rights
Percentage increase in number of women registered to vote	2007: 0% of women registered to vote (women were not allowed to vote)	20% annual increase in percentage of eligible women registered to vote
Percentage increase in number of indigenous people registered to vote	2007: 30% of eligible minorities registered to vote	20% annual increase in percentage of eligible minorities registered to vote
Ratio of voter registration centres per population in rural areas	2006: 1 centre to 11,000 people	2010: 1 centre to 4,000 people
OUTPUT 1: Draft new policy on electoral reform formulated and submitted to Cabinet		
Progress made in drafting new policy	2008: Agreement reached between major political parties on need to redraft electoral legislation	2009: 5 major public consultations held and white paper prepared on new policy
OUTPUT 2: National electoral management agency has systems, procedures and competencies to administer free and fair elections		
Percentage of electoral centres using multiple forms of voter identification measures	2006: 0% of centres used multiple forms of voter identification	2009: 70% of centres use two or more forms of voter identification, including fingerprint identification (annual targets may be set)
Number of centres that are headed by trained, publicly recruited professional staff	2006: 20% of centres were run by publicly recruited professional staff (based on study done by [specify] agency)	2009: 80% of centres run by professional staff recruited through public recruitment process
Percentage of electoral management office staff who believe that their agency is more professional and better run than 1 year ago	No baseline exists; survey to be introduced for the first time in 2008	2009: 70% of staff believe their agency is more professional and better run than 1 year ago
Percentage of electoral management office staff and volunteers trained in techniques to reduce voter fraud	2006: 0%	2009: 80%

Identifying means of verification should take place in close coordination with key stakeholders. Evidence on outcomes (let alone impact) will need to be provided by the target group, beneficiaries or development partners. Therefore, it is important that in planning programmes and projects, such stakeholders are involved in thinking about how evidence on progress will be obtained during implementation and after completion of the initiative. Clear means of verification thus facilitates the establishment of monitoring systems and contributes significantly to ensuring that programmes and projects are evaluation-ready.

Based on this guidance, the team of stakeholders should refine or finalize the results framework for either the programme or project being developed.

Table 12. Sample results framework with means of verification			
Indicator	**Baseline**	**Target**	**Means of Verification**
IMPACT: Increased public participation in national and local elections, particularly by women, indigenous populations and other traditionally marginalized groups			
Overall proportion of eligible voters who vote in the national (or local) elections	2006: 42% of eligible voters voted in national elections	2010: 70% of eligible voters vote in national elections	Office of Electoral Administration's final report on elections
OUTCOME: Electoral administrative policies and systems reformed to ensure freer and fairer elections and to facilitate participation by marginalized groups			
Percentage of public that believe that the electoral management process is free and fair	2006: 30% (based on last survey conducted)	2010: 80%	Special survey to be undertaken as part of the electoral assistance project in 2008 and 2010
Percentage increase in number of women registered to vote	2007: 0% of women registered to vote (women were not allowed to vote)	2010: 20% annual increase in percentage of eligible women registered to vote	Office of Electoral Administration's database
Ratio of voter registration centres per population in rural areas	2006: 1 centre to 11,000 people	2010: 1 centre to 4,000 people	To be computed based on number of centres (Electoral Office database) in relation to population in rural areas (National Planning Agency's 2010 demographic survey)
OUTPUT 1: Draft new policy on electoral reform formulated and submitted to Cabinet			
Progress made in drafting new policy	2008: Agreement reached between major political parties on need to redraft electoral legislation	2009: 5 major public consultations held and white paper prepared on new policy	Report from government agency organizing workshops Record of Parliamentary proceedings (for submission of white paper) to be obtained from Office of Public Sector Information
OUTPUT 2: National electoral management agency has systems, procedures and competencies to administer free and fair elections			
Percentage of electoral centres using multiple forms of voter identification measures	2006: 0% of centres used multiple forms of voter identification	2009: 70% of centres use two or more forms of voter identification, including fingerprint identification (annual targets may be set)	Electoral Office database

The formulation of a results framework is a participatory and iterative process. Participation is key to ensuring that stakeholders understand and support the initiative and are aware of the implications of all elements of the results framework. In developing a results framework, the definition of new elements (such as formulating outputs after identifying outcomes, or defining indicators after defining a particular result, or specifying the means of verification after defining indicators) should be used to test the validity of previously defined elements.

RELATIONSHIP BETWEEN THE RESULTS FRAMEWORK AND UNDP RBM SYSTEMS

The data created in the planning exercise may appear at different times in various planning documents and systems. For example:

- The impacts and/or national priorities appear in the relevant sections of the UNDAF or global, regional or country programme results framework when these are developed.

- The impact developed in a global, regional or country programme would also be entered in the RBM platform (home.undp.org) in the global, regional or national goal field.

- Impact indicators are normally entered in national strategy documents and plans and in the UNDAF results framework. Reference can also be made to these indicators in the situation analysis and statements of objective in a CPD or CPAP.

- The analysis of what is causing the problems would normally be reflected in the situation analysis section of the respective programme or project document.

- The analysis of what needs to happen or be in place to achieve the goals and impact would also be reflected in the programme or project document, along with any government or UNDP action needed to influence partners and non-partners to take desired actions. This would be captured in the objectives and strategy sections of the respective documents.

- The specific outcomes that UNDP will support would be entered in the relevant sections of the UNDAF.

- The UNDP outcomes identified in the UNDAF are used to formulate the CPD that is approved by the UNDP Executive Board.

- The same outcomes (or slightly revised outcomes based on the CPAP process but with the same intention) would be entered into Atlas as part of the programme's project tree. These outcomes would then appear on the programme planning and monitoring page of the RBM platform.

- Outcome indicators would be entered in the relevant sections of the programme documents and the same indicators (or slightly revised indicators based on the CPAP refinement process) would be entered into the RBM platform at the start of the programme.

- Baselines and targets would be entered for the outcome indicators in both places as well.

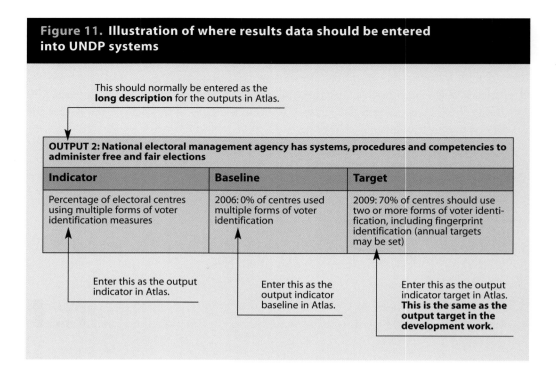

Figure 11. Illustration of where results data should be entered into UNDP systems

This should normally be entered as the **long description** for the outputs in Atlas.

OUTPUT 2: National electoral management agency has systems, procedures and competencies to administer free and fair elections

Indicator	Baseline	Target
Percentage of electoral centres using multiple forms of voter identification measures	2006: 0% of centres used multiple forms of voter identification	2009: 70% of centres should use two or more forms of voter identification, including fingerprint identification (annual targets may be set)

Enter this as the output indicator in Atlas.

Enter this as the output indicator baseline in Atlas.

Enter this as the output indicator target in Atlas. **This is the same as the output target in the development work.**

- The UNDAF and CPD would normally include a set of outputs that the programme intends to produce.

- These outputs are normally refined in the CPAP process as stakeholders obtain greater clarity on the implementation details for the programme. This may occur months after the UNDAF or CPD has been finalized.

- The CPAP outputs would be created as output projects in Atlas, together with their indicators, baselines and targets. This information would then appear in the RBM platform to facilitate monitoring and reporting against these outputs. **As far as possible, the project outputs in Atlas should have, as their long description, the same wording as the outputs created in the results framework. Likewise, the indicators and baselines for the outputs are the same as should be entered in Atlas. The output targets are also the same as the annual output targets that are used in Atlas and are normally entered when offices prepare their development work plans and set targets for the year.** This is illustrated in Figure 11.

- The risks and assumptions would be documented in the relevant column of the programme results and resources table. The risks would also be entered in Atlas and related to an Award (the Award is a collection of outputs). These would then be reflected in the RBM platform for monitoring purposes.

- Information on partners would be entered in the results framework, and the programme document would explain the efforts of both partners and non-partners in contributing to the outcomes and impact. The role of partners should be included in the formal monitoring and evaluation process (such as in a joint evaluation of an UNDAF). The efforts of non-partners can be monitored informally through meetings with them or other means.

Atlas and the RBM platform should serve as tools to enter the information contained in the results framework and to conduct transactions and monitor progress. The development work plan component of the platform is therefore a monitoring tool for the global, regional and country programmes (or CPAPs), as it captures the outcomes, outcome indicators, outputs, output indicators, budgets and key risks related to projects. The data should be entered by either the UNDP programme or project manager, with quality assurance conducted by the designated quality assurance officer. (See the POPP for more information on the roles and responsibilities in programme and project formulation.)

At the end of the planning process, stakeholders should therefore have as their **eighth deliverable**—a **results framework** that may look like the one in Table 13.

Table 13. Sample results framework				
National Goal/Priority	**"Improved public confidence and involvement in national and local processes of governance" or "More vibrant democratic processes that involve a wider cross-section of citizens"**			
UNDAF Outcome A1	**Wider participation by citizens in national and local elections by 2015**			
Programme Outcomes	**Outcome Indicators, Baselines and Targets**	**Programme Outputs**	**Role of Partners**	**Financial Resources**
1.1.1 Electoral administrative policies and systems reformed to ensure freer and fairer elections and to facilitate participation by marginalized groups	1.1.1 Public perception of capacity of electoral management authority to administer free and fair elections (disaggregated by gender, population group, etc.) **Baseline:** 40% of public had confidence in electoral management authority as of 2008 (50% men, 30% women, 20% indigenous populations) **Target:** 70% of overall population has confidence in electoral management authority by 2016 (75% men, 65% women, 60% indigenous populations)	1.1.1 Advocacy campaign aimed at building consensus on need for electoral law and system reform implemented 1.1.2 Adequate staff recruited and systems implemented in the electoral management authority to administer free and fair elections 1.1.3 Training programme on use of new electoral management technology designed and implemented for staff of electoral management authority	UNDP, Department for International Development (DFID), European Union (EU), US Agency for International Development (USAID) and the World Bank (all working on institutional reform of electoral management authority)	
1.2.1 Increased participation by women and indigenous populations in national and local electoral processes in five regions by 2016	1.2.1 Percentage of eligible women registered to vote in 5 regions **Baseline:** 30% of eligible women registered in the 5 regions as of 2008 **Target:** 60% registration of eligible women in the 5 regions by 2016	1.2.1 Revised draft legislation on rights of women and indigenous populations to participate in elections prepared	UNESCO working on culturally relevant communications programme targeting women and indigenous populations	

In the UNDAF, all the relevant indicators for the UNDAF outcomes would also be included, along with the outputs of the different UN organizations contributing to those outcomes. Likewise, the national priorities would have their related indicators and outputs in the government's development strategies. UNDP staff (both programme and operations) should be familiar with these higher level results and performance targets in order to better manage for results in their own programmes and projects.

In UNDP and many other agencies, the information obtained from the planning process is normally used to develop not only the results framework, but also a narrative programme or project document. This document may have requirements that go beyond the issues dealt with in this Handbook. Users of the Handbook should therefore consult with their respective agency policies and procedures manuals for guidance.

2.5   PREPARING TO OPERATIONALIZE

The previous sections covered the steps for preparing a results map and the specific results framework that would be included in a UNDP-supported programme or project document. To realize the results envisaged in the framework, it has to be communicated, implemented, monitored and evaluated. In the absence of effective monitoring and evaluation, it will not be possible for UNDP, its stakeholders and partners to know whether the intended results are being achieved or if they should take corrective action to support the delivery of the intended results. Monitoring and evaluation are essential for effective programme and project implementation and to support UNDP accountability and learning. Chapter 3 covers the important steps in planning to monitor and evaluate. This section briefly examines arrangements for operationalizing the results framework.

At the end of the planning process, the stakeholders should devote time to strategizing how the framework will be implemented and how the goals and objectives will be reinforced. A results framework that is operationalized is:

- Broadly communicated to all stakeholders

- Regularly and formally reviewed and updated

- Clear on who is responsible and accountable for what components

- Used for decision making

- Consistent with the incentives systems in the organization

COMMUNICATION AND PARTNERSHIP BUILDING

In the last planning meeting, stakeholders should reflect on what methods will be used to communicate the major objectives contained in the framework. The purpose is to increase awareness of the programme and generate support for it.

Either an individual or a subteam should be tasked with developing the communication plan. For large programmes it could be useful to engage a communications firm to provide support. Box 16 and 17 include ideas for communication plans and an example of how one organization is executing its plan.

Box 16. Suggestions for communications plans

- In some situations, flyers and publicity material, such as the MDG flyers and videos, are created to capture the main objectives and targets in simple terms. These are then circulated to stakeholders.
- In other cases, there is an ongoing communication programme (radio, newspapers, etc.) on the main goals and targets. This is used to keep the plan and its objectives constantly in the minds of stakeholders, maintaining commitment and ensuring clarity on the common goals.
- In some private and public sector offices, open spaces and notice boards are used to present the main objectives of the plan, while meeting rooms often have whiteboards, flipcharts and other tools capturing the main goals and targets.
- In many organizations, meetings are held with slides showing the targets and progress against them.

It is frequently helpful to discuss in the last planning meeting how to build partnerships and teams to carry the work forward. For example, within development agencies (government, international and other) there is a tendency for staff to see programmatic work as the purview of the programme team. Operations staff sometimes do not feel ownership of the plan and are only involved in processing administrative transactions. This can rob the team of the broader energies, ideas and support it may need to move forward efficiently. Spending time to brainstorm creative ways of engaging both internal and external partners can therefore be quite useful.

Box 17. Sharing the vision

In one large U.S. hospital, every notice board carries key elements of the values, mission and objectives of the hospital. Additionally, different units have large boards displaying the performance indicators relevant to the unit and achievements of the unit in relation to those indicators. The hospital has consistently received some of the highest scores in client satisfaction and boasts some of the lowest error rates in patient treatment. It proudly displays its numerous awards and citations beside its mission statement and performance indicators.

ACCOUNTABILITY AND INCENTIVES

Stakeholders should similarly reflect on who will be accountable for what elements of the framework and what types of incentives or sanctions could be used to encourage behaviour consistent with the framework.

Accountability

Often once the results framework or map is developed, the group moves on to discuss who will be responsible for coordinating the development of the various programmes and interventions. In some cases this may be an organization (United Nations or other), or an individual within an office.

- Stakeholders should review the results map or framework to identify areas where concrete actions will be needed to get things going. Individuals or agencies should be designated to lead on those actions.

- These agreements should be documented and used to form part of a simple implementation plan.

- The plan would also address issues such as approvals or policy decisions needed and the strategy for obtaining these.

- A smaller group can be asked to examine in greater detail elements of the results framework that may require focused action by specific stakeholders.

- Chapter 3 will address setting up the arrangements for monitoring and evaluation.

Incentives and sanctions

Stakeholders should brainstorm possible incentive arrangements and sanctions (if appropriate) that could promote implementation of the framework. Again, it may be possible to ask one or more persons to review the framework and come up with suggestions for the group. However at the initial stage, it may be worthwhile hearing a range of ideas from the group. These ideas should then be documented as part of the implementation plan.

2.6 PUTTING IT TOGETHER: PLANNING FOR CHANGE

Planning for real results requires thinking critically about desired change and what is required to bring it about. The process involves asking a series of questions:

- What precisely do we want to see changed?

- How will this change occur? What will make change happen?
  - Who needs to be involved?
  - What resources are needed?
  - What conditions need to be in place, and what will influence these conditions?

- How will we monitor and evaluate the changes?

- How will we use the information obtained from monitoring and evaluation?

The process should define all the building blocks required to bring about the desired long-term goal, and monitor and evaluate the extent to which progress is being made. Done in this manner, planning can become a powerful process that helps to:

- Achieve stakeholder consensus and commitment

- Communicate clearly with all stakeholders about the desired changes

- Motivate actions and mobilize resources

- Better define all the internal and external resources and partnerships needed to achieve results

- Better understand the interests, needs and concerns of different groups of stakeholders, including men, women and traditionally marginalized groups

- Set clearer performance indicators for monitoring and evaluation

- Allocate responsibilities

Box 18. Recap of key considerations in planning for results

- Planning should be focused on results—real development changes that help to improve people's lives. It should not be done merely to meet the requirements of supervisors or Headquarters.

- Planning should always be seen as a process, of which the actual plan is only one product.

- The planning process should extend beyond only looking at results and performance measures. It should include a plan and mechanisms for managing, monitoring and evaluating and well-developed ideas for partnering and collaborating to achieve the desired results.

- The planning process should be highly participatory and very open, and should encourage frankness, creativity and innovation.

- Planning must be guided by core principles of development effectiveness. It should not lead to a neutral or generic plan but one that is based on lessons of what works or does not work in development programming.

- The most important outcomes of the planning process are: clarity on goals, objectives and a vision of the future; commitment and motivation of stakeholders; and clarity on the process to implement and manage the plan. The planning document can serve as a useful record of what has been agreed and a tool for communicating to new stakeholders.

PLANNING FOR MONITORING AND EVALUATION

Chapter 2 illustrated how a shared vision coupled with an inclusive planning process could produce a realistic results framework or a 'development plan' to bring about desired development changes. Monitoring and evaluation play critical roles in realizing the results envisaged in this development plan. Planning for monitoring and evaluation should be part of the overall planning process. It concerns setting up the systems and processes necessary to ensure the intended results are achieved as planned. This chapter provides guidance on the planning and preparations for effective monitoring and evaluation of such development plans in the UNDP context: country, regional and global programmes.

3.1   INTRODUCTION

WHY MONITOR AND EVALUATE?

Monitoring and evaluation serve several purposes. In the absence of effective monitoring and evaluation, it would be difficult to know whether the intended results are being achieved as planned, what corrective action may be needed to ensure delivery of the intended results, and whether initiatives are making positive contributions towards human development. Monitoring and evaluation always relate to pre-identified results in the development plan. They are driven by the need to account for the achievement of intended results and provide a fact base to inform corrective decision making. They are an essential management tool to support the UNDP commitment to accountability for results, resources entrusted to it, and organizational learning. Furthermore, both feed into the overall programme management processes and make an essential contribution to the ability to manage for development results.[22]

---

22 Adopted from: UNDP, 'The Evaluation Policy of UNDP', Executive Board Document DP/2005/28, May 2006, available at: http://www.undp.org/eo/documents/Evaluation-Policy.pdf; and UNEG, 'Norms for Evaluation in the UN System', 2005, available at: http://www.unevaluation.org/unegnorms.

Monitoring, as well as evaluation, provides opportunities at regular predetermined points to validate the logic of a programme, its activities and their implementation and to make adjustments as needed. Good planning and designs alone do not ensure results. Progress towards achieving results needs to be monitored. Equally, no amount of good monitoring alone will correct poor programme designs, plans and results. Information from monitoring needs to be used to encourage improvements or reinforce plans. Information from systematic monitoring also provides critical input to evaluation. It is very difficult to evaluate a programme that is not well designed and that does not systematically monitor its progress.

The key questions that **monitoring** seeks to answer include the following:

- Are the preidentified outputs being produced as planned and efficiently?

- What are the issues, risks and challenges that we face or foresee that need to be taken into account to ensure the achievement of results?

- What decisions need to be made concerning changes to the already planned work in subsequent stages?

- Will the planned and delivered outputs continue to be relevant for the achievement of the envisioned outcomes?

- Are the outcomes we envisaged remaining relevant and effective for achieving the overall national priorities, goals and impacts?

- What are we learning?

Like monitoring, **evaluation** is an integral part of programme management and a critical management tool. Evaluation complements monitoring by providing an independent and in-depth assessment of what worked and what did not work, and why this was the case. After implementing and monitoring an initiative for some time, it is an important management discipline to take stock of the situation through an external evaluation.

The benefits of using evaluations are multiple. A quality evaluation provides feedback that can be used to improve programming, policy and strategy. Evaluation also identifies unintended results and consequences of development initiatives, which may not be obvious in regular monitoring as the latter focuses on the implementation of the development plan. Information generated from evaluations contributes to organizational learning as well as the global knowledge base on development effectiveness.

In fast evolving development contexts or in emerging, ongoing or post-crisis environments, the development plan needs to be dynamic and revised and improved over time. Whenever development plans are updated during implementation, it is necessary to document the rationale for such changes. Effective monitoring and evaluation is important as it provides evidence to base such changes through informed management decisions.

Effective and timely decision making requires information from regular and planned monitoring and evaluation activities. **Planning for monitoring and evaluation must start at the time of programme or project design, and they must be planned together.** While monitoring provides real-time information on ongoing programme or project implementation required by management, evaluation provides more in-depth assessments. The monitoring process can generate questions to be answered by evaluation. Also, evaluation draws heavily on data generated through monitoring, including baseline data, information on the programme or project implementation process, and measurements of progress towards the planned results through indicators.

Planning for monitoring must be done with evaluation in mind: The availability of a clearly defined results or outcome model and monitoring data, among other things, determine the 'evaluability'[23] of the subject to be evaluated.

3.2 MONITORING AND EVALUATION FRAMEWORK

A clear framework, agreed among the key stakeholders at the end of the planning stage, is essential in order to carry out monitoring and evaluation systematically. This framework serves as a plan for monitoring and evaluation, and should clarify:

- What is to be monitored and evaluated
- The activities needed to monitor and evaluate
- Who is responsible for monitoring and evaluation activities
- When monitoring and evaluation activities are planned (timing)
- How monitoring and evaluation are carried out (methods)
- What resources are required and where they are committed

In addition, relevant risks and assumptions in carrying out planned monitoring and evaluation activities should be seriously considered, anticipated and included in the M&E framework.

In general, the M&E framework has three main components:

1. Narrative component—This describes how the partners will undertake monitoring and evaluation and the accountabilities assigned to different individuals and agencies. For example, at the UNDAF or national result level, it is necessary to engage with national monitoring committees or outcome level groups (e.g. sector arrangements) as well as with UN interagency monitoring working groups. If these do not exist, there might be a need to establish such structures for effective monitoring and evaluation. In addition the narrative should also reflect:

    a. Plans that may be in place to strengthen national or sub-national monitoring and evaluation capacities

---

23 Evaluability can be defined by clarity in the intent of the subject to be evaluated, sufficient measurable indicators, accessible reliable information sources, and no major factor hindering an impartial evaluation process.

b. Existing monitoring and evaluation capacities and an estimate of the human, financial and material resource requirements for its implementation

2. Results framework—This should be prepared in the planning stage as described in Chapter 2.

3. Planning matrices for monitoring and evaluation—These are strategic and consolidate the information required for monitoring and evaluation for easy reference.

The planning matrix for monitoring in Table 14 is illustrative for UNDP and could be used at the country, regional and global programme level to determine what needs to be monitored. (A completed example of Table 14 is given in Table 15.) This matrix should be adapted as determined by local circumstances and conditions. In some cases, the columns could be modified to cover results elements such as outcomes, outputs, indicators, baselines, risks and assumptions separately.

The need for an M&E framework applies for both programmes and projects within a programme. Therefore both programmes and projects should develop M&E frameworks in their planning stages. The project-level M&E framework should cascade from the programme level M&E framework and could contain more detailed information on monitoring and evaluation tasks that apply specifically to respective projects. Conversely, the programme-level framework builds upon the project-level frameworks. Monitoring and evaluation activities should be seen as an integral component of programme and project management. They take place throughout the programme and project cycles and should be reviewed and updated regularly (at least annually, for example at the time of annual reviews).

Table 14. Planning matrix for monitoring[24]

Expected Results (Outcomes & Outputs)	Indicators (with Baselines & Indicative Targets) and Other Key Areas to Monitor	M&E Event with Data Collection Methods	Time or Schedule and Frequency	Responsibilities	Means of Verification: Data Source and Type	Resources	Risks
Obtained from development plan and results framework.	From results framework. Indicators should also capture key priorities such as capacity development and gender. In addition, other key areas need to be monitored, such as the risks identified in the planning stage as well as other key management needs.	How is data to be obtained? Example: through a survey, a review or stakeholder meeting, etc.	Level of detail that can be included would depend on the practical needs. In UNDP, this information can also be captured in the Project Monitoring Schedule Plan from Atlas.	Who is responsible for organizing the data collection and verifying data quality and source?	Systematic source and location where you would find the identified and necessary data such as a national institute or DevInfo.	Estimate of resources required and committed for carrying out planned monitoring activities.	What are the risks and assumptions for carrying out the planned monitoring activities? How may these affect the planned monitoring events and quality of data?

---

24 The format in Table 14 primarily applies to programme-level monitoring. UNDP country offices are expected to attach a table with the above information to their CPAP, which is needed to operationalize the country programmes.

Table 15. Illustrative example of planning matrix for monitoring: Enhanced capacity of electoral management authority

Expected Results (Outcomes & Outputs)	Indicators (with Baselines & Indicative Targets) and Other Key Areas to Monitor	M&E Event with Data Collection Methods	Time or Schedule and Frequency	Responsibilities	Means of Verification: Data Source and Type	Resources	Risks
Outcome 1: Enhanced capacity of electoral management authority to administer free and fair elections	Public perception of capacity of electoral management authority to administer free and fair elections (disaggregated by gender, population group, etc.)	1. Surveys	1. All surveys will be completed six months prior to the completion of activities	1. National Office of Statistics will commission survey; external partners, UNDP, and the World Bank will provide technical resources as needed through their assistance for capacity development	1.1 Data and analysis of surveys will be available in (a) report for public And (b) on websites of National Office of Statistics and Elections Authority	1. Resources estimated at USD 0.2 million for the survey will be provided by the European Union	1. It is assumed that capacity development activities within National Office of Statistics required for carrying out the survey will be completed one year in advance to actual survey; if there are delays, then a private company could be contracted to carry out the survey
1.1. Advocacy campaign aimed at building consensus on need for electoral law and system reform implemented	**Baseline:** 40% of public had confidence in electoral management authority as of 2008 (50% men, 30% women, 20% indigenous populations)	2. Annual Progress Reviews	2. Progress reviews on achievement of all connected outputs will be held jointly in the fourth quarter	2. Progress Reviews will be organized by Elections Authority	2.1 Annual Progress Reports 2.2 Minutes of Annual Progress Reviews	2. Resources for M&E activities will be made available in World Bank assistance project 3. Cost of external partners' participation will be met by each respective partner. Other logistical costs will be funded from World Bank project	
1.2. Electoral management authority has adequate staff and systems to administer free and fair elections	**Target:** 70% of overall population have confidence in electoral management authority by 2016	3. Joint field visits to five regions	3. Two field visits will be held prior to the final survey and three more afterward	3. Field visits will be organized by Elections Authority; Elections Authority will ensure meetings with a representative cross section of stakeholders; at least two external partners will participate in a given joint field visit	3. Records of joint field visits will be available on website of Elections Authority		
1.3. Training programme on use of new electoral management technology designed and implemented for staff of electoral management authority	(75% men, 65% women, 60% indigenous populations)	4. ...	4. ...	4. ...	4. ...	4. ...	
Outcome 2: Increased participation by women and indigenous populations in national and local electoral processes in five regions by 2016	Percentage of eligible women registered to vote in five regions **Baseline:** 30% of eligible women registered in the five regions as of 2008						
2.1. Revised draft legislation on rights of women and indigenous populations to participate in elections prepared	**Target:** 60% registration of eligible women in the five regions by 2016						

Table 16. Evaluation plan

Evaluation Title	Partners (Joint Evaluation)	Strategic Plan Results Area	CPD/ CPAP Outcome	Planned Completion Date	Key Evaluation Stakeholders	Source of Funding for Evaluation	Mandatory Evaluation (Y/N)
Outcome Evaluations							
Midterm Outcome Evaluation of the Poverty Reduction Programme	N/A	Poverty Reduction & MDGs	1	June 2010	Ministry of Planning, civil society groups, donors, UNDP, communities	M&E Project	Y
Midterm Outcome Evaluation of the Governance Programme	DFID (donor)	Democratic Governance	2	June 2010	Election Authority, Parliament, Ministry of Law, DFID, UNDP	DFID, related UNDP projects	Y
Outcome Evaluation: Energy and Environment Portfolio	Ministry of Environment	Environment and Sustainable Development	3	December 2011	Ministry of Environment, NGOs, donors, UNDP, communities	Biodiversity Project, Sustainable Energy Project	Y
Project Evaluations							
Microfinance Sector Pilot Project	UNCDF	Poverty Reduction: Promoting Inclusive Growth	1.3	March 2010	Microfinance Apex Org., Ministry of Finance, UNCDF, UNICEF	Project budget	N
Biodiversity Project (Global Environment Facility)	N/A	Environment: Mobilizing Environment Financing	3.2	May 2011	Ministry of Environment, NGOs, donors, UNDP, communities	Project budget	Y
Strengthening of the Electoral Process Project	N/A	Democratic Governance: Inclusive participation	2.4	September 2009	Election Authority, donors, UNDP, public	Project budget	Y
Mainstreaming Disaster Risk Reduction Project	N/A	Crisis Prevention and Recovery	4.2	June 2011	Ministry of Disaster Management, implementing NGOs, European Community (donor), UNDP	Project budget	Y
Other Evaluations							
UNDAF Midterm Evaluation	All resident UN organizations	N/A	All	December 2009	Government, UN organizations	M&E Project	N

Note: DFID stands for Department for International Development (UK); UNCDF, United Nations Capital Development Fund; UNICEF, United Nations Children's Fund.

SPECIFIC CONSIDERATIONS FOR PLANNING EVALUATIONS

It is mandatory for UNDP to present an evaluation plan to its Executive Board with each country, regional and global programme document considered for approval. The evaluation plan is a component of the M&E framework and should include those evaluations that can be foreseen at the end of the programme planning stage. The plan should be strategic, including a selection of evaluations that will generate the most critical and useful information for UNDP and its partners in decision making.

The initial evaluation plan should, at a minimum, include **all mandatory evaluations**. For programme units in UNDP, outcome evaluations and project evaluations required by partnership protocols such as the Global Environment Facility are mandatory. The evaluation plan is not a static document. It should be reviewed as part of the M&E framework and refined as needed during programme implementation. For example, as new projects are designed and the needs for evaluations are identified, these new evaluations should be added to the evaluation plan.

After a country, regional or global programme is approved, the respective programme unit enters the evaluation plan in the Evaluation Resource Centre (ERC) for tracking.[25] As the units exercising oversight responsibility, the regional bureaux use the evaluation plan submitted by the programme units as the basis for assessing compliance. The Evaluation Office reports on evaluation compliance directly to the UNDP Executive Board in its Annual Report on Evaluation.

UNDP programme units are required to select and commission evaluations that provide substantive information for decision making. In deciding what to evaluate, the programme units should first determine the purpose of the evaluation and other factors that may influence the relevance and use of proposed evaluations. In general, for accountability purposes, at least **20 percent to 30 percent of the entire programme portfolio** should be subject to evaluation.

Evaluations generally require significant resources and time. Therefore, every evaluation must be justified and used in an optimal way. Programme units together with key stakeholders should consider the following points in developing an evaluation plan:

- Uses, purpose and timing of evaluation—Evaluations should be proposed only when commissioning programme units and stakeholders are clear at the onset about **why the evaluation is being conducted (the purpose), what the information needs are (demand for information), who will use the information, and how the information will be used.** Such information can be derived from a shared vision of success, as expressed in the results or outcome model at the planning stage. The intended use determines the timing of an evaluation, its methodological framework, and level and nature of stakeholder participation. The timing of an evaluation should be directly linked to its purpose and use. To ensure the relevance

---

25 The Evaluation Resource Centre (ERC) is the UNDP information management system to support management accountability for evaluation. Available at: http://www.erc.undp.org.

of an evaluation and effective use of evaluation information, the evaluation should be made available in a timely manner so that decisions can be made informed by evaluative evidence.[26]

■ Resources invested—An area (thematic or programmatic area, outcome or project) in which UNDP has invested significant resources may be subject to an evaluation as there may be greater accountability requirements.

■ The likelihood of future initiatives in the same area—Evaluations are an important means of generating recommendations to guide future work. An evaluation enables the programme unit to take stock of whether the outputs have contributed to the outcome and whether UNDP has crafted an effective partnership strategy. When selecting an initiative to be evaluated, look for one in an area that UNDP will continue to support.

■ Anticipated problems—Evaluations can help prevent problems and provide an independent perspective on existing problems. When selecting an outcome for evaluation, look for those with problems or where complications are likely to arise because the outcome is within a sensitive area with a number of partners.

■ Need for lessons learned—What kinds of lessons are needed to help guide activities in this country or other countries or regions in the region?

■ Alignment and harmonization—Planned evaluations should be aligned with national, regional and global development priorities and UNDP corporate priorities (for example, the UNDP Strategic Plan), and should be harmonized with evaluations of UN system organizations and other international partners. This ensures that proposed evaluations will generate important information to help UNDP and its partners better manage for results in a changing context. Opportunities for joint evaluations with governments and partners should be actively pursued. Evaluations commissioned by UNDP should be useful for national partners. In determining the timing of an evaluation, UNDP should consider various decision-making points that exist in the partner government, such as budget decision making, development framework or strategy setting, and existing review processes for development programmes and projects. For instance, if the government is undertaking an evaluation of a national development strategy or framework to which UNDP projects are contributing, the UNDP-managed evaluations should enhance complementarities and minimize duplicated efforts.

Once the outcome evaluations are selected, the programme unit identifies the projects that are designed to contribute to the outcome and indicates them as relevant projects for the evaluation plan. This gives notice to the concerned projects and allows them to

---

26 When determining the timing of outcome evaluations, it is important to keep in mind that the Evaluation Office is mandated to conduct evaluations of the global and regional programmes and selected country programmes (Assessments of Development Results) before the new programmes are submitted to the Executive Board for approval. The evaluation process normally starts in year four of the programme. Since outcome and project evaluations commissioned by the programme units provide the substantive basis for independent evaluations, they should be completed during the early to middle stages of the programme cycle, before the conduct of the Evaluation Office's independent evaluations.

take account of the outcome evaluation in their monitoring and work planning. It also helps the UNDP programme officers and relevant national partners in outcome monitoring prepare for the outcome evaluation.

The same criteria for selecting outcomes should be applied to selecting **project evaluations**. Some partnership protocols require their related projects to be evaluated. It is strongly recommended that evaluations should be completed for pilot projects before replication or upscaling, projects that are going into a next phase, and projects ongoing for more than five years for accountability and learning purposes. As part of the regular updating process of the evaluation plan, any newly identified project evaluations should be included in the plan.

In crisis settings, extra time should be allocated to evaluations, as there is a need for flexibility in order to respond to changing situations. This means being flexible when scheduling field visits and interviews and anticipating delays in data collection and last-minute changes in data collection methods if relationships between different groups change. Further, more preparation is required when working with vulnerable groups and those affected by conflict, as greater care and ethical considerations are required.

3.3 RESOURCES FOR MONITORING AND EVALUATION

Inadequate resources lead to poor quality monitoring and evaluation. To ensure effective and quality monitoring and evaluation, it is critical to set aside adequate financial and human resources at the planning stage. The required financial and human resources for monitoring and evaluation should be considered within the overall costs of delivering the agreed results and not as additional costs.

Financial resources for monitoring and evaluation should be estimated realistically at the time of planning for monitoring and evaluation. While it is critical to plan for monitoring and evaluation together, resources for each function should be separate. In practice, each project should have two separate budget lines for its monitoring and evaluation agreed in advance with partners. This will help UNDP and its partners be more realistic in budgeting. It will also reduce the risk of running out of resources for evaluation, which often takes place towards the end of implementation.

Monitoring and evaluation costs associated with projects can be identified relatively easily and be charged directly to the respective project budgets with prior agreement among partners through inclusion in the project budget or Annual Work Plan (AWP) signed by partners.

Sourcing and securing financial resources for monitoring and evaluation of outcomes or programmes can pose additional challenges, as there is not one project where these costs can be directly charged. The most commonly observed financing mechanism is to draw resources together from relevant projects. Some additional possibilities include:

■ Create a separate monitoring and evaluation fund, facility or project associated with an outcome or a programme to which all the constituent projects would contribute through transfer of some project funds. This facility could be located in the same entity that manages the outcome or programme.

- Mobilize funds from partners directly for an outcome or programme monitoring and evaluation facility.

- Allocate required funds annually for each outcome on the basis of planned costs of monitoring and evaluation from overall programme budget to the facility or fund.

It is important that partners consider the resources needed for monitoring and evaluation and agree on a practical arrangement to finance the associated activities. Such arrangements should be documented at the beginning of the programme to enable partners to transfer necessary funds in accordance with their procedures, which could take considerable time and effort.

Human resources are critical for effective monitoring and evaluation, even after securing adequate financial resources. For high-quality monitoring and evaluation, there should be:

- Dedicated staff time—For effective monitoring and evaluation, staff should be dedicated for the function. The practices of deployment of personnel for monitoring vary among organizations. Some UNDP country offices have established monitoring and evaluation units with specific terms of references (ToRs), dedicated skilled staff, work plans and other resources.

- Skilled personnel—Staff entrusted with monitoring should have required technical expertise in the area. A number of UNDP country offices have a dedicated monitoring and evaluation specialist. Where necessary, skill levels should be augmented to meet the needs and with ongoing investments in developing such capacity within the office as necessary.

Each monitoring and evaluation entity that functions at different levels, for example at the project, programme or outcome level, should have a clear ToR outlining its role and responsibilities. In general, these responsibilities should include:

- Setting up systematic monitoring frameworks and developing an evaluation plan

- Meeting regularly with key partners and stakeholders to assess progress towards achieving the results

- Conducting joint field monitoring and evaluation missions to assess achievements and constraints

- Identifying any lessons or good practices

- Reflecting on how well the results being achieved are addressing gender, and the interests and rights of marginalized and vulnerable groups in the society

- Identifying additional capacity development needs among stakeholders and partners

- Reporting regularly to the lead individuals or agencies for the particular result areas and seeking opportunities to influence policy and decision-making processes

- Ensuring the quality of monitoring and evaluation work and providing guidance as needed

- Assessing the relevance of the M&E framework on a regular basis based on emerging development priorities and changing context

SPECIFIC CONSIDERATIONS FOR BUDGETING AND FINANCING FOR EVALUATION

Programme units should estimate and indicate financial requirements and financing means for each evaluation in the evaluation plan. When estimating the cost for an evaluation, the **duration and scope** of the evaluation should be considered. The duration of an evaluation will be determined by its purpose. An evaluation conducted

---

Box 19. Key issues to be considered in costing an evaluation

- **Evaluators and external advisers, and expenses related to their duties**
  Evaluation consultants and expert advisory panel members (if any)
  - One evaluator or a team? How many in a team? What is the composition (national or international)?
  - How many days will be required for each consultant and adviser?
  - What would be the daily rate range for each one of them?
  - Any cost associated with hiring?
  - Are the advisory panel members paid (daily fees, honorarium)?

  Travel requirements
  - What types of travel expenses will be incurred? For example, how many times does the team need to travel to the country or field? What travel requirements exist for briefings in UNDP offices, interviews with stakeholders, data collection activities, stakeholder meetings, etc.?
  - What would be the primary mode of travel (air, project vehicle, etc.)? Is there a need for special modes of transportation due to accessibility and security considerations?
  - For how many days and what are the allowances?

- **Requirements for consultations with stakeholders**
  - Are there regular meetings with the steering committee members to discuss the progress of the evaluation? Will there be a meeting with wider stakeholders to discuss the findings and recommendations of the evaluation? How many and who will be invited? What would be the cost associated with renting venues, and bringing in stakeholders (allowances and travel expenses) and refreshments?

- **Data collection and analysis tools and methods**
  - What are methods of data collection? If surveys and/or questionnaires will be used, what is the target population and area to be covered? What resources are required (fees for enumerators, including their travel expenses, etc.)? Is there a need for researchers to complete a detailed analysis of data collected?

- Any **supplies** needed? For example, office supplies, computer software for data analysis, etc.

- **Communication costs**
  - What are the phone, Internet and fax usage requirements?
  - If surveys or questionnaires are conducted, how will they be administered (mail, Internet, telephone, etc.)?

- **Publication and dissemination** of evaluation reports and other products, including translation costs, if needed.

- Are there any resources allocated for incidentals?

- Are there partners for the evaluation? Is this evaluation cost-shared? What would be the cost to UNDP?

early in implementation, which tends to focus on programme or project design issues, is apt to be less complex and entail a smaller scope, hence requiring less data than would a 'heavier' exercise conducted at the end of the project or the programming cycle. The greater the complexity and scope of an evaluation, the longer time and more detailed work will be needed by the evaluation team to collect required data. This may increase evaluators' total fees. Programme units should be realistic in terms of the scope and complexity of the evaluation *vis-à-vis* available resources.

In addition, **the availability and accessibility of primary and secondary data** (monitoring, regular reporting and evaluation) and data collection methods influence the cost of the evaluation exercise. In the absence of reliable data, the evaluators need to spend more time and resources to locate or generate information. The appropriateness of allocated resources should be assessed together with the commissioned external evaluators based on the work programme submitted by them.

If an evaluation is carried out jointly with government or donors in the context of a larger outcome or government evaluation, the programme unit should agree on resourcing modalities with potential donors or government counterparts at the outset. Box 19 outlines the key items that are required for the evaluation. The programme unit responsible for the evaluation should ensure that every item is considered.

3.4 ENGAGEMENT OF STAKEHOLDERS IN MONITORING AND EVALUATION

The engagement of stakeholders enlisted during planning and described in Section 2.2 continues to be relevant for monitoring and evaluation stages for the following reasons:

- The stakeholders, who set the vision and the prioritized results to realize that vision during the planning stage, have the best ideas on how the results would continue to remain relevant to them. They must therefore be involved in identifying the **information or feedback that is needed during implementation**, which determines the parameters for monitoring and evaluation.

- Having set the vision, priority results and initial parameters for monitoring and evaluation, the key stakeholders are best placed to ensure that the programmatic initiatives planned would deliver what was intended and the way it was intended.

Stakeholder participation in monitoring and evaluation can produce effective communication for various other objectives. These include: facilitate communication of 'early wins' to increase support and enlist engagement of those who are not yet engaged, ensure access of early products and services of initiatives for intended beneficiaries, mobilize additional resources to fill resource gaps, and ensure effective use of lessons learned in future decision making.

Stakeholder participation throughout the programming cycle ensures ownership, learning and sustainability of results. **Continued stakeholder participation in monitoring and evaluation cannot be assumed. It must be institutionalized.** Specific measures have to be built into programme and project management processes to ensure continued and effective involvement of stakeholders. The UNDP practice of institutionalizing stakeholder engagement is summarized in Box 20.

Box 20. Stakeholder involvement in monitoring and evaluation: Practice of UNDP

The programme management approach used by UNDP is designed to ensure that: A programme contributes to the achievement of the outcomes covered in the programme; a programme and its projects are coordinated within the national development framework; and agreed outputs are generated through projects and programme funds. This involves three levels: **the programme level,** which would cover one or more outcomes and provide linkage to overall national results; **the sectoral or outcome level;** and **the project level,** which relates to operational level of delivery of outputs by implementing activities using resources. The responsibilities for monitoring and evaluation are different at each programming level. (See Chapter 4 for further details.)

The participation of stakeholders is institutionalized in the management arrangements by boards or committees at the programme, sectoral/outcome and project levels. **These boards or committees should not duplicate existing mechanisms but instead use existing national structures and mechanisms. If no mechanisms exist, efforts should be made to constitute groups that fulfil such functions.** Each board or committee should have representatives of the owners, the beneficiaries and suppliers of technical services.

Sectoral or outcome level: There is a need to coordinate UNDP contributions to outcomes and provide feedback into the overall UNDP programme management. UNDP often participates in national sectoral coordination mechanisms to make explicit the link between UNDP contributions and national priorities. The sectoral or outcome level coordination mechanisms: promote partnerships bringing together all projects concerned within a single shared outcome; ensure synergy and reinforce a common strategy among partners towards results; and monitor the achievement of outcomes. Also, the UNDP programme manager should ensure that UNDP-supported outputs are coordinated at the outcome level.

Programme and Project Boards: Programme and Project Boards meet at a minimum annually to review annual progress of results, agree on any changes as required, and set new annual targets. These boards are management entities of the UNDP programme and focus on the UNDP contribution to national development results.

3.5 CAPACITY FOR MONITORING AND EVALUATION

In UNDP assisted programmes, national programme partners are jointly responsible with UNDP for carrying out certain planned monitoring and evaluation activities. In line with the principles of MfDR, national ownership and use of country systems, monitoring and evaluation efforts in UNDP should capitalize, be aligned to, and build on existing national monitoring and evaluation systems and capacities whenever feasible (see Box 21). When appropriate, monitoring and evaluation efforts of UNDP

Box 21. Examples of alignment with national systems

- National budgeting process
- National medium-term or long-term development strategic plan or framework
- Sector strategy, policy, programme or projects and national coordination bodies tasked to coordinate such activities
- National M&E systems for national development strategy, plan or framework and a sector strategy, policy, programme or projects
- Existing review mechanisms (poverty reduction strategy reviews, New Partnership for Africa's Development [NEPAD], peer-review, etc.)

should indicate where the organization's programmatic support requires further strengthening, including that of national systems. The analytical process and data used for planning provides initial opportunities and insights to discern future monitoring and evaluation requirements in comparison to existing data sources and quality. This also identifies areas where capacity to monitor and evaluate can be further developed in national partners at their request and when relevant.

At the higher levels of results (national goals, sector goals and outcomes), key stakeholders should typically form sector-wide or inter-agency groups around each major outcome or sector. Whenever there are existing national structures such as sector-wide coordination mechanisms, the United Nations and UNDP should ideally engage them and participate in these rather than setting up parallel systems. Sectoral or outcome-level coordinating mechanisms should not be a United Nations or UNDP management arrangement, but an existing national structure that is already charged with the coordination of the sector from a development perspective within the national context. These groups should have adequate capacity to be responsible for the following:

- Agree on an M&E framework for the outcomes and oversee their implementation. They ensure continuous outcome assessment and can enhance progress towards results.

- Promote partnerships and coordination within a single shared outcome. All projects that are generating relevant outputs to the corresponding outcome should be included in the outcome group to ensure inclusive discussions. This gives partners a common vision of the outcome to which different projects or outputs are contributing.

- Ensure synergy and coordination by reinforcing a common strategy among partners working towards common results.

- Monitor and evaluate, where appropriate, the achievement of outcomes and their contribution to national development goals. Outcome-level mechanisms are expected to determine who is responsible for monitoring and data collection, how often it will be collected, who will receive it and in what form. The results frameworks and the M&E framework serve as the basis for joint monitoring and evaluation by these groups.

- Carry out, participate in, and assure the overall quality of project, outcome, thematic and other types of reviews and evaluations and ensure that the processes and products meet international standards.

- Ensure effective use and dissemination of monitoring and evaluation information in future planning and decision making for improvements.

Capacities for monitoring and evaluation, like for most technical areas, exist on three levels: the enabling environment, the organizational level, and the individual level. Capacities at these levels are interdependent and influence each other through complex codependent relationships. Change in capacity generally occurs across four domains: institutional arrangements, including adequate resources and incentives; leadership; knowledge; and accountability mechanisms. Addressing only one of these levels or domains in a programme or project is unlikely to result in developing sustainable monitoring and evaluation capacities. Therefore, an outcome group needs to take a more holistic view in identifying and addressing the capacities needed to monitor and evaluate the results being pursued.

The relevant sector-wide or outcome-level coordinating mechanism may begin by undertaking a high-level or preliminary capacity assessment to understand the level of existing and required monitoring and evaluation capacities of a given entity.[27] Benchmarks for the three levels and four domains mentioned above are limited. However, the subsections below offer possible lines of questioning for the preliminary assessment. The insights generated by these questions and others may help a programme team formulate a capacity development response.

INSTITUTIONAL ARRANGEMENTS

- Is there a documented institutional or sector programme monitoring and evaluation policy that clarifies the mandates of monitoring and evaluation entities and programme or project teams, their responsibilities, and accountability measures for effective data collection and data management of public programmes or projects?

- Does the institutional and sector policy mandate require: establishing standard tools and templates, aligning organizational data with the national data collection and management, defining standards for monitoring and evaluating skills, and ensuring proper training?

- Are sufficient resources, including availability of skilled staff and financial resources, allocated for monitoring and evaluation activities in respective monitoring and evaluation entities? Do monitoring staff have proper statistical and analytical skills to compile and analyse sample and snapshot data?

- Is there an independent evaluation entity? Is the institution responsible for evaluation truly 'independent' from management and subject to evaluation? What is the reporting line of those responsible for carrying out evaluations? What mechanisms are there to safeguard the independence of the evaluation function?

LEADERSHIP

- Does high-level management support evidence-based decision making throughout the organization?

KNOWLEDGE

- Can high-quality information be disaggregated by relevant factors (such as gender, age and geography) to assess progress and analyse performance?

- Do the respective monitoring and evaluation entities have access to all relevant programme or project information to be gathered? Do the stakeholders have access to data collected and analysed (for example through the Internet)?

- Do the monitoring and evaluation entities have easy-to-understand formats for data collection and reporting? Is there a systematic and documented process of ensuring data quality control at all levels of collection, analysis and aggregation?

- Is there sufficient evaluation technical expertise in the national system? Are there national professional evaluation associations?

---

27 See UNDP, 'Practice Note on Capacity Assessment', October 2008, for a full discussion of UNDP capacity assessment methodology.

ACCOUNTABILITY

- Can the information from the monitoring and evaluation entities be provided to decision makers and other relevant stakeholders in a timely manner to enable evidence-based decision making?

Based on the above considerations and the insights generated from a high-level capacity assessment, one of four broad approaches would be selected to meet the monitoring and evaluation requirements of the results being pursued (see Figure 12). This high-level capacity assessment may also lead to more in-depth capacity assessments for particular areas.

It may be important for the sector-wide or outcome group to document the analysis from Figure 12 in a simple capacity development matrix (see Table 17). This matrix can help determine what monitoring and evaluation facilities exist in national partner institutions that can be used and identify gaps. The last column could be used to indicate how capacity development efforts—including detailed capacity assessments—may be addressed through other UNDP programmatic support, when relevant national demand and need arise.

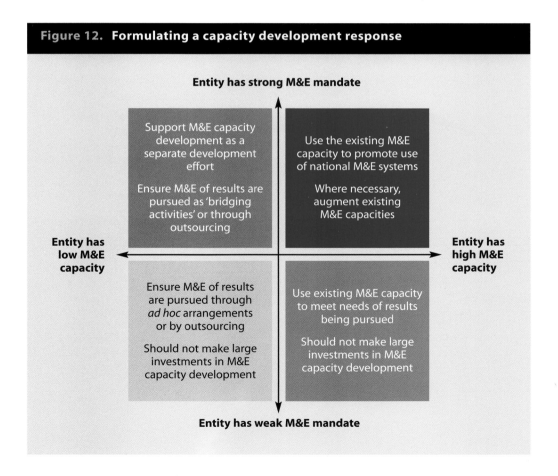

Figure 12. Formulating a capacity development response

Entity has strong M&E mandate

Support M&E capacity development as a separate development effort

Ensure M&E of results are pursued as 'bridging activities' or through outsourcing

Use the existing M&E capacity to promote use of national M&E systems

Where necessary, augment existing M&E capacities

Entity has low M&E capacity

Entity has high M&E capacity

Ensure M&E of results are pursued through *ad hoc* arrangements or by outsourcing

Should not make large investments in M&E capacity development

Use existing M&E capacity to meet needs of results being pursued

Should not make large investments in M&E capacity development

Entity has weak M&E mandate

Table 17. Monitoring and evaluation capacity matrix

Key Partner or Stakeholder of the Outcome Group Contributing to Result	Specific Component of Result or Outcome for Which the Partner is Directly Associated	Existing M&E Mechanisms and Capacities of Partner (institutional arrangements, leadership, knowledge, accountability)	Potential Areas for Developing M&E Capacities of Partner in Line with Its Mandate	Recommended Action for Developing M&E Capacities
Elections Authority	■ Organizing progress reviews, field visits ■ Collection and analysis data ■ Reporting	Limited to Headquarters level only.	Field monitoring, especially skills at the regional level to assess inclusion of disadvantaged and those in remote locations.	Initial capacity development support should be focused on developing monitoring skills pertaining to achieving the outcome. Funds available within the outcome may also be used to carry out a capacity assessment for the Elections Authority.
National Office of Statistics	All surveys will be completed by National Office of Statistics.	National Office of Statistics is a key national institute that is expected to provide high quality national surveys, analyses and reporting of findings.	Capacity development of National Office of Statistics is a national priority.	The Outcome Group should promote a national effort to develop capacity of National Office of Statistics for conducting, analysing and reporting on surveys.
Monitoring and Evaluation Division, Ministry of Planning	Government unit responsible for monitoring and evaluating major development projects and coordination of sector-level monitoring and evaluation (including the election project) at the national outcome level, and to build the national capacity in monitoring and evaluation.*	Monitoring and Evaluation Division is politically independent and is staffed with civil servants competent in monitoring and evaluation.	Monitoring and Evaluation Division has never worked directly with staff members of the Election Authority or National Office of Statistics regarding monitoring and evaluation in this particular area. This is at high risk to be politicized.	Support the efforts of the Monitoring and Evaluation Division to train the Election Authority Electoral Commission staff and National Office of Statistics staff on the development of specific indicators, baselines and targets and data collection methods for the work of the Elections Authority. Support the efforts of the Monitoring and Evaluation Division to promote the culture of evaluation within the Elections Authority.

* Units responsible for monitoring and evaluation of independent institutional bodies, such as a Monitoring and Evaluation Division, vary from country to country.

MONITORING FOR RESULTS

The previous chapter provided guidance on how to plan for monitoring and evaluation including developing an M&E framework and effectively addressing other planning needs, such as securing resources and capacities for implementing monitoring and evaluation activities. This chapter provides step-by-step guidance on how to implement planned monitoring activities. It also presents useful tools and tips for effective monitoring and use of monitoring evidence in decision making.

The chapter follows the general steps of implementation of monitoring:

1. Have a clear common understanding of the following:

   a. The **monitoring policies** applicable to the respective monitoring entity

   b. Relevant **roles and responsibilities** and how they are applied in monitoring for both outcomes and outputs, and management entities in projects and programmes

   c. Commonly used monitoring tools and approaches

2. Reinforce and elaborate the initial monitoring framework (described in Chapter 3) with detailed information needed to implement monitoring actions. This includes finalizing reference points for periodic monitoring such as indicators, baselines, risks, and annual targets, and locking them in monitoring information systems.

3. Implement monitoring actions: organize, plan and implement monitoring actions, using selected tools for collection and analysis of data and reporting.

4. Use monitoring data objectively for management action and decision making.

These steps are depicted in Figure 13.

There is no blueprint for monitoring that can be applied to all monitoring situations. The monitoring approach an organization uses in a given situation—for example, in a

Figure 13. General steps for implementing monitoring

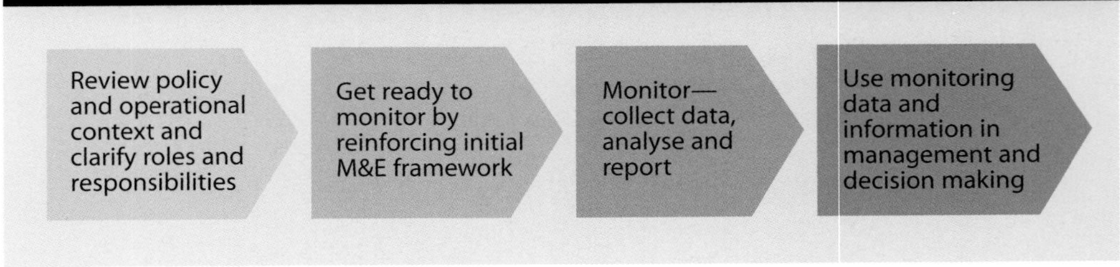

Review policy and operational context and clarify roles and responsibilities → Get ready to monitor by reinforcing initial M&E framework → Monitor—collect data, analyse and report → Use monitoring data and information in management and decision making

country, regional or global programme, or in a development project—depends on many factors. They include corporate accountability requirements (both organizational and developmental), and the complexity, scope and context of the results being pursued. The substance of monitoring and approaches used by organizations such as UNDP, its subunits, programmes and projects depend to a great extent on corporate monitoring policies. This chapter presents these elements in the operational context of UNDP.

TIP Monitoring is part of programme and project management not an addition to it. Monitoring should not be regarded as merely a management or reporting requirement. Rather, it should be regarded as an opportunity to:

- Engage beneficiaries so that they feel ownership of results being achieved and are motivated to sustain them.
- Demonstrate achievement of development results, how they benefit the intended people, and leverage support of the beneficiaries and other stakeholders to address any operational challenges faced.
- Nurture an inclusive and purposeful monitoring culture to make implementation and management effective and interesting as well as to ease gathering of data and evidence objectively to back achievements and make decisions.

4.1 MONITORING POLICY OF UNDP, ITS OPERATIONAL CONTEXT AND ROLES AND RESPONSIBILITIES

POLICY CONTEXT FOR MONITORING

Any organization that strives for results requires a robust, continuous and effective monitoring system. This requirement becomes even more relevant for UNDP, as the organization is aiming for results that: are nationally owned and form part of the multi-stakeholder framework, such as the UNDAF or national development plan; cover global, regional and country levels; are defined and achieved through the engagement of a broad range of stakeholders; and have to be accounted for. UNDP works towards a robust monitoring system through effective policies, tools, processes and systems so that it can meet the multiple monitoring challenges it faces.

The monitoring policy of UNDP is stated in the POPP and notes that all results—outcomes and outputs—to which UNDP is contributing must be monitored, regardless of budget and duration. Each programme supported by UNDP must be monitored to ensure that:

- The outcomes agreed in each programme (country, regional and global) and their constituent projects are being achieved. This is a collective responsibility among UNDP and its partners. However, UNDP is responsible for monitoring its contribution towards the outcome by ensuring that the outputs being generated with UNDP assistance are contributing towards the outcome.

- Each constituent project of the respective programme produces the envisaged outputs in an efficient manner as per the overall development plan and the corresponding annual workplan. This is a specific UNDP responsibility.

- Decisions of programmes and projects are based on facts and evidence.

- Lessons learned are systematically captured for knowledge and improving future programmes and projects.

The UNDP Strategic Plan 2008-2011 further emphasizes that outcomes must be nationally owned, hence the first line of accountability rests with national authorities. UNDP will contribute to those outcomes. Therefore, its chief accountability must be for its contributions to national development impact. The on-the-ground performance of UNDP should be assessed first at the country level, as part of a joint process with governments and other partners, and second at the corporate level by senior management and the Executive Board, based on monitoring and evaluation data. UNDP is directly accountable for the corporate services and global and regional programmes that support country programmes.

OPERATIONAL CONTEXT FOR MONITORING

The key reference for monitoring is the M&E framework associated with each programme (see Chapter 3). Within this, the results frameworks (sometimes referred to as 'results and resources frameworks') of the corresponding planning documents—such as the UNDAF, Global Programme Document, Regional Programme Document, CPD and constituent project documents—further indicate what is to be monitored. The results frameworks state: the selected national, regional and global development results towards which UNDP contributes, including UN level outcomes as applicable (based on the UNDAF); outcomes more specifically addressed by UNDP support at the country level (in CPDs), regionally (in regional programme documents) and globally (in global programme documents); and outputs associated with each outcome. The results frameworks also give indicators, baseline and targets for each outcome and output as applicable.

While the prime objective of monitoring in UNDP is achievement of results, it is also necessary to monitor the appropriate use of resources at all levels. UNDP does this through monitoring at three levels: outputs and projects, outcomes and programme.

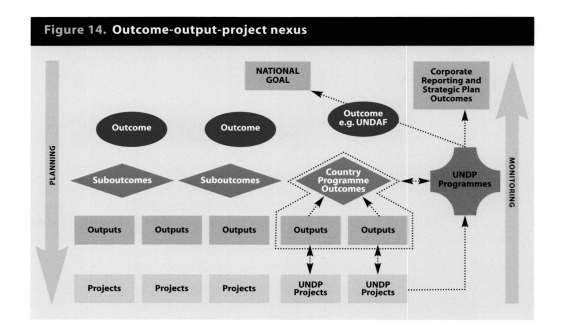

Figure 14. Outcome-output-project nexus

Figure 14 depicts the nexus among:

- The results continuum: outcomes and outputs
- The management arrangements and entities of projects and programmes
- The interrelationships at the three levels of projects, programmes and results (both outcomes and outputs)

From Figure 14, the following can be noted.

Project and output level

The project is the entity that uses inputs and resources and converts them to activities and outputs. It is also the entity from which monitoring actions begin. Outputs generated by projects are always connected directly to an outcome.[28] UNDP projects normally operate in complex development settings and it is important to be clear on each project's role, deliverables and outputs, and their connections to other projects to avoid mix ups.

There is a critical responsibility at each project level with regards to the generation of the planned output through a carefully planned set of relevant and effective activities, and proper use of resources allocated for those activities. Both these aspects must be monitored. The primary responsibility for monitoring at the project or output level lies

---

28 In some cases, it is also possible that an output may be connected to more than one outcome. For example, a database on displaced communities generated by one project could serve not only an outcome on safety of the displaced, but also other outcomes relating, *inter alia*, to their education and nutrition and health standards, etc.

with the project manager. Primary monitoring tools used at the project level by UNDP are: the corporate project management system (Atlas); field visits, consultations and reviews with stakeholders; Annual (and quarterly) Project Reports; and the Annual Project Review Process.

Outcome level

The outcomes are achieved by the generation of outputs through projects (and other related activities such as soft advocacy). These projects and related activities could be supported by UNDP or others.

In UN and UNDP operating environments, there are normally more than one outcome hierarchies: UNDAF outcomes and UNDP country programme outcomes. In Figure 14, higher level outcomes, such as UNDAF or national outcomes, are depicted by oval shapes. The country programme outcomes are depicted by diamond shapes. They could also be conceived as suboutcomes that lie within a higher level national or UNDAF outcome as depicted.

> **NOTE** There could be a number of suboutcomes associated with a broad national outcome or an UNDAF outcome. They serve the purpose of convenience of communication and presentation, particularly in complex results frameworks and multi-agency environments such as UN and UNDP cycles. Sub-outcomes may be referred to differently, for example, as 'intermediary outcomes'. Note also that in some cases they may not be needed. For example, an output generated by a national agency or a single donor (for example, World Bank) could be directly connected to a national-level outcome without necessarily a sub-outcome level. Sub outcomes or country programme outcomes encourage UNDP to remain focused on its mandate and comparative advantage while addressing a UNDAF or national outcome.

Monitoring at a given outcome level requires a clear understanding of all contributory outputs to the outcome from all partners and the connections of the sub-outcomes to other levels of outcomes. Each partner is responsible for its own contribution toward the outcome, but the responsibility for monitoring the overall outcome is shared among all partners. For practical purposes, one of the partners should be assigned the responsibility to coordinate among the partners. Given the primacy of national ownership for all development results, primary responsibility for monitoring at the outcome level should be with the government or a national institution. UNDP supports this monitoring function of national institutions and focuses on developing their capacities for monitoring. This focus can extend to developing national monitoring systems. However, such capacity development activities should be elaborated within overall capacity development approaches as stated in the UNDP approach for capacity development[29] (referred to in Chapter 3).

---

29 UNDP, 'Supporting Capacity Development: The UNDP Approach', and UNDP, 'Practice Note on Capacity Development'.

Primary monitoring tools used at the outcome level by UNDP are: the corporate results management system (RBM Platform); field visits, consultations and reviews with stakeholders; findings from project and programme monitoring; Annual Reports; and the Annual Programme and UNDAF Review Process. For outcome monitoring, UNDP systems should be augmented by links to national systems and those of other development partners. UNDP should always seek to engage existing national processes in this regard.

UNDP programme level

Depicted by the cross shape in Figure 14, UNDP programmes support several projects and outcomes. Programme-level monitoring entails:

- Oversight of all constituent projects

- Monitoring for each outcome that is being supported by programme funds

- Accountability of the programme for UNDAF, contribution to national results, and achieving the corporate outcomes in the Strategic Plan

The primary responsibility with UNDP at the programme level rests with the programme manager. The monitoring tools used at the programme level by UNDP are generally the same as those used at the outcome level.

It is important to understand that while outputs and outcomes are intrinsic elements of the results chain, projects and programmes are, in effect, arrangements to manage the generation of the outputs towards achieving outcomes. UNDP monitoring covers all the above elements.

ROLES AND RESPONSIBILITIES FOR MONITORING

Monitoring of development results takes place at different levels—typically the national, programme, outcome and project output. There are specific individual and collective monitoring responsibilities at each level for partner organizations.

While some monitoring functions can be assigned to specific entities or functionaries, such as project managers at the project or output level, monitoring responsibilities at outcome and higher result levels are collective efforts. Successful monitoring and achievement of results depends on each partner being clear on their individual and shared roles and responsibilities. The respective roles and responsibilities associated at each point at which monitoring takes place and how they apply to UNDP programmes and projects are indicated in Table 18.

4.2 PREPARING TO MONITOR BY REINFORCING THE INITIAL M&E PLAN

Once there is clear understanding on the monitoring policy, operational context and roles and responsibilities, one can prepare to implement monitoring actions. The first activity in implementing monitoring activities is to ensure that the M&E framework is up to date. The M&E framework prepared at the end of the planning stage of a programme or project (described in Chapter 3), forms the basis for this purpose. It should be carefully reviewed and elaborated as necessary.

Table 18. Roles and responsibilities for monitoring

Who: Actors and Accountability	What: Roles and Responsibilities	How: Timing and Methodology

National authorities
Main responsibilities:
■ Lead and oversee national programmes to determine progress towards intended results
■ Identify and manage partnerships
	Monitoring for programme level results
	■ To ensure nationally owned results-based monitoring and evaluation
	■ To provide clear basis for decision making and guide development initiatives
	■ To use partner monitoring systems based on their comparative advantages
	■ To link results with resources and ensure accountability in the use of resources
	■ To ensure quality and the appropriate use of monitoring evidence and lessons learned
	■ To resolve key bottlenecks to implementation in order to improve the chances of achieving results (outcomes)
		1. At initial planning stages
		  ■ Through active participation in development and approval of M&E frameworks for national programmes and UNDAF
		2. Annual reviews (of progress towards results) by
		  ■ Reviewing progress, issues, and trends in the achievement of results given in documents for the annual review
		  ■ Making decisions on changes as needed
		  ■ Approving future work including M&E tasks
		3. Participating in joint monitoring (selectively as decided by prior agreement with partners)

Senior managers of UNDP programmes
Main responsibilities:
■ Lead, implement and monitor the progress of country programmes, together with governments, UN organizations and other partners
■ Collaborate with national partners to determine the focus and intended results of UNDP assistance to the country
■ Identify and manage partnerships
■ Assess the overall performance of UNDP assistance to the country (progress towards and achievement of results)
■ Ensure the strategic and cost-effective use of UNDP resources
	Monitoring for programme level results
	■ To forge strong coalitions for results
	■ To provide clear basis for decision making and guide development initiatives
	■ To ensure active and results-based monitoring
	■ To ensure quality and the appropriate use of monitoring evidence and lessons learned
	■ To resolve key bottlenecks to implementation in order to improve the chances of achieving results (outcomes)
	■ To link results with resources and ensure accountability in the use of resources
	■ To adjust UNDP assistance in view of emerging changes as required
	■ To position UNDP strategically within the framework of development cooperation with the country
	■ To approve M&E framework for the programme (for UNDP CPAP M&E Plan) in line with UNDAF and national M&E plans as applicable
	■ To use project and outcome level monitoring data and feed it into programme discussions
		1. At initial planning stages
		  ■ Through active participation in the development and approval of M&E framework
		2. Participate in joint monitoring (see above)
		3. Prior to annual reviews by
		  ■ Determining strategic contribution being made by programme towards results through review of outcome group reviews and Annual Project Reports
		  ■ Deciding on strategic changes needed in programme results and resources, if needed
		  ■ Finalizing evidence-based contribution of programme as a whole to annual review
		4. Participate in annual reviews

Table 18 (cont-d). Roles and responsibilities for monitoring

Who: Actors and Accountability	What: Roles and Responsibilities	How: Timing and Methodology

UNDP portfolio managers
 	
Main responsibilities:
 	
■ Contribute to sectoral/outcome level coordination mechanisms
 	
■ Manage UNDP portfolio of programmes and projects in a thematic area such as governance or poverty, in other words, UNDP contribution to outcomes
	At outcome level
	■ To analyse progress towards achievement of outcomes
	■ To assess the efficacy of partnership strategies and take related actions (e.g., better coordination with partners)
	■ To monitor the effectiveness of implementation strategies in tackling the constraints to the achievement of results (outcomes) and take related actions
	■ To ensure effective use of resources, deploying them to maximize the possibility of achieving results (outcomes)
	■ To discern and promote capacity development in monitoring and evaluation
	■ To use project-level monitoring data and feed it into outcome-level discussions
		1. At initial planning stages
		  ■ Through active participation in development and approval of M&E framework for respective outcomes
		2. Throughout programme cycle by carrying out monitoring activities and joint monitoring
		3. Prior to annual reviews by determining:
		  ■ Progress towards the achievement of outcomes
		  ■ Progress of the partnership strategies for achieving outcomes
		  ■ Rate and efficiency of resource use
		  ■ Issues that require decisions at the annual reviews
		  ■ Inputs to programme reviews and annual reviews
		4. Participate in annual reviews at the outcome level

Project managers and staff
 	
Main responsibilities:
 	
■ Manage UNDP-assisted projects to help produce outputs
 	
■ Contribute to project management and project performance
	At project level, monitoring outputs
	■ To ground the project in the larger context
	■ To take steps towards achieving output targets
	■ To ensure effective collaboration with partners
	■ To interface with beneficiaries
	■ To ensure efficient use of resources
	■ To feed information of project data to higher level monitoring (outcome and programme-level monitoring)
		1. At initial planning stages
		  ■ Development of and agreement on M&E framework for project through an inclusive process
		2. Throughout programme cycle by carrying out monitoring activities connected with the project
		3. Prior to annual reviews by determining:
		  ■ Progress towards the achievement of outputs and contribution related outcomes
		  ■ Rate and efficiency of resource use
		  ■ Issues that require decisions at the annual reviews
		  ■ Inputs to programme reviews and annual reviews in the Annual Project Reports
		4. Ensure holding annual reviews of the project

There is no artificially fixed time for elaborating the M&E framework, except that it should be done prior to implementing programme initiatives and as close as possible to when actual implementation starts. For UNDP country, regional and global programmes, the detailed programme-level M&E framework should be prepared after the submission of the respective programme documents for Executive Board approval.

The period of six to nine months prior to the beginning of the programme implementation cycle is often opportune to do this. For country programmes, this period is when the CPAP and its constituent projects and their AWPs are prepared. Such timing helps forge better linkages and mutual reinforcement between programmes and projects, thereby not only increasing the overall coherence of the programmes, but also enabling monitoring to be focused on a coherent set of programmatic activities and targets.

As noted in Chapter 3, the M&E framework comprises three components: a narrative component, a results framework and a planning matrix for monitoring and evaluation. Any changes that might be needed to the narrative component are unlikely to be substantial, and updating of that component would be relatively straightforward. However, there might be a need to refine the results map and the planning matrix for monitoring and evaluation on the basis of new (and more accurate) information that emerges during the development of specific projects. Detailed information on the outcomes, outputs and related indicators, baselines, risks, and assumptions becomes clearer during the development stages of the CPAP and specific constituent projects, which take place subsequent to the initial overall programme planning stage. Data that emerges during detailed project development stages could significantly improve the initial descriptions of outputs, indicators, baselines, risks and assumptions, and thereby enhance the effectiveness and quality of monitoring. Moreover, the M&E framework is first prepared at the end of the planning process, which is focused on planning for results. Detailed information pertaining to implementation or monitoring (for example, type or scheduling of monitoring events, methods to be used, and so forth) could not have been easily accessible or accurately predicted at that time. Therefore, it should be carefully reviewed and incorporated at this stage.

Elaborating the M&E framework provides the opportunity for the M&E framework to be a more realistic and effective tool for monitoring. An example of the planning matrix is given in Table 14 based on the sample results table on the enhanced capacity of electoral management authority discussed in Chapter 2.

For UNDP, at the country level, the CPAP is the overall instrument for managing results. The M&E framework for the CPAP should be prepared and finalized along with the CPAP and ideally be seen as a constituent component to the latter. Similarly, for regional and global programmes, M&E frameworks should be prepared mirroring the respective programme approved by the Executive Board.

Updating the M&E framework is not a one-time event. Each time a significant change to the results framework is effected, for example when existing projects are completed or new projects are added to the CPAP, both the CPAP and the M&E framework should be revised and approved. Annual work planning is the most pertinent point for this continuous updating of the CPAP and M&E framework.

The finalization of the CPAP and the M&E framework is a critical point in initiating monitoring. The following four actions should take place in this phase:

- **At the individual project level, develop detailed M&E frameworks** for projects in accordance with the generation of project specific outputs. The project-level outputs should be the same as those in overall planning documents of programmes (CPDs, CPAPs, and regional and global programme documents) and their M&E frameworks. Furthermore, the project results matrices and the project M&E plans should be synchronized with the programmes and their M&E plans. Initial data needed for setting up monitoring should be gathered during the formulation stage of each project. The project results and monitoring information should then be entered into relevant national, corporate, project or programme management information systems (for UNDP, this is Atlas).

- As projects are implemented through AWPs, it is critical to **set annual targets for outputs and clearly reflect them in the AWPs** of projects for monitoring purposes at the end of the year. (See Section 4.3 for further details on AWPs.) Unlike outcomes, each partner responsible for an output has to generate the entire output that is contributing towards the outcome. Therefore, what matters most in project-level monitoring is to have clear means to indicate progress towards generating the entire output through annual targets.

- **Once agreed upon, lock annual output targets in AWPs** for performance monitoring in any existing national or corporate results management or outcome monitoring systems. For UNDP, the annual output targets in AWPs of projects would also serve as the reference points in the corporate results monitoring systems. They are therefore first entered in Atlas and then captured by the RBM Platform.

- **At the programme level, ensure that the elaborated programme-level M&E framework** and the constituent projects flow from outputs to outcomes (results logic) and from projects to country programme (management entities).

Once these activities have been completed, the monitoring actions can be systematically implemented.

4.3   MONITOR: COLLECTION OF DATA, ANALYSIS AND REPORTING

SCOPE OF MONITORING

Monitoring aims to identify progress towards results, precipitate decisions that would increase the likelihood of achieving results, enhance accountability and learning. All monitoring efforts should, at a minimum, address the following:

- Progress towards outcomes—This entails periodically analysing the extent to which intended outcomes have actually been achieved or are being achieved.

- Factors contributing to or impeding achievement of the outcomes—This necessitates monitoring the country context and the economic, sociological, political and other developments simultaneously taking place and is closely linked to risk management.

- Individual partner contributions to the outcomes through outputs—These outputs may be generated by programmes, projects, policy advice, advocacy and other activities. Their monitoring and evaluation entails analysing whether or not outputs are in the process of being delivered as planned and whether or not the outputs are contributing to the outcome.

- Partnership strategy—This requires the review of current partnership strategies and their functioning as well as formation of new partnerships as needed. This helps to ensure that partners who are concerned with an outcome have a common appreciation of problems and needs, and that they share a synchronized strategy.

- Lessons being learned and creation of knowledge products for wider sharing.

Partners may add additional elements where needed for management or analysis, while keeping a realistic scope in view of available capacities. Monitoring usually provides raw data that requires further analysis and synthesis prior to reporting for decision making. Using information gained through monitoring, programme managers must analyse and take action on the programme and project activities to ensure that the intended results—results that are in the agreed results and resources frameworks—are being achieved. Managers of programmes also monitor and document the contributions of soft development initiatives and strategic partnerships.

PRIORITIZING MONITORING

In practice, it is necessary to prioritize monitoring. Two factors can help assign monitoring priority: **criticality** of a UNDP contribution to the attainment of the overall result; and the severity of **risks** it faces. As the criticality and severity of risks change, the corresponding priority attached monitoring of an initiative also changes.

Criticality of a UNDP project or an initiative is considered high when: it is connected with a tight time-bound high national priority; there is critical reliance on relevant UNDP comparative strengths, expertise and competencies for the achievement of planned results; or it involves a critical UNDP coordination role entrusted by government and other partners.

Risks are initially identified in the results frameworks with their potential impacts. However, during programme and project implementation, additional risks may arise from a changing operational environment (such as a crisis) that may have to be factored in when prioritizing monitoring.

Based on the two criteria of criticality and risks, as indicated in Figure 15, it is possible to determine four broad categories to assign priority in monitoring. It is also possible to identify which of the two aspects should be followed more closely.

MONITORING IN CRISIS SETTINGS

Standard processes of planning, monitoring and evaluation that apply in 'normal' developmental contexts need to be modified in order to be sensitive to crisis situations. In crisis contexts, monitoring approaches and processes should include:

- Reference in the M&E framework to conflict-sensitive measures that need to be considered in implementing monitoring actions. These actions should flow from the situation analysis that applies to a given programme or project.

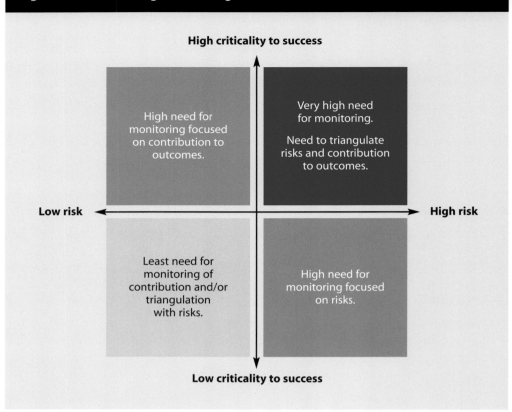

Figure 15. Prioritizing monitoring

High criticality to success

High need for monitoring focused on contribution to outcomes.

Very high need for monitoring.

Need to triangulate risks and contribution to outcomes.

Low risk ← → High risk

Least need for monitoring of contribution and/or triangulation with risks.

High need for monitoring focused on risks.

Low criticality to success

- Monitoring should continually feed back to the conflict analysis—and the big picture—in order to make sure understanding of the crisis is up to date. Monitoring should also inform any changes that may be required to results maps.

- Crisis situations are normally very fluid. Therefore, monitoring actions should be sensitive to changing circumstances. For example, monitoring schedules and data gathering methods may require frequent review and changes.

- Take additional measures to make monitoring processes inclusive of the most vulnerable groups. Interviews, field visits, documents consulted, and all information gathered should be triangulated as much as possible to prevent bias. Furthermore, officials should be consulted regularly to ensure their ownership of results as well as to maintain credibility and balance in monitoring.

- Monitoring can help address intragroup disparities—**particularly gender-related disparities**—that can result from development initiatives. This applies particularly to vulnerable groups, such as internally displaced people, minorities and indigenous groups. Particular attention should be paid to disaggregating monitoring data by sex, age, location and so forth in order to ensure programming initiatives meet the well being of marginalized people, especially women, youth and the elderly.

- Capacity development for monitoring should be pursued even in crisis situations. However, it is necessary to execute monitoring, even if desired capacity development efforts fall behind the planned targets.

- If direct monitoring of projects in crisis situations is difficult or impossible, capacity development of local partners and civil society organizations for monitoring should be given serious consideration. Where project staff cannot conduct regular field visits, monitoring should still be done using secondary information from credible informants. However, use of such methods should be clearly stated in reporting data, without necessarily disclosing informants' identities as that may place them at risk.

- Monitoring should also factor in security risks and build adequate safeguards and resources to manage such risks.

SELECTING THE MONITORING APPROACH AND TOOLS

There is a range of approaches and tools that may be applied to monitoring projects, programmes, outcomes and any other programmatic activity. Those who manage programmes and projects must determine the correct mix of monitoring tools and approaches for each project, programme or outcome, ensuring that the monitoring contains an appropriate balance between:

- Data and analysis—This entails obtaining and analysing documentation from projects that provides information on progress.

- Validation—This entails checking or verifying whether or not the reported progress is accurate.

- Participation—This entails obtaining feedback from partners and beneficiaries on progress and proposed actions.

Table 19 lists a variety of common monitoring tools and mechanisms, divided into three categories according to their predominant characteristic.

Table 19. Selecting the right mix of monitoring mechanisms		
Purpose		
Data and Analysis	**Validation**	**Participation**
■ M&E framework ■ AWPs ■ Progress and quarterly reports on achievement of outputs ■ Annual Project Report ■ Project delivery reports and combined delivery reports ■ Substantive or technical documents: MDG Reports, National Human Development Reports, Human Development Reports ■ Progress towards achieving outcomes and Standard Progress Reports on outcomes	■ Field visits ■ Spot-checks ■ Reviews and assessments by other partners ■ Client surveys ■ Evaluations ■ Reviews and studies	■ Sectoral and outcome groups and mechanisms ■ Steering committees and mechanisms ■ Stakeholder meetings ■ Focus group meetings ■ Annual review
← **Learning** takes place through all monitoring tools and mechanisms →		

It is not realistic to expect that any one monitoring tool or mechanism will satisfy all needs. Different stakeholders may use different tools or may use the same tools differently. For partners who are actively involved in managing for results, monitoring data and gathering information begins at the project level. The most common tools and events used for systematic monitoring, data gathering and reporting applicable to projects used by partners are AWPs, field visits and Annual Project Reports (APRs). Monitoring of outcomes typically requires a different mix of tools than those traditionally used at the project level. Instruments such as project visits or bilateral meetings may be insufficient because the scope of a given project is too narrow or the range of partners involved is too limited. Instead, more useful tools may include reviews by outcome groups, analyses and surveys. (Further information on such tools is available in Chapters 5 through 8.)

Annual work plans (AWPs)

AWPs detail the activities to be carried out by a programme or project—including who is responsible for what, time frames, planned inputs and funding sources—in order to generate outputs in relation to the outcome. AWPs also serve as good references for monitoring progress later in the year. Therefore AWPs and their accompanying monitoring tools are among the most important tools in monitoring, especially for programmes and projects that are normally multi-year and multi-partner efforts. In order to plan, manage and monitor a programme for a given period (typically a calendar year), most partners—including UNDP—use AWPs.[30] There are numerous formats and ways to prepare AWPs. Usually AWPs are produced at the beginning of the year as a planning tool, and their monitoring versions are prepared later in the year separately. One possible AWP format, which has the advantage of combining both annual planning and reporting elements, is given in Table 20. All information except the last two columns should be given at the beginning of the year. The last two columns should be completed at the end of the year.

The project manager who is responsible for delivering the outputs should prepare the AWP. Depending on the complexity and nature of the results being pursued, the AWP preparation could be a collective effort. The institution managing the project ensures the interface between the desired results and the expectations of the target beneficiaries, thus promoting a sense of ownership among all partners. Project management should also contribute to developing the required partnerships among the partners through the AWP preparation process.

AWPs have multiple uses in monitoring:

- To understand the contributions and targets set and agreed by the partners for the year to achieve a planned result in a transparent way

- To review ongoing progress against the plan and identify bottlenecks

- To use as a basis for reporting at the end of the year (annual report) and planning future work

---

30 Annual Work plans should not cover more than a 12-month period. However, usually at the start-up of the programme, these may cover less than one year.

Table 20. Example of an Annual Work Plan format with monitoring component

Outcome:

Expected Outputs	Planned Activities	Time-frame				Responsible Party	Budget				Monitoring Framework	
		Q1	Q2	Q3	Q4		Funding source	Budget description	Amount	Expenditures	Progress towards outputs
Output 1											*Status of progress to target contribution to country programme outcome*
Targets:											
Output 2											
Targets:											
Output 3											
Targets:											
Total											

Notes:

1. The above is only illustrative. It may be adapted for practical use as appropriate.

2. The format is based on the UNDG AWP format and its related monitoring tool (currently used as two separate formats).

3. Outputs in column 1 should also give baselines, associated indicators and annual targets as applicable

4. All activities including monitoring and evaluation activities to be undertaken during the year towards the stated outputs must be included in the Activities column

5. Actual expenditures against activities completed should be given in the Expenditures column.

6. The last column should be completed using data on annual indicator targets to state progress towards achieving the outputs. Where relevant, comment on factors that facilitated or constrained achievement of results including: whether risks and assumptions as identified in the country programme M&E framework materialized or whether new risks emerged; and internal factors such as timing of inputs and activities, quality of products and services, coordination and other management issues.

Field visits

Field visits are essential for any field-based project. Field visits should be planned well in order to be of maximum use. The following considerations may help plan an effective field visit.

- What is the purpose of the visit in terms of monitoring?—Field visits serve the purpose of validation. They validate the results reported by programmes and projects. They are of particular importance to large, key programmes and projects that are essential for outcomes. They involve an assessment of progress, results and problems and may also include visits to the project management or directorate.

- Timing—A field visit may take place at any time of the year. If undertaken in the first half of the year, just after the annual review, it may be oriented towards the validation of results. If undertaken in the latter part of the year, the field visit should provide the latest information on progress towards annual and outcome review processes. The reports of field visits should be action-oriented and brief, submitted within a week of return to the office to the members of the respective Project Board, Programme Board and the Outcome Group for consideration and appropriated action if required.

- Who should participate and be involved?—Visits are increasingly joint monitoring efforts of several partners working on a cluster of programmes and projects targeting an outcome or result. Joint visits also support ownership of the results. A team of staff from one or more partners may make visits to projects that are contributing to one particular outcome or in a specific geographical area addressing a specific development condition, for example displaced persons, post-natural disaster or a vulnerable community. Such joint efforts are often an efficient way to obtain a comprehensive overview of progress. In planning such visits, it is important to focus on what specific issues are to be addressed and to ensure that relevant national partners and beneficiaries would be available, involved and participate as required.

- Dialogue and consultations—The emphasis should be on observing and ascertaining credible information on progress being made towards the attainment of results—outputs and outcomes—as well as their quality and sustainability. Those undertaking the field visit should discern other initiatives, for example soft assistance or gaps in strategy that may need to be addressed. Field visits should not be used for lengthy discussions on detailed implementation issues. Such issues, if raised during field visits, may be noted for discussion with relevant partners who can resolve them.

- Findings of field visits—These should be forwarded to appropriate partners and stakeholders for effective action. A format for field visit reports is given in Annex 2.

Box 22. UNDP policy on field visits and good implementation practice

A representative from the UNDP country office must visit each programme and project contributing to results in the CPD and CPAP at least once a year. Field visits may be undertaken by the Programme Manager, Policy Adviser or a team from the country office (particularly when dealing with a complex outcome). The Resident Representative and other country office management staff are also encouraged to undertake field visits.

Annual Project Report (APR)

The APR is a self-assessment by the project management that serves as the basis for assessing the performance of programmes and projects in terms of their contributions to intended outcomes through outputs. The APR should provide an accurate update on project results, identify major constraints and propose future directions. As a self-assessment report by project management to the country office, it can be used to spur dialogue with partners.

Content, format and preparation of the APR

The basic APR should reflect the assessment of the AWP, discussed earlier. The APR is a report from the project to other stakeholders through the board or steering committee. APRs should be objective and may reflect views not agreed to by all stakeholders. The APR should be brief and contain the basic minimum elements required for the assessment of results, major problems and proposed actions. These elements include:

- An analysis of project performance over the reporting period, including outputs produced and, where possible, information on the status of the outcome

- Constraints in progress towards results, that is, issues, risks and reasons behind the constraints

- Lessons learned and indications of how these will be incorporated

- Clear recommendations for the future approach to addressing the main challenges

Beyond the minimum content, additional elements may be added as required by the project management or other partners. In the spirit of the principles of harmonization

---

Box 23. Assurance role

UNDP has introduced the concept of programme and project assurance, which, *inter alia*, enhances the quality of monitoring. Managers of projects and programmes have the primary responsibility for ensuring that the monitoring data is accurate and of high quality. The assurance role is additional and is part of the responsibility of the programme and project board, as referred to in Box 20 in Chapter 3. It is normally delegated to a UNDP staff member who is not directly involved in the management of the project or programme. Typically, the programme assurance role is assigned to the M&E Focal Point in the office, and the project assurance role is assigned to a Programme Officer. The assurance function is operational during all stages of formulation, implementation and closure of projects and programmes. With regard to monitoring, the assurance role plays the following functions:

- Adherence to monitoring and reporting requirements and standards
- Ensure that project results elements are clear and captured in management information systems to facilitate monitoring and reporting
- Ensure that high-quality periodic progress reports are prepared and submitted
- Perform oversight activities, such as periodic monitoring visits and 'spot-checks'
- Ensure that decisions of the project and programme board and steering committee are followed and changes are managed in line with the required procedures

and simplification, the partners should agree on harmonized reporting formats (to the extent possible) to eliminate multiple reports and minimize work. From a monitoring perspective, it is critical for the APR to flow from the AWP and for it to serve the objectives of the overall M&E framework and hence the achievement of the planned results.

The project management is responsible for preparing and circulating the APR. The APR is prepared by project staff with specific attention to outputs and is considered by donors, other partners and stakeholders. Since project staff members are often experts in their fields, monitoring at the project level may also entail some expert assessment of the status of progress towards the achievement of the outcome.

The person responsible for project assurance (see Box 23 on page 115) should review and make observations on the validity, reliability and quality of monitoring data collected and compiled by the project.

Use of the APR

The APR is part of oversight and monitoring of projects and a key building block of the annual review. Normally, it also feeds into the annual reporting by donor partners on the results that they support. Once the APR has been prepared and distributed, the next step is to hold consultations, which may take place at the project board or steering committee, or through written observations from partners. Depending on its content and approach, the APR can be used for the following:

- Performance assessment—When using mechanisms such as outcome boards, groups or steering committees to review project performance, the APR may provide a basis for consensus-building and joint decision making on recommendations for future courses of action. Key elements of the APR are fed into higher levels of reviews, for example the UNDAF annual review, sectoral reviews and reviews of national development results and plans. The APR should be used as a basis for feedback on project performance.

- Learning—The APR should provide information on what went right or what went wrong, and the factors contributing to success or failure. This should feed into the annual review, learning and practitioners networks, repositories of knowledge and evaluations. It is recommended that the APR of the final year of the project include specific sections on lessons learned and planning for sustainability (exit strategy). APRs may address the main lessons learned in terms of best and worst practices, the likelihood of success, and recommendations for follow-up actions where necessary. APRs may also be used to share results and problems with beneficiaries, partners and stakeholders and to solicit their feedback.

- Decision making—The partners may use the APR for planning future actions and implementation strategies, tracking progress in achieving outputs, approaching 'soft assistance', and developing partnerships and alliances. The APR allows the project board, steering committee and partners to seek solutions to the major constraints to achievement of the planned results. As a result of this consultative process, necessary modifications could be made to the overall project design and to the corresponding overall results frameworks in the planning documents.

Joint monitoring

Monitoring of development results cannot be carried out in isolation or on an *ad hoc* basis. Whenever possible, monitoring should be carried out as joint or collaborative efforts among key stakeholders. Primary stakeholders—including multiple UN organizations working towards a given results as well as representatives of identified beneficiary groups and key national partners—should be involved to the extent possible. Such joint monitoring should also manifest in joint field visits. Ideally, joint monitoring should be organized and coordinated through the national outcome groups or sector-wide mechanisms. Joint monitoring should lead to joint analysis and precipitating decisions, for example to agree formally at annual reviews.

Where national institution-led joint monitoring is constrained, the UNCT could form interagency groups around each UNDAF outcome. These groups would use the results matrix and M&E framework as the basis for joint monitoring with relevant programme partners. Results of such monitoring should be used to report to the UNCT about progress and for joint analysis. These UNDAF outcome groups should augment any monitoring information that could be generated by UN organizations and partners separately.

In practical terms, joint monitoring would involve the following:

- Meeting regularly with partners to assess progress towards results already stated in the M&E framework and sharing information gathered by one or more partners

- Planning and conducting joint field monitoring missions to gauge achievements and constraints

- Identifying lessons or good practices, sharing them, promoting their use by partners and developing knowledge products

- Identifying capacity development needs among partners, particularly related to data collection, analysis, monitoring and reporting

- Reporting regularly to the respective stakeholders and steering committee or board

- Bringing lessons and good practices to the attention of policy makers

- Contributing to common annual progress reports for consideration at outcome level reviews and annual reviews

> **TIP** Start thinking about monitoring data and capacities needed for monitoring early in the programme planning process. It may be too late to think about them during implementation stages.

Obtaining reliable data and information for monitoring

Monitoring is part of a comprehensive programming continuum that starts with an in-depth analysis of the development situation. Normally, this analytical phase that precedes planning provides early insights into monitoring considerations. For example, the availability and quality of data that is needed for analysis for developing a new programme or project would indicate the scope and possibilities for use of existing capacities and resources for monitoring. It would also indicate critical gaps that may need to be addressed in order to ensure effective monitoring in the future. Therefore, recognizing that there is an important opportunity during the analytical phase preceding planning can ensure effective monitoring later in the programme cycle.

Ideally, monitoring data should originate or be collected from national sources. However, this depends on the availability and quality of data from those sources. In an increasing number of countries, analytical data does come from national development information systems, which are also the repositories of important monitoring data and information. External partners should identify and build on what data and systems already exist in the country. Specific attention should be given to establish baselines, identify trends and data gaps, and highlight constraints in country statistical and monitoring systems. Many UNDP country offices have assisted in setting up data collection systems. Some examples are given in Box 24.

In addition, UNDG can provide support related to **DevInfo**[31], which is a database system for monitoring human development. It is a tool for organizing, storing and presenting

---

Box 24. Good practices of data collection supported by UNDP

■ UNDP Pakistan has successfully supported a data collection system called the Participatory Information System under one of its institutional and capacity development projects in Balochistan Province. The system has two prominent features: the community collects household and services information through Community Information Committees, which are composed of community members; and the system provides the communities with a graphical look at their social and economic status, facilitates the planners and service providers in filling the service gaps, and makes the existing services better. The type of information collected facilitates monitoring progress towards the achievement of MDGs.

■ The first 'Atlas of Human Development in Brazil', launched in 1998, pioneered calculation of the human development index at the municipal level. For the first time, the human development index and its components were calculated for all the municipalities of a country. (Brazil had 4,491 municipalities at the time.) In 2003, a new edition of the Atlas (available only in Portuguese) was released, using data from the 2000 Demographic Census. This can be downloaded from http://www.pnud.org.br/atlas/ by clicking on the link "Clique aquipara instalar o Atlas de Desenvolvimento Humano no Brasilemse u computador." (Translation: "Click here to install the Atlas of Human Development in Brazil on your computer.")

   The Atlas allows a multi-dimensional approach to human development measurement, since it provides a host of indicators on access to basic services, educational attainment, social vulnerability, and other themes. Special geo-referenced software was developed to allow for easy manipulation of the database, which in the current version comprises 200+ indicators for the 5,500+ Brazilian municipalities. The software has features to perform elaborate queries, create thematic maps, and generate fact sheets, and some simple statistical functions (such as creation of histograms, correlation plots and descriptive statistics). The software played a key role in the Atlas' success, allowing non-statistically trained people to make their own analyses.

---

31 Please see http://www.devinfo.org for more details on DevInfo.

data in a uniform way to facilitate data sharing at the country level across government departments, UN organizations and development partners. In 2004, the UNDG endorsed the use of DevInfo to assist countries in monitoring achievement of the MDGs. At present, more than 100 countries use DevInfo as a platform to develop a national socio-economic database. More than 80 national statistics organizations and other agencies have officially launched and adapted the DevInfo database with their user-specified requirements. The software is available royalty-free and there is a DevInfo Support Group providing technical assistance to the countries and supporting national capacity development efforts.

Arrangements and formats for reporting results should be agreed upon in advance in order to meet the needs of partners. Where possible, a common monitoring format should be adopted by all partners in order to minimize the workload, especially for national partners, and to meet the commitments of simplification and harmonization agreed upon in international forums.

UN organizations have developed several harmonized reporting formats. They include:

- A format for AWPs with a monitoring framework, which could be used to report at project level (discussed in Table 20)

- Several UN organizations use the Standard Progress Report[32] format for progress and donor reporting, which shows how resources were used and the results that were achieved. This could be used at the outcome level. It is linked to the other standard formats used by UN organizations such as the AWP, CPAP, CPD and UNDAF results matrix.

The above form a good basis for adopting common reporting formats. They can also be adapted by partners to meet specific requirements.

4.4 USE OF MONITORING DATA FOR MANAGEMENT ACTION AND DECISION MAKING

Data and information on progress towards results are gathered, reviewed and used at the project, outcome, sectoral and programme levels. These entities are interconnected and reinforce each other. There is a two-way flow of information among them with the following common objectives:

- Clarifying and analysing progress, issues, challenges and lessons

- Precipitating actions and decisions including effecting changes in plans and resources as required

PROJECT LEVEL

Monitoring data normally aggregates from project level to higher level results. At the project level, the use of monitoring information can be summarized as follows.

---

32 UNDG, 'Standard Progress Report'. Available at: http://www.undg.org/index.cfm?P=261.

The first monitoring action at the project level is to be clear of what is expected in terms of project-specific results and what is to be done with respect to monitoring actions. At the beginning, projects should: have a clear scope (that continues to be clear throughout the project); expected deliverables and how these contribute to the higher level results; ensure that cumulative annual targets are adequate to produce the envisaged outputs; and ensure that they lead to the delivery of planned outputs in the agreed time frame. This information is initially captured in the project results framework and its M&E framework. This process should be repeated at each annual project review to continuously validate that delivery of outputs is on schedule and remains relevant. If this is not the case, higher level boards or committees should be notified so that any implications on the overall planned results can be reviewed for modifications, new time frames and costs.

Monitoring data should be collected according to the AWP, and in the case of UNDP, by using Atlas-generated quarterly progress reports. The project should review the data to:

▪ Revalidate if the project and programme results logic remain valid in light of the operational experience and evidence.

▪ Discern what issues have emerged during implementation: Have the foreseen risks and assumptions materialized? Have other unforeseen challenges, opportunities and risks materialized? Are these being managed?

Progress towards generating outputs and their continued relevance to the outcome and issues should be synthesized and forwarded to the agency to which the project reports and to the respective outcome or sectoral monitoring mechanism. On the basis of that monitoring data, the project management and board or steering committee should re-confirm that the delivery of outputs is on schedule and that the project is contributing towards the desired outcomes. If not, they should determine what changes are needed. If revisions to plans are needed, then the project management should draft the revisions, including the results framework with new cost estimates, annual targets and so forth, to facilitate decision making at higher levels. Such information could be provided at agreed intervals such as quarterly, semi-annually, annually or on an as-needed basis.

OUTCOME LEVEL

Sectoral and outcome-level coordinating mechanisms play a critical role in results monitoring and developing capacities for monitoring. They forge partnerships around initiatives supported by partners to achieve common results, provide oversight in a collective spirit, make linkages to national systems and national development goals, and promote the development of monitoring capacities.

At the beginning of the programme or project implementation, the existence of such outcome-level monitoring and oversight mechanisms should be verified. If such mechanisms do not exist, then arrangements should be made to set up such groups through engagement with national partners. As interim measures, UN Theme Groups could be set up in accordance with UNDG (CCA and UNDAF) Guidelines. The outcome and sectoral monitoring mechanisms should take the following actions:

- Ensure that all those who are contributing to the outcome are included in the group. For UNDP, this should answer the question whether UNDP is engaged with the right partners to deliver outputs and to achieve outcomes.

- Agree on regular interactions and a plan of action to ensure that coordination and monitoring mechanisms remain efficient and effective.

- Review the components of the outcome (outputs and other activities) and ensure that outputs to be produced are sufficient to bring about the outcome and sustain the benefits.

- Ensure that the results plan for outcome indicators, targets, risks and assumptions are valid, adequate and managed.

- Promote development of national capacities in monitoring.

- Agree on a practical arrangement to coordinate the functioning of the outcome group. The outcome group should ideally be led by a national entity. However, UNDP may also offer such services.

The sectoral or outcome coordinating mechanism should continually assess the status of outputs and related initiatives by partners—all of which contribute to an intended outcome. It does so by examining information from all relevant projects, national reports, donor reports and other sources. It should review the findings of quarterly and annual reviews pertaining to the outcomes and identify lessons that are to be fed back into programming, and serve as a vehicle for ensuring documenting and disseminating lessons learned. It also serves as the focal team for outcome evaluations. Specifically it should:

- Review and assess connected projects and provide feedback to all relevant partners upon receipt of relevant reports, notably the APRs from each contributing project.

- Consider any changes needed in each constituent project and in overall approach in order to achieve the outcomes, consider the consequences of the necessary changes, and take appropriate action to ensure achievement of the outcomes.

It is important to keep in mind that the outcome and sector-level coordinating mechanisms are 'larger' than the United Nations and UNDP programme, as they focus on the achievement of the national outcomes. Hence, the United Nations and UNDP are one of many contributors towards the achievement of these outcomes. Ideally, the outcome and sector-level coordinating mechanisms should not be a UN or UNDP management arrangement but an existing national structure that is charged to coordinate the sector within the national context.

PROGRAMME LEVEL

Each partner (such as UNDP) that contributes to one or more outcome typically has its own arrangements to plan, implement and monitor the contributions it is making to results. For UNDP at the country level, this is the function of the CPAP and its monitoring and annual review. The M&E framework, which is the CPAP monitoring framework, forms the basis for this purpose.

The primary question to address at the programme level is: Does UNDP, as a partner, ensure that its programme is effectively contributing to the planned UNDP country programme, UNDAF and national results within the agreed partnership arrangements? The same principle applies for UNDP regional programmes, the global programme and the Strategic Plan. Furthermore, it should also ascertain whether or not country programmes, regional programmes and the global programme are contributing to the objectives and envisaged outcomes of the Strategic Plan.

The following steps are necessary to organize programme-level monitoring:

- Obtain monitoring information for each UNDP funded project through the respective quarterly progress report (if used), APRs and other related activities, such as soft assistance relevant for a given outcome. This should answer the questions: What progress has UNDP made in delivering the agreed CPAP outputs in the reference period? What progress has UNDP as a whole made towards achieving the CPAP outcomes? What are the programme-level issues that require action? What are we learning as a programme?

- Determine if outputs being generated with UNDP support remain valid and contribute to achieving corresponding outcomes.

- Participate in dialogue with relevant stakeholders at the outcome, sector and national level.

- Determine if other partners are contributing as planned and identify gaps to be addressed and opportunities for forging stronger partnerships.

- Triangulate monitoring information to obtain a more objective assessment of the UNDP contribution to each outcome. Identify issues and changes that are necessary to further dialogue at the respective outcome monitoring mechanism. Analyse to what extent UNDP has integrated key concerns such as capacity development, gender equality, national ownership and South-South cooperation.

- Summarize key relevant points for the programme as a whole for corporate reporting purposes and decision making at the annual programme review.

- A separate annual review meeting on the UNDP country programme may not be necessary if issues pertaining to the UNDP programme and related decisions could be covered at the UNDAF annual review. It might be helpful to hold a one-day UN programme review at the annual review, where one half day focuses on the UNDAF and the other half day focuses on respective agency programmes.

- Implement the necessary changes agreed at annual reviews.

The same analytical work should feed the corporate learning and reporting processes. For UNDP, this means that the managers of country, regional and global programmes should feed the findings of this analysis into the RBM Platform to report on progress against the Strategic Plan.

ANNUAL REVIEW WITH KEY STAKEHOLDERS

The annual review with the participation of all key stakeholders is a key monitoring event at the national programme or UNDAF level. It is the culmination of monitoring activities that started at the project level and cascaded upwards through the outcome and individual partner programme level during the year. The annual review facilitates a dialogue among senior managers to assess progress towards results (outputs and outcomes). It is also a forum that is used for building a stronger mutual understanding and consensus among partners on the issues directly relevant to achieving the planned results and for making key high-level decisions. Annual reviews are ideally held towards the end of the year, and the discussions are meant to guide and approve plans for the following year.

Annual reviews have to be well planned in order to extract the best results from them. The following should be considered in the preparation for the annual review:

- It is essential that the annual review is conducted based on objective monitoring data and analyses prepared by all connected projects (for example APRs) and finalized after consultations with relevant stakeholders. The following actions could be helpful:

  - Based on the APRs and project board or steering committee and outcome groups' or boards' findings and recommendations, each partner organization should present a synthesis of its own key points—including an assessment of its contribution to the outcomes and other issues that need to be discussed at the annual review. These syntheses should be succinct and made available to annual review participants prior to the meeting.

  - Given the time constraints at the annual review meeting, if deemed necessary, organize prior consultations among relevant partners to ensure deliberations at the annual review will be efficient, avoid potential conflicts, and lead to decisions and clear follow-up actions on the subsequent year's work programme.

- The annual review should be organized by the relevant national partner and carried out in an inclusive and practical manner. Depending on national capacities, and in consultation and with the leadership of the key national partners, another partner (for example UNDP) may organize or assist in the organization of the annual review. The participants should be at the decision-making level of each participating partner. Its success often depends on how well the partners have been involved in the lead up to the annual review and are informed on the issues to be discussed. Ideally, many of the issues to be addressed at the annual review should already have been discussed, for example, in regular monitoring events such as field visits or in prior discussions on the APRs at the project or outcome level. A focused approach is recommended for the annual review so that the key issues and outcomes are addressed. The following actions may help in this respect:

  - The agenda of the annual review should be prepared carefully, giving priority to those items that require collective review and decision making by the partners at the annual review meeting. Ensure sufficient time for dialogue and provide background information for each agenda item in advance.

  - Ensure that the annual review process will lead to decisions and agreements on: the current status of the achievement of the results being pursued; any changes to overall results frameworks; and an updated AWP for the forthcoming year.

Global and regional programmes (of UNDP)

At a minimum, an annual review of the global programme and of each regional programme must be held. These annual reviews are informed by a variety of information sources, including APRs of constituent projects.

Box 25. Typical UNDAF annual review process and lessons learned

At the country level:

The UNDP annual review process is linked to the UNDAF annual review, which is the once-a-year opportunity for all agencies and national partners to review the UNCT contribution to achievement of national goals based on the UNDAF Results Matrix. In consultation with national partners, the UNCT decides on the meeting's scope and modalities.

The UNDAF annual review should provide the UNCT and national partners with:

- A yearly update of overall progress *vis-à-vis* the UNDAF Results Matrix
- Validation of conclusions and recommendations that should feed into annual planning processes

UNDP contributes to the annual UNDAF review through the annual results reporting in CPAP. The annual report of CPAP is prepared from: analyses that originate from project APRs and the project boards; coordinated comments on each outcome by sectoral or outcome coordinating mechanisms (including national coordination mechanisms and UN Theme Groups) to reflect progress towards outcome at outcome levels; and project and outcome evaluations or any other relevant outcome and project reviews that have been carried out during the year, including those carried out by other partners.

Substantively, UNDP contribution to the UNDAF annual review—a synthesis of the CPAP annual report—includes: a brief assessment of the achievement of annual targets of all UNDP funded activities in the context of achieving UNDAF outcomes; operational issues of the CPAP implementation; and any modifications to the existing CPAP that would require agreement of non-UNDP partners.

Some general lessons learned from conducting UNDAF annual reviews, based on the experience of the Solomon Islands:

- **Use the government's National Development Plan as the organizing principle for the review**—Organize reporting and deliberations on the basis of the National Development Plan. This may require additional work on the part of the UN system and other partners, but the extra effort is highly justified by the resulting increased national ownership.
- **Be strategic**—Presentations on individual UN organization programmes would be uninteresting. Avoid long lists of outputs by individual partners. Such information could be presented as background documents and referred to in the meeting. Focus on the likely development changes in relation to development indicators.
- **Repetition makes things easier**—As each agency has its own reporting formats, timelines and terms, at first, it is difficult for many organizations to cooperate on annual planning and review exercises. Cooperation becomes easier when coordinated efforts are repeated.
- **Standard formats should be devised and discussed at the earliest possible date**—While it is tempting to focus more on the structure of the meeting and agenda, it is the finalization of the annual reports and AWPs that make up most of the work of the review exercise. Thus, the earlier this work is started, the better.
- **Reduce transaction costs**—Use video and Web-conferencing for consultations among UN partners.
- **The United Nations is stronger together than separate**—Taken as a whole, aggregated support of the UN system in a country could be on par with other major external partners. This enhances the UN system's position and also underpins the principle of Delivering as One.

Follow up to annual review

- Agendas and records of annual review meetings should be documented, circulated among all partners and agreed upon by them.

- Revise the AWP subsequent to, and in line with, the decisions of the annual reviews. It should be approved, preferably in writing, by all the partners involved, typically at the project board level. The M&E frameworks at programme (CPAP) and project levels and the accompanying AWP monitoring tool should be prepared thereafter in readiness for monitoring purposes in the subsequent year.

- For UNDP, when the annual review is completed and new work targets for the subsequent year are agreed upon, the following processes are triggered: updated AWPs for projects are finalized with the new annual targets and signed; results of the review year is updated in the RBM Platform for corporate annual reporting; and newly agreed targets are set using the RBM Platform for subsequent annual reviews.

- Coordinate any changes with the outcome or sector-level committee to ensure that all stakeholders are aware of any changes.

USE OF MONITORING DATA IN EVALUATIONS

Effective monitoring generates a solid data base for evaluations. Data, reports, analysis and decisions based on monitoring evidence should be retained with a view to making them easily accessible to evaluations.

EVALUATING FOR RESULTS

This chapter presents a holistic view of the UNDP evaluation function in order to help managers and staff of programme units and partners make strategic decisions about evaluations. The chapter describes why evaluation is important for UNDP and how evaluative information should be used, then briefly presents the UNDP evaluation policy, types of evaluations that are commonly conducted in UNDP, key roles and responsibilities in evaluation, and evaluation requirements as stipulated in the evaluation policy.

5.1 WHY EVALUATE? USES OF EVALUATION

Evaluation is critical for UNDP to progress towards advancing human development. Through the generation of 'evidence' and objective information, evaluations enable managers to make informed decisions and plan strategically. UNDP success depends, in part, on the ability of UNDP and its counterparts to carry out credible evaluations and use them to make evidenced-based decisions. The effective conduct and use of evaluation requires adequate human and financial resources, sound understanding of evaluation and most importantly, **a culture of results-orientation, learning, inquiry and evidence-based decision making**. Everyone in UNDP and its stakeholders have to share the same vision and be open to change.

When evaluations are used effectively, they support programme improvements, knowledge generation and accountability.

Supporting programme improvements—Did it work or not, and why? How could it be done differently for better results?

The interest is on **what works, why and in what context**. Decision makers, such as managers, use evaluations to make necessary improvements, adjustments to the implementation approach or strategies, and to decide on alternatives. Evaluations addressing these questions need to provide concrete information on how improvements could be made or what alternatives exist to address the necessary improvements.

Building knowledge for generalizability and wider-application—What can we learn from the evaluation? How can we apply this knowledge to other contexts?

The main interest is in the development of knowledge for global use and for generalization to other contexts and situations. When the interest is on knowledge generation, evaluations generally apply more rigorous methodology to ensure a higher level of accuracy in the evaluation and the information being produced to allow for generalizability and wider application beyond a particular context.

Evaluations should not be seen as an event but as part of an exercise whereby different stakeholders are able to participate in the continuous process of generating and applying evaluative knowledge. UNDP managers, together with government and other stakeholders, decide who participates in what part of this process (analysing findings and lessons, developing a management response to an evaluation, disseminating knowledge) and to what extent they will be involved (informed, consulted, actively involved, equal partners or key decision makers). These are strategic decisions for UNDP managers that have a direct bearing on the learning and ownership of evaluation findings. An evaluation framework that generates knowledge, promotes learning and guides action is an important means of capacity development and sustainability of results.

Supporting accountability—Is UNDP doing the right things? Is UNDP doing things right? Did UNDP do what it said it would do?

The interest here is on determining the merit or worth and value of an initiative and its quality. An effective accountability framework requires credible and objective information, and evaluations can deliver such information. Evaluations help ensure that UNDP goals and initiatives are aligned with and support the Millennium Declaration, MDGs, and global, national and corporate priorities. UNDP is accountable for providing evaluative evidence that links UNDP contributions to the achievement of development results in a given country and for delivering services that are based on the principles of human development. By providing such objective and independent assessments, evaluations in UNDP support the organization's accountability towards its Executive Board, donors, governments, national partners and beneficiaries.

The intended use determines the timing of an evaluation, its methodological framework, and level and nature of stakeholder participation. Therefore, the use has to be determined at the planning stage. Box 26 provides a set of questions to guide UNDP and its stakeholders in assessing the potential use of evaluations.

These uses are not mutually exclusive and evaluation, in general, has multiple uses. Throughout the evaluation process, the identified use has to be revisited and redefined, as necessary, in consultation with stakeholders. This inclusive process ensures the credibility and ownership of the evaluation process and products, hence resulting in its optimal use.

Box 26. Assessing the use of an evaluation

What information is needed? Examples:

- Information on the relevance of intended outputs or outcomes and validity of the results framework and results map
- Information about the status of an outcome and factors affecting it
- Information about the effectiveness of the UNDP partnership strategy
- Information about the status of project implementation
- Information on the cost of an initiative relative to the observed benefits
- Information about lessons learned

Who will use the information? The intended users of evaluation are those individuals or groups who have a vested interest in the evaluation results and are in a position to make decisions or take action based on the evaluation results. Users of evaluation are varied but generally fall within the following categories in the UNDP context:

- UNDP management and programme or project officers and managers, others involved in design and implementation
- National government counterparts, policy makers, strategic planners
- Development partners
- Donors and other funders
- Public and beneficiaries
- The UNDP Executive Board and other national oversight bodies

How will the information be used? Examples:

- To design or validate a development strategy
- To make mid-course corrections
- To improve project or programme design and implementation
- To ensure accountability
- To make funding decisions
- To increase knowledge and understanding of the benefits and challenges of development programmes and projects intended for the enhancement of human development

5.2   EVALUATION POLICY: PRINCIPLES, NORMS AND STANDARDS FOR EVALUATION

The evaluation policy was adopted in 2006 to strengthen the evaluation function in UNDP. The guiding principles, norms and standards as expressed in the policy and the UNEG Norms and Standards for Evaluation in the UN system[33] guide the practice and use of evaluation in UNDP. Norms for evaluation—how evaluation should be conducted in order to meet the required quality standards and its intended role—are summarized in Box 27.

The remaining evaluation section of this Handbook aims to provide practical guidance on how these norms and principles can be applied throughout the evaluation process.

---

33 UNEG, 'Norms for Evaluation in the UN System', 2005, available at: http://www.unevaluation.org/unegnorms; and UNEG, 'Standards for Evaluation in the UN System', 2005, available at: http://www.unevaluation.org/unegstandards.

Box 27. Norms for evaluation

Evaluation in UNDP should be:

- **Independent**—Management must not impose restrictions on the scope, content, comments and recommendations of evaluation reports. Evaluators must be free of conflict of interest (see Box 34, page 155).
- **Intentional**—The rationale for an evaluation and the decisions to be based on it should be clear from the outset.
- **Transparent**—Meaningful consultation with stakeholders is essential for the credibility and utility of the evaluation.
- **Ethical**—Evaluation should not reflect personal or sectoral interests. Evaluators must have professional integrity, respect the rights of institutions and individuals to provide information in confidence, and be sensitive to the beliefs and customs of local social and cultural environments.
- **Impartial**—Removing bias and maximizing objectivity are critical for the credibility of the evaluation and its contribution to knowledge.
- **Of high quality**—All evaluations should meet minimum quality standards defined by the Evaluation Office (see Annex 3).
- **Timely**—Evaluations must be designed and completed in a timely fashion so as to ensure the usefulness of the findings and recommendations
- **Used**—Evaluation is a management discipline that seeks to provide information to be used for evidence-based decision making. To enhance the usefulness of the findings and recommendations, key stakeholders should be engaged in various ways in the conduct of the evaluation.

Source: UNDP, 'The Evaluation Policy of UNDP', Executive Board Document DP/2005/28, May 2006. Available at: http://www.undp.org/eo/documents/Evaluation-Policy.pdf.

5.3   TYPES OF EVALUATION IN UNDP

INDEPENDENT AND DECENTRALIZED EVALUATIONS

UNDP support and services consist of **programmes, projects, partnerships** and '**soft assistance**' such as advocacy, policy advice and coordination support, which may or may not be delivered within a project framework. Programmes and projects have results frameworks that detail the results map and intended results at the output and outcome levels. Evaluations in UNDP are carried out to adequately cover this wide range of UNDP initiatives in order to assess their worth and merit and support the organization's learning efforts and accountability. The architecture of evaluation in UNDP, therefore, corresponds to the UNDP programmatic structure and its components.

There are two categories of evaluations in UNDP: independent and decentralized evaluations. The UNDP Evaluation Office is mandated by the Executive Board to carry out **independent evaluations**. They are referred to as independent since the Evaluation Office is independent from programme management and is not part of subsequent decision-making processes regarding the subject of an evaluation. The Evaluation Office is also required to conduct country programme evaluations (known as Assessments of Development Results or ADRs), regional and global programme evaluations, and thematic evaluations in accordance with the programme of work that is approved by the Executive Board.

The programme units carry out various types of **decentralized evaluations** and ensure that they provide adequate information about the overall performance of UNDP support in a given context. In doing so, the programme units draw from a range of evaluation types that are based on business units of their development assistance at the country, regional or global levels. These include: UNDAF; country, regional or global programmes; outcomes; thematic areas; and projects. The most common decentralized evaluations are **project and outcome evaluations**. The programme units do not conduct these evaluations themselves, but rather commission external evaluation consultants to do so.

Together, these two categories of evaluations are intended to provide comprehensive information about UNDP performance at the project, programme, corporate and UN system levels, with a view to supporting sound management of UNDP initiatives and strategic direction.

Relationship between independent and decentralized evaluations

Although the institutional arrangements—including mandates, lines of accountability and operational modalities—of independent and decentralized evaluations are different, they complement and reinforce each other. For example, decentralized evaluations, particularly outcome evaluations, carried out in a given country provide a substantive basis for an independent evaluation of the country programme or the ADRs that are conducted by the Evaluation Office. Therefore, outcome evaluations and their associated project evaluations should be completed before the ADRs. Moreover, in conducting country case studies of a thematic or regional programme evaluation, the Evaluation Office may apply a meta-evaluation approach[34] and draw extensively from country or region-specific decentralized evaluations. In the absence of adequate and credible decentralized evaluations, independent evaluations may have a limited evaluative basis and may require more time to collect necessary data. Similarly, evaluators for decentralized evaluations may use the analysis provided in the relevant independent evaluations and case studies as a building block for their analysis. Table 21 documents the main types of evaluations carried out in UNDP, including responsible parties mandated for carrying them out and main users of these evaluations.

OUTCOME EVALUATION

Outcome evaluations in UNDP assess UNDP contributions towards the progress made on outcome achievements. These outcomes are generally identified in the programme or project results frameworks to which UNDP initiatives contribute.

Outcome evaluations are undertaken to:

- Provide evidence to support accountability of programmes and for UNDP to use in its accountability requirements to its investors

- Provide evidence of the UNDP contribution to outcomes

---

34 **Meta-evaluation** is an evaluation of evaluations. It uses findings from a series of evaluations and requires a robust quality assurance mechanism to ensure that the evaluations used as secondary data are credible and of good quality.

Table 21. Examples of different types of evaluations carried out by the Evaluation Office and programme units

Evaluation Type

Programme Evaluations (Global Programme, Regional Programme, Country Programme)

Mandated Responsibility for Evaluation	Strategic Plan	Programme Areas (e.g. governance, South-South cooperation)	Thematic Areas or Topics (gender, capacity building, RBM)	Global Programme	Regional Programme	Country Programme	Global, Regional or Country Programme Outcomes	UNDAF Outcomes	Projects
Evaluations Conducted by Evaluation Office*									
Evaluation Office		Thematic evaluations		Evaluation of Global Cooperation Framework	Evaluation of Regional Cooperation Framework	Assessment of Development Results			
Primary users		Executive Board, UNDP management		Executive Board, UNDP management, BDP	Executive Board, UNDP management, regional bureaux	Executive Board, UNDP management, country office, national partners			
Evaluations Commissioned by Programme Units**									
BDP	Cross-programme area evaluations	Outcome or outcome-oriented thematic evaluations	Outcome or outcome-oriented thematic evaluations	Midterm evaluation			Outcome or outcome-oriented evaluations (see section 5.3)		Project evaluations
BCPR									
Regional bureaux					Midterm evaluation				
Other units***									
Country offices						Midterm or end of cycle evaluation			Project evaluations (e.g., Global Environment Facility terminal evaluations)
UNCT								UNDAF evaluation	
Primary users		Management and partners					Management and partners		Management, partners, and donors

*The Evaluation Office is required to conduct all evaluations outlined in the programme of work approved by the Executive Board. **Programme units are required to conduct all evaluations planned in their evaluation plan. *** Other units with programmatic responsibilities such as the Bureau of Management and the Partnership Bureau, as relevant.

- Guide performance improvement within the current global, regional and country programmes by identifying current areas of strengths, weaknesses and gaps, especially in regard to:
  - The appropriateness of the UNDP partnership strategy
  - Impediments to the outcome
  - Midcourse adjustments
  - Lessons learned for the next programming cycle
- Inform higher level evaluations, such as ADRs and evaluations of regional and global programmes, and subsequent planning
- Support learning across UNDP about outcome evaluation

Outcome evaluations are strategic, addressing: broad-based linkages with development; partnerships across agencies; analysis of the external local, regional and global environment in the analysis of success; and the comparative value of UNDP and significance in development. Another distinct characteristic of outcome evaluations is that they explicitly recognize the role of partners in the attainment of those outcomes and provide critical information for the purpose of enhancing development effectiveness and assisting decision and policy making beyond a particular project or initiative. Outcome evaluations also provide a substantive basis for higher level evaluations (e.g., UNDAF evaluations) and independent evaluations conducted by the Evaluation Office. Therefore, the conduct of outcome evaluations during the programme cycle is mandatory for all programme units in UNDP.

As UNDP works in a wide range of development contexts and situations, the requirements for outcome evaluations can be fulfilled through different arrangements. For instance, joint evaluations, focusing on themes, large projects or geographical areas that address specific outcomes as predefined in planning documents (such as country, regional and global programme documents) may be considered as fulfilling requirements for outcome evaluations.

Whatever the arrangements may be, in order to meet the requirements for outcome evaluations, **the evaluation must be outcome oriented**. Outcome evaluations must meet the objectives to assess the following:

- Progress towards achieving the outcome, including unintended effects of activities related to this outcome
- The contributing factors to the outcomes
- The contribution the UNDP has made to the outcomes
- The effectiveness of the partnership strategy in achieving the outcomes

In consultation with relevant partners, UNDP programme units may decide which outcomes to choose and what modality to use in evaluation. The existing partnerships on the ground, the nature of the programme, planned evaluations by partners and government (so as to seek opportunities for joint evaluations) and other programme-specific factors may influence such decisions. For more details, please refer to the compendium on outcome evaluations.

PROJECT EVALUATION

UNDP programme units may commission evaluations of their respective projects as needed. Managing for results requires, as a starting point, a good knowledge of projects, their effectiveness, internal and external factors affecting effectiveness, their added value and their contribution to higher level outcomes. A project evaluation assesses the performance of a project in achieving its intended results. It yields useful information on project implementation arrangements and the achievement of outputs. It is at this level that direct cause and attribution can be addressed given the close causal linkage between the initiatives and the outputs.

The primary purpose of a project evaluation is to make improvements, to continue or upscale an initiative, to assess replicability in other settings, or to consider alternatives. Therefore, although project evaluations are mandatory only when required by partnership protocols, **programme units are strongly recommended to commission evaluations, particularly of pilot programmes, before replication or upscaling, projects that are going into a next phase, and projects more than five years in duration**. Increasingly, project evaluations play an important role in accountability to donors and governments involved in financing projects. For their own accountability reasons, donor agencies and other cost-sharing partners[35] may request UNDP to include evaluation requirements in the UNDP-donor partnership agreements. Mid-term and final evaluations of Global Environment Facility projects are examples of project evaluations, as they are carried out within the clearly defined scope of a single project.[36]

When a project is undertaken in partnership with other development actors, the evaluation needs to take into consideration the objectives, inputs and contributions by each partner. The overall evaluation conclusions need to highlight how these different elements integrate to achieve the intended outputs, and what can be learned from the added value of the collaboration. Therefore, it is of central importance that UNDP and the partners involved in a project work together, voice their expectations and issues, and own the evaluation from the planning phase throughout the whole process.

PROJECT VERSUS OUTCOME EVALUATIONS

There are several important differences between project evaluations and outcome evaluations, as illustrated in Table 22.

The increasing focus on outcome evaluations in UNDP does not mean that outcome evaluations have replaced project evaluations. Many programme units continue to undertake project evaluations because they yield useful information on project implementation arrangements, administrative structures and the achievement of outputs. Further, project evaluation provides a basis for the evaluation of outcomes and programmes, as well as for programme and thematic evaluations conducted by the Evaluation Office, and for distilling lessons from experience for learning and sharing knowledge.

---

35 See section on mandatory evaluations on page 142.

36 The Global Environment Facility, 'Monitoring and Evaluation Policy', February 2006. Available at: http://www.undp.org/gef/05/documents/me/GEF_ME_Policies_and_Precedures_06.pdf.

Table 22. Differences between project and outcome evaluations

	Project Evaluation	Outcome Evaluation
Focus	Generally speaking, inputs, activities and outputs (if and how project outputs were delivered within a sector or geographic area and if direct results occurred and can be attributed to the project)*	Outcomes (whether, why and how the outcome has been achieved, and the contribution of UNDP to a change in a given development situation)
Scope	Specific to project objectives, inputs, outputs and activities Also considers relevance and continued linkage with outcome	Broad, encompassing outcomes and the extent to which programmes, project, soft assistance, partners' initiatives and synergies among partners contributed to its achievement
Purpose	Project based to improve implementation, to re-direct future projects in the same area, or to allow for upscaling of project	To enhance development effectiveness, to assist decision making, to assist policy making, to re-direct future UNDP assistance, to systematize innovative approaches to sustainable human development

Source: UNDP, Guidelines for Evaluators, 2002

*Large projects may have outcomes that can be evaluated. Further, small projects may also make tangible contributions to the achievement of CPD outcomes or even project-specific outcomes. In such instances, these project evaluations may be considered to be fulfilling requirements for outcome evaluations.

To ensure the relevance and effective use of evaluation information, evaluations should be made available in a timely manner so that decision makers can make decisions informed by evaluative evidence.

THEMATIC EVALUATIONS

In addition to project and outcome evaluations, senior managers of programme units may choose to commission thematic evaluations to assess UNDP performance in areas that are critical to ensuring sustained contribution to development results. They may focus on one or several cross-cutting themes that have significance beyond a particular project or initiative. Examples of thematic evaluations commissioned by programme units include the evaluation of UNDP initiatives in a particular results area, such as democratic governance, and the evaluation of a cross-cutting theme, such as capacity development or gender mainstreaming in UNDP programming in a given country.

COUNTRY, REGIONAL OR GLOBAL PROGRAMME EVALUATION

Country offices may commission a country programme evaluation to assess UNDP attainment of intended results and contributions to national development results in a given country. The evaluation examines key issues that are similar to those in the ADRs, such as UNDP effectiveness in delivering and influencing the achievement of development results and UNDP strategic positioning. The country programme evaluation contributes to the greater accountability of UNDP and the quality assurance of UNDP initiatives at the country level. As in the ADR, it allows findings and recommendations to feed into the preparation of subsequent programmes. It can be used to facilitate dialogue with the government and other national partners and may also provide lessons that are useful for the government in its aid management work and its relationship with other development partners. Despite a number of similarities, country programme evaluations commissioned by country offices are distinct from the ADRs in terms of their scope and management arrangements. They are usually focused on a given programme cycle with a greater focus on performance at the project level. Further, decentralized country programme evaluations are commissioned by those responsible for programme management, as opposed to the independent Evaluation Office.

Similarly, regional bureaux and policy and practice units may decide to carry out mid-term evaluations of their respective regional and global programmes. These mid-term programme evaluations allow for mid-course adjustment of programmes and also feed into the regional and global programme evaluations that the Evaluation Office is mandated to conduct towards the end of the programme period.

IMPACT EVALUATION

An impact evaluation is an evaluation of the effects—positive or negative, intended or not—on individual households and institutions, and the environment caused by a given development activity such as a programme or project. Such an evaluation refers to the final (long-term) impact as well as to the (medium-term) effects at the outcome level.

By identifying if development assistance is working or not, impact evaluation also serves the accountability function. Hence, impact evaluation is aligned with RBM and monitoring the contribution of development assistance towards meeting the MDGs. An impact evaluation is useful when:

▪ The project or programme is functioning long enough to have visible effects

▪ The project or programme has a scale that justifies a more thorough evaluation

Impact evaluation does not simply measure whether objectives have been achieved or assess direct effects on intended beneficiaries. It includes the full range of impacts at all levels of the results chain, including ripple effects on families, households and communities; on institutional, technical or social systems; and on the environment. In terms of a simple logic model, there can be multiple intermediate (short and medium term) outcomes over time that eventually lead to impact—some or all of which may be included in an evaluation of impact at a specific moment in time.

This definition emphasizes the need for understanding the consequences of development initiatives in the longer term. Another important issue connected to impact evaluation is attribution—that is, determining to what extent an initiative, rather than other external factors, has contributed to observed impacts. There are many methods that can be applied to deal with the attribution issue. It is important that this issue be taken into account in the design of the initiative, as well as the evaluation ToR and design.[37]

---

37 Further materials on impact evaluation can be found on the World Bank website sections on Impact Evaluation (www.worldbank.org/impactevaluation) and Network of Networks on Impact Evaluation (www.worldbank.org/ieg/nonie/).

UNDP programmes, projects and operations operate in concert to support **UNDAF objectives and outcomes** that address national priorities. The UNDAF describes the collective response of all UN operations in a country. While UNDP outcome evaluations focus on CPD outcomes, **UNDAF evaluations** focus on UNDAF outcomes, their contributions to national priorities and the coherence of UNCT support. The UNDAF evaluation is timed to provide inputs to the preparation of the next UNDAF, country programmes and projects by individual agencies. The UNDAF evaluation should take place at the beginning of the penultimate year of the programme cycle and build on UNDAF annual reviews as well as major studies and evaluations that have been completed by individual agencies. Although the results of the UNDAF evaluation are meant to contribute to managing for results, it is an external function, which should be separated from programme management. UNDAF monitoring and evaluation should always be aligned with existing national monitoring and evaluation systems or focus on their development and institutionalization if they are premature or absent.

The scope of the UNDAF evaluation depends on the previous evaluations and studies already conducted during the cycle and on the nature of UNCT operations in a country. UNDAF evaluations are jointly commissioned and managed by the heads of UN organizations and national governments. They are conducted by external consultants selected by mutual agreement between the United Nations and the government through a transparent and thorough selection process. The 2007 CCA and UNDAF Guidelines[39] should be consulted for more information.

Box 28. Categorizing evaluations by timing

Evaluations can be defined in terms of different modalities of UNDP support, such as project and programme, and also different levels or frameworks of results such as outcome, UNDAF and themes. Evaluations can also be defined by when they are carried out:

- **Ex-ante evaluation** is a forward-looking assessment of the likely future effects of new initiatives and support such as policies, programmes and strategies. It takes place prior to the implementation of an initiative.

- **Midterm evaluation** generally has a *formative* nature as it is undertaken around the middle period of implementation of the initiative. **Formative evaluation** intends to improve performance, most often conducted during the implementation phase of projects or programmes.

- **Final or terminal evaluations** normally serve the purpose of a *summative* evaluation since they are undertaken towards the end of the implementation phase of projects or programmers. **Summative evaluation** is conducted at the end of an initiative (or a phase of that initiative) to determine the extent to which anticipated outcomes were produced. It is intended to provide information about the worth of the programme.

- **Ex-post evaluation** is a type of summative evaluation of an initiative after it has been completed; usually conducted two years or more after completion. Its purpose is to study how well the initiative (programme or project) served its aims, to assess sustainability of results and impacts and to draw conclusions for similar initiatives in the future.

Evaluations defined by the modality of development initiatives or level of results can be further defined by the timing. For example, a programme unit may undertake a final project evaluation or a midterm UNDAF evaluation.

---

38 UNDG, 'CCA/UNDAF Monitoring and Evaluation Guidelines', 2007. Available at: http://www.undg.org/index.cfm?P=259.

39 Ibid.

REAL TIME EVALUATIONS

Real time evaluations are often undertaken at an early stage of an initiative to provide managers with timely feedback in order to make an immediate difference to the initiative. They are commonly applied in humanitarian or post-conflict contexts to provide implementing staff with the opportunity to analyse whether the initial response or recovery is appropriate in terms of desired results and process. They can also be used in crisis settings where there may be constraints in conducting lengthier evaluations. These constraints include the absence of baseline data, limited data collection efforts due to a rapid turnover of staff members (for example, lack of institutional memory) and difficulty conducting interviews and surveys due to security issues.

JOINT EVALUATION

Joint evaluation is one modality of carrying out an evaluation to which different partners contribute. Any evaluation can be conducted as a joint evaluation. Increasingly, UNDP is engaged in joint evaluations and there are various degrees of 'jointness' depending on the extent to which individual partners cooperate in the evaluation process, merge their evaluation resources and combine their evaluation reporting.[40]

The joint evaluation approach became popular in the 1990s with the promotion of the approach through the DAC Principles for Evaluation of Development Assistance, which

---

Box 29. Benefits and challenges of joint evaluations

Benefits

- Strengthened evaluation harmonization and capacity development: shared good practice, innovations and improved programming
- Reduced transaction costs and management burden (mainly for the partner country)
- Improved donor coordination and alignment: increase donor understanding of government strategies, priorities and procedures
- Objectivity and legitimacy: enables greater diversity of perspectives and a consensus must be reached
- Broader scope: able to tackle more complex and wider reaching subject areas
- Enhanced ownership: greater participation
- Greater learning: by providing opportunities for bringing together wider stakeholders, learning from evaluation becomes broader than simply for organizational learning and also encompasses advancement of knowledge in development

Challenges

- More difficult subjects to evaluate (complex, many partners, etc.)
- Processes for coordinating large number of participants may make it difficult to reach consensus
- Lower-level of commitment by some participants

Source: Adopted from OECD, 'DAC Guidance for Managing Joint Evaluations', Paris, France, 2006; and Feinstein O and G Ingram, 'Lessons Learned from World Bank experiences in Joint Evaluation', OECD, Paris, France, 2003.

---

40 OECD, 'Glossary of Key Terms in Evaluation and Results-based Management', Development Assistance Committee (DAC), Paris, France, 2002. Available at: http://www.oecd.org/dataoecd/29/21/2754804.pdf.

stated, "Joint donor evaluation should be promoted in order to improve understanding of each others' procedures and approaches and to reduce the administrative burden on the recipient."[41] The Paris Declaration also reinforced the joint evaluation approach through the commitment made by development agencies and partner countries to find more effective ways of working together.[42] Joint evaluations can be characterized by a number of benefits and challenges as shown in Box 29.

At the country level, one of the most obvious examples of a joint evaluation is the UNDAF evaluation, in which a number of UN organizations and the government participate. In addition, a UNDP country office may jointly carry out, together with the partner government or with a donor, a joint outcome evaluation that looks where both parties are mutually and equally responsible for the evaluation exercise. For guidance on how to organize and manage a joint evaluation process, see Chapter 6.

5.4   ROLES AND RESPONSIBILITIES IN EVALUATION

The UNDP evaluation policy outlines the roles and responsibilities of key constituents of the organization in evaluation. Programme units and the UNDP Evaluation Office in Headquarters carry out different types of evaluations in order to objectively assess UNDP contributions to development results.

Senior managers of the programme units are responsible for commissioning **decentralized evaluations** in the programmatic areas for which they are responsible and using the information in managing for results. In order to enhance the impartiality and objectivity of decentralized evaluations, the programme units hire external experts and institutions to carry out an evaluation. Decentralized evaluations help ensure that UNDP remains accountable to the relevant programme country and its people and is responsible for contributing to development results in the most relevant and efficient way.

In programme units, there has been an increase in the number of dedicated **M&E specialists** who contribute to the enhanced quality of the monitoring and evaluation function at the decentralized level. As successful evaluation requires the involvement of all stakeholders, this function entails close communication and coordination with all involved in various stages and aspects of results-based programme management, including UNDP country office management, programme and project officers, national counterparts, partners, UN organizations, regional bureaux and the Evaluation Office. At the individual project and programme level, the primary responsibility for planning for monitoring and evaluation and implementation rests with the implementers and UNDP programme officers. M&E specialists are expected to provide those responsible for monitoring and evaluation planning, implementation

---

41 OECD, 'DAC Principles for Evaluation of Development Assistance', Development Assistance Committee (DAC), Paris, France, 1991, p.8. Available at: http://www.oecd.org/dataoecd/21/32/41029845.pdf.

42 OECD, 'DAC Guidance for Managing Joint Evaluations', Development Assistance Committee (DAC), Paris, France, 2006. Available at: http://www.oecd.org/dataoecd/28/14/37484787.pdf.

and follow up with technical guidance, and support to enhance the quality of their work. In terms of evaluation, to enhance its independence and technical rigour, it is advised that the M&E specialists manage the evaluation in close consultation with programme staff who are responsible for the subject of evaluation.

Due to different organizational and programme structures at the decentralized level, organizational relationships cannot be generalized and prescribed to all programme units. However, it is recommended that **the M&E specialists report to senior management on evaluation-related matters in order to ensure effective coherence, coordination and independence of the function**.

UNDP M&E officers, programme officers, partners, stakeholders and evaluators all play different roles in the evaluation process. Their respective roles and responsibilities are described in relevant sections of Chapter 6.

In the case of independent evaluations conducted by the Evaluation Office, programme units concerned (for example, a country office subject to an ADR or the case study of a thematic evaluation) are expected to play certain roles such as providing necessary documentation, arranging meetings, supporting logistics and providing feedback on the draft evaluation report.

As the custodian of the evaluation function, the **UNDP Evaluation Office** conducts independent evaluations (see Section 5.3); sets standards and guidelines; manages the systems for quality assurance and evaluation planning and use, such as the ERC (see Box 30); and develops products to support organizational learning, knowledge management and evaluation capacity development. The Evaluation Office also participates in the UNEG, which works to strengthen the objectivity, effectiveness and visibility of the evaluation function across the UN system. The Evaluation Office hosts and supports the UNEG Secretariat.

Box 30. Evaluation Resource Centre (ERC)

The ERC, available online at erc.undp.org, is the UNDP information management system to support management accountability for evaluation. It provides timely data on the status of evaluations in the evaluation plans, management responses and follow-up. The Evaluation Office reports on evaluation practices and compliance, using the data in the ERC in its Annual Report on Evaluation to the Executive Board. Regional bureaux and other oversight units also use the ERC data. ERC is a public website.

Detailed roles and responsibilities of key actors in decentralized evaluations are outlined in Table 23.

Table 23. Roles and responsibilities in decentralized evaluations

Who: Actors and Accountability	What: Roles and Responsibilities	When
Senior Management of Programme Units ■ UNDP contribution towards national goals ■ Progress, problems and trends in the achievement of UNDAF level and programme results ■ Patterns and efficiency of resource use ■ Use of evaluative knowledge for learning and accountability	■ Ensure the development of an evaluation plan (see Chapter 3) ■ Promote joint evaluation work with the UN system and other partners ■ Ensure evaluability of UNDP initiatives, clear and comprehensive results frameworks are in place, and effective monitoring is implemented ■ Safeguard the independence of the evaluation exercise and ensure quality of evaluations ■ Prepare a management response to all evaluations and ensure the implementation of committed actions in the management response	Planning Planning and monitoring Commissioning of evaluation Post-evaluation and follow-up
Heads of Thematic Units and Programme Officers/Project Staff Heads of Thematic Units: ■ UNDP portfolio of programmes and projects in a thematic area—UNDP contribution to particular outcomes within a programme Programme Officers or Project Staff: ■ Progress towards and achievement of outputs and outcomes ■ Problems and issues related to implementation ■ Practical project-level collaboration with and monitoring of partners' contribution, as well as resource mobilization	■ Participate and involve relevant stakeholders in developing an evaluation plan ■ Ensure evaluability of UNDP initiatives in a given thematic or results area ■ Facilitate and ensure the preparation and implementation of relevant management responses ■ Facilitate and ensure knowledge sharing and use of sectoral or thematic evaluative information in programming	Planning Planning and monitoring Post-evaluation and follow-up
M&E Specialists/Advisers and Regional Evaluation Advisers ■ Coherent M&E framework and systems in place and implemented at the programme and project levels ■ Enhanced quality of planning, monitoring and evaluation	■ Support programme evaluability by facilitating the development of a coherent results framework and a monitoring system, and providing programme and project staff with tools, guidance and training ■ Support evaluation planning and upload and maintain the evaluation plan in ERC ■ Provide guidance in drafting evaluation ToR, selecting evaluators, mapping stakeholders, reviewing draft evaluation reports, and identifying evaluation questions and methodologies ■ Facilitate the preparation of timely management responses to all evaluations ■ Ensure management response tracking through ERC and support M&E capacity development and knowledge sharing	Planning Planning and ongoing implementation Post-evaluation and follow-up
Stakeholders and Partners	■ Actively participate in the development of the evaluation plan for UNDP ■ Participate, as relevant, in evaluations as a member of the reference group	Planning implementation and follow-up
Oversight Units: **Regional Bureaux and the Executive Office**	■ Regional bureaux: provide oversight to ensure that the relevant country offices fulfil the requirements as outlined above[43] ■ The Executive Office provides oversight for evaluations carried out by the regional bureaux and other corporate units such as BDP, BCPR and Partnership Bureau	Planning, monitoring, implementation and follow-up
Evaluation Office	■ Provide norms, standards, guidelines and tools to support the quality enhancement of evaluations ■ Maintain and improve management systems for evaluation, known as the ERC	

43 The Evaluation Resource Centre or ERC provides timely information to support the regional bureaux oversight responsibilities in evaluation.

5.5 MANDATORY REQUIREMENTS FOR PROGRAMME UNITS

Since the 2002 version of the Handbook on Monitoring and Evaluation for Results, requirements for evaluation practices have been adjusted in many ways. Table 24 lists the policy requirements before and after the introduction of the Evaluation Policy in 2006. As discussed in Chapter 3, each evaluation plan should indicate, at a minimum, mandatory evaluations. The implementation status of the evaluation plan and committed actions in management responses will be monitored by responsible oversight units in ERC.

Table 24. Mandatory evaluation-related requirements		
Tool	**Before the Evaluation Policy (2001 – May 2006)**	**After the Evaluation Policy (May 2006 on)**
Project Evaluation	Optional	Only mandatory when required by a partnership protocol (including Global Environment Facility) and included in the project document. Strongly recommended to evaluate pilot projects before replication or upscaling, projects that are going into a next phase, and projects more than five years for accountability and learning purposes.
Outcome Evaluation	A certain number of them are required during the programme period, depending on the size of the total programme.	Outcome evaluations or outcome-oriented evaluation planned in the evaluation plan. For more information on outcome information requirements, see the evaluation section in the POPP.
Evaluation Plan	Country-level evaluation plan is prepared by country offices electronically, and submitted to the Evaluation Office for approval.	All programme units are required to prepare a plan for the programme period. It is made available to the Executive Board along with the programme document before its approval. It is uploaded in the ERC to monitor and report on evaluation compliance. The Evaluation Office no longer reviews or approves the evaluation plan.
Management Response	Optional	All evaluations require a management response. It is entered in the ERC to monitor and report on the status of committed follow-up actions.
Information Disclosure in the ERC	It contains evaluation plans and reports for UNDP country offices. It is accessible to UNDP account holders only. It is optional for programme units to upload information.	Programme units are required to upload evaluation plans, ToRs, reports, and management responses. ERC also contains summary reports, information on evaluation focal points in each programme unit, and various reporting tools for all programme units. It is a publicly accessible site.

EVALUATION REQUIREMENTS FOR ASSOCIATED FUNDS AND PROGRAMMES

The evaluation units of the Associated Funds and Programmes—United Nations Capital Development Fund (UNCDF), United Nations Development Fund for Women (UNIFEM) and United Nations Volunteers (UNV); their programme units, such as regional, subregional and country offices; as well as Headquarters-based thematic units carry out evaluations of their respective initiatives. Box 31 outlines their respective mandatory evaluation requirements.

Box 31. Mandatory evaluation requirements for UNDP associated funds and programmes

- **UNCDF**—Midterm and final evaluation of all programmes of a duration of five years or more and a budget of USD 2.5 million or more, or when stipulated in a partnership agreement. Project evaluations of UNCDF funded (or UNCDF and UNDP joint projects) should be included in the relevant UNDP country office evaluation plan. UNCDF also carries out strategic, thematic and outcome evaluations.

- **UNIFEM**—One thematic assessment every two years and one evaluation during the lifecycle for all programmes with a budget of between USD 1 million and USD 3 million. A mid-term and final evaluation is required for all programmes with a budget of USD 3 million or more.

- **UNV**—Evaluation of programmatic initiatives financed from the Special Voluntary Fund, thematic assessments in accordance with organizational priorities, and project evaluations as required by a partnership protocol.

INITIATING AND MANAGING AN EVALUATION

This chapter introduces key steps in the process of preparing for and managing an evaluation for UNDP programme units, who are responsible for commissioning evaluations that are planned in their respective evaluation plans. The chapter presents the involvement of stakeholders and partners in evaluation as one of the guiding principles in UNDP evaluation, describes their important role in ensuring ownership and high quality of evaluation, and discusses how UNDP can ensure their meaningful and optimal involvement in the process. The chapter also introduces tools such as the ToR and evaluation report templates and quality standards, which are intended to help programme units carry out their tasks effectively. Finally, this chapter discusses key elements of the joint evaluation process.

6.1 INVOLVEMENT AND ROLES OF STAKEHOLDERS AND PARTNERS IN MANAGING AN EVALUATION

The evaluation process should involve key government counterparts, donors, civil society and UN organizations, as well as beneficiaries of initiatives and 'informants', who may not necessarily have a direct stake in the subject of an evaluation. Such broad-based involvement of national stakeholders will enhance not only the ownership of and mutual accountability for results, but also the credibility and transparency of the evaluation exercise.

The evaluation process described in Section 6.2 adheres to the principles of national ownership (see Box 32). All parties concerned should be consulted and take part in decision making at every critical step of the process. Stakeholders of the evaluation, as identified in the stakeholder mapping exercise, should be consulted and engaged, when appropriate, in developing an evaluation plan, drafting the evaluation ToR, appraising the selection of evaluators, providing the evaluators with information and guidance, reviewing the evaluation draft, preparing and implementing the management response, and disseminating and internalizing knowledge generated from the evaluation.

In conflict settings, conducting an evaluation in an inclusive manner is critical for bringing different factions together to hear each other's viewpoints, while being transparent and ensuring that a balance of views is represented between the different groups. This allows UNDP to remain transparent and to ensure that one group does not feel (rightly or mistakenly) excluded or discriminated against, which may heighten tensions or vulnerabilities. It may be difficult to maintain this inclusive approach in conflict settings because of typically high staff turnover and mobility, and the need for fast results that may make it 'easier' to do an evaluation without much involvement of others rather than taking time to involve and capacitate national partners. However, despite the challenges, capacity development through an inclusive manner is an important part of the recovery process.

Box 32. National ownership of evaluation

UNDP emphasizes the centrality of national ownership in evaluating results. The achievement of the outcome is dependent upon contributions from a range of partners, including UNDP. To this effect, the involvement of stakeholders and partners in the planning, management, conduct and use of evaluation is critical. The degree and modalities of their involvement will vary at different stages of the process. Some need only be informed of the process, while it would be important for others to be involved in a decision-making capacity. In each evaluation, a thorough assessment should be done in order to determine who the stakeholders are and how they should be involved in the evaluation process. The following are several ways of carrying out evaluations that reflect various degrees of national ownership:

- **Country-led evaluations** where the evaluative exercise is led largely by independent evaluation institutions operating within national monitoring and evaluation systems
- Evaluations of UNDP contributions conducted solely by an independent non-governmental **national entity** (e.g. research institution, think-tank or academic institution)
- **Joint-evaluations** with government and/or other national implementing partners where UNDP and partners are mutually and equally responsible for the evaluation exercise
- In partnership with government and other stakeholders or partners, **UNDP commissions evaluations** to international, or a combination of international and national, institutions and consultants

In order to pursue these various modalities, UNDP programme units and relevant key partners should first assess and develop, when needed, the evaluation capacity of existing national monitoring and evaluation systems and determine the role of independent evaluation institutions. These are necessary steps in order to ensure independence and enhance credibility of the evaluation exercise. UNDP globally supports evaluation capacity development of governments and national institutions through developing their data and statistical capacity. This includes capacity to establish performance measures and baselines and develop systems for data collection for analysis in the context of Poverty Reduction Strategies and the MDGs. Similarly, UNDP supports capacity development at the local and community level to map and monitor poverty incidence and vulnerabilities, and link results to planning and budgeting processes. Such programmatic support of UNDP in the area of evaluation capacity development has an additional advantage as it presents future opportunities for evaluations with greater ownership at the national and local level.

6.2 KEY STEPS IN DECENTRALIZED EVALUATIONS

The process for decentralized evaluations, commissioned by programme units, include the following key steps (see Box 33 and the checklist on page 148).

Box 33. Steps in decentralized evaluations

Step 1:	Step 2:	Step 3:	Step 4:
Initiating the evaluation process	Preparation	Managing the evaluation	Using the evaluation

Step 1: Pre-evaluation: Initiating the evaluation process
- Checking the 'evaluability,' or readiness, for evaluation

Tools: Evaluation plan template (Chapter 3)

Step 2: Preparation
- Agreeing on the management structure of an evaluation and roles and responsibilities
- Drafting the ToR
- Organizing the relevant documentation
- Selecting the evaluation team

Tools: Template and quality criteria for ToR (Annex 3), selection criteria for evaluators (Annex 5)

Step 3: Managing the conduct of the evaluation (while external evaluators conduct evaluation)
- Briefing and supporting the evaluation team
- Reviewing the inception report prepared by the evaluation team
- Reviewing the draft evaluation report

Tools: Template and quality criteria for evaluation reports (Annex 7)

Step 4: Using the evaluation: Management response, knowledge sharing and dissemination
- Preparing the management response and implementing follow-up actions
- Preparing and disseminating evaluation products and organizing knowledge sharing events
- Reviewing evaluations prior to new planning processes

Tools: Management response template (Annex 6), practical steps for developing knowledge products and dissemination

---

STEP 1: PRE-EVALUATION: INITIATING THE EVALUATION PROCESS

Checking the evaluability, or readiness, for evaluation

Before formally initiating an evaluation process, UNDP programme units and stakeholders who were involved in the development of an evaluation plan (see Chapter 3) should assess whether the subject of evaluation is ready for evaluation. This entails determining whether the proposed evaluation is: still relevant and feasible as planned, designed to be complementary to the previous analysis, and likely to add value to existing information and other planned and future evaluations by government and other partners.

Further, UNDP programme units and stakeholders should review the results matrix, which forms the basis of evaluations. Since the model was completed at the planning stage (see Chapter 2), there may have been changes in the development context or partnership strategy during implementation. Therefore, before the evaluation is formally commissioned, programme units and key partners and stakeholders may revise and update the model and add emerging information that reflects the changes that have occurred over a period of the initiative. The results map should be updated throughout the life of the programme as it helps evaluators and others understand the outcome, changes that have occurred and the factors that are understood to contribute to outcomes.

The checklist below is intended to help UNDP programme units and stakeholders determine the degree of readiness for evaluation.

QUICK CHECKLIST FOR ASSESSING THE READINESS FOR EVALUATION	YES	NO
✓ Does the subject of evaluation have a **clearly defined results map**? Is there common understanding as to what initiatives will be subject to evaluation?		
✓ Is there a **well-defined results framework for initiative(s)** that are subject to evaluation? Are goals, outcome statements, outputs, inputs and activities clearly defined? Are indicators SMART?		
✓ Is there sufficient capacity for the initiative(s) to provide **required data for evaluation**? For example, is there baseline data? Is there sufficient data collected from monitoring against a set of targets? Are there well-documented progress reports, field visit reports, reviews and previous evaluations?		
✓ Is the planned evaluation still **relevant**, given the evolving context? In other words, is there still a demand for evaluation? Is the purpose of the evaluation clearly defined and commonly shared amongst stakeholders?		
✓ Will **political, social and economic factors** allow for an effective conduct and use of evaluation as envisaged?		
✓ Are there **sufficient resources** (human and financial) allocated to evaluation?		

If political and socio-economic situations do not allow the team to carry out an evaluation in a meaningful manner, UNDP management, together with national stakeholders, may decide to wait until an environment that is conducive to evaluation is secured. In conflict settings, such a decision should be made based on good and current analyses of the setting so that the evaluation will be relevant to fast changing crisis situations. Factors such as security situations (safety of evaluators, UNDP staff involved and interviewees) and potential impact of the evaluation on existing tensions should be carefully assessed.

If the results map or the results framework needs improvements, UNDP may organize a session with relevant stakeholders to enhance it by reviewing and clearly articulating the intended outcomes, outputs and indicators and also initiate a quick exercise to gather primary data through surveys and a desk review. This also presents an opportunity to establish baselines, which may not have been made available at the time of planning.

If a decision to carry out an evaluation is taken, all parties concerned should be informed of the decision to ensure buy-in, credibility and transparency of the evaluation. In conflict settings, getting the correct officials involved, visited and acknowledged at the outset of the evaluation process is critical to ensure ownership of the future process.

STEP 2: PREPARATION

Agreeing on the management structure of an evaluation and roles and responsibilities

There should be a clearly defined organization and management structure for an evaluation and established roles and responsibilities for key players. Table 25 outlines key roles and responsibilities of the commissioner of the evaluation (UNDP), partners, evaluators and stakeholders in the evaluation process and Figure 16 shows the management structure.

UNDP and evaluation stakeholders should appoint an **evaluation manager**, who will assume the day-to-day responsibility for managing the evaluation and serve as a central person connecting other key players. Whenever available, an evaluation or M&E specialist in the programme unit should assume this role to enhance the independence of the exercise from those directly responsible for the subject of an evaluation. To ensure the substantive linkage between the programme or project being evaluated and the evaluation exercise, the designated manager should work closely with a relevant programme or project staff. In the absence of a specialist, a UNDP Programme Officer may assume this role.

National ownership means that key partners and stakeholders must play an integral part in the evaluation process from the outset. For every evaluation, there should be a **reference group** comprised of key stakeholders to work closely with the evaluation manager to guide the process. In most UNDP managed programmes and projects, there is already an existing mechanism and structure to ensure an adequate level of engagement and ownership by national stakeholders and partners. If such an entity— for example, a steering group, programme, outcome or project board or thematic group—already exists, members of such boards and additional key stakeholders for a

Table 25. Key roles and responsibilities in the evaluation process

Person or Organization	Roles and Responsibilities
Commissioner of the Evaluation (UNDP)	■ Determine which outcomes and projects will be evaluated and when ■ Provide clear advice to the evaluation manager at the onset on how the findings will be used ■ Respond to the evaluation by preparing a management response and use the findings as appropriate ■ Take responsibility for learning across evaluations on various content areas and about evaluation ■ Safeguard the independence of the exercise ■ Allocate adequate funding and human resources
Co-commissioner of the Evaluation (In the case of joint evaluations, governments, other UN organizations, development partners, etc.)	Same as commissioner
Evaluation Manager appointed by the commissioner and partners; often a UNDP Programme Officer or an M&E specialist, when available	■ Lead the development of the evaluation ToR ■ Manage the selection and recruitment of the external evaluators ■ Manage the contractual arrangements, the budget and the personnel involved in the evaluation ■ Provide executive and coordination support to the reference group ■ Provide the evaluators with administrative support and required data ■ Liaise with and respond to the commissioners and co-commissioners ■ Connect the evaluation team with the wider programme unit, senior management and key evaluation stakeholders, and ensure a fully inclusive and transparent approach to the evaluation ■ Review the inception report and the draft evaluation report(s); ensure the final draft meets quality standards
Representatives of the Stakeholders, including beneficiaries who make up the Reference Group	■ Define or confirm the profile, competencies and roles and responsibilities of the evaluation manager and co-evaluation manager (for a joint evaluation); if applicable, particularly in a joint evaluation, for the evaluation and review and, clear candidates submitted for this role ■ Participate in the drafting and review of the draft ToR ■ Assist in collecting required data ■ Oversee progress and conduct of the evaluation ■ Review the draft evaluation report and ensure final draft meets quality standards
Evaluation Team (Consultants)	■ Fulfil the contractual arrangements in line with the UNEG norms and standards and ethical guidelines; this includes developing an evaluation matrix as part of the inception report, drafting reports, and briefing the commissioner and stakeholders on the progress and key findings and recommendations, as needed
Quality Assurance Panel Members, external to the evaluation exercise and can be M&E advisers in the regional centres, bureaux or national evaluation experts (see Annex 4 for the list of national evaluation associations)	■ Review documents as required and provide advice on the quality of the evaluation and options for improvement, albeit for another evaluation ■ Be a critical friend

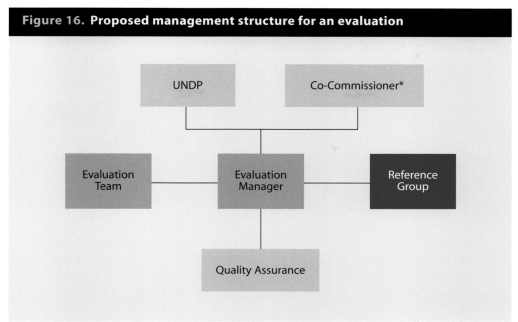

Figure 16. Proposed management structure for an evaluation

* The presence of a Co-commissioner is applicable in the case of a joint evaluation.

particular evaluation can constitute the group of evaluation stakeholders, that is, the reference group. As long as an existing structure allows for an adequate level of stakeholder participation throughout the evaluation process, there is no need to create a new structure. If such a structure does not exist, a mapping exercise should be carried out to identify key stakeholders for a particular evaluation. In crisis settings, a formal functional structure is unlikely to exist. When creating one in such circumstances, it is important to ensure representation is balanced, so that one particular group of people will not be dominant in the structure, which can heighten existing tensions amongst different groups of people or individuals.

For each evaluation, there should also be a mechanism for **assuring the quality of the process and outputs of evaluation**, such as ToRs and evaluation reports. Senior managers of UNDP programme units are ultimately responsible and accountable for the quality of the evaluation process and products. Relevant expertise may be drawn from evaluation advisers in UNDP regional centres, within the UN system in the country or neighboring countries, and in regional and national evaluation associations and research institutions (see Annex 4 for a list of these).

Drafting the Terms of Reference (ToR)

The ToR defines the scope, requirements and expectations of the evaluation and serves as a guide and point of reference throughout the evaluation. While the initial draft of the ToR is usually the responsibility of the commissioning office, an evaluation ToR should be developed in consultation with key stakeholders and evaluation partners to ensure that their key concerns are addressed and that the essential audience for the evaluation will view the evaluation results as valid and useful. Regional evaluation advisers and others with necessary expertise may comment on the draft ToR to ensure it meets the corporate quality standards.

A quality ToR should be explicit and focused and provide a clear mandate for the evaluation team about what is being evaluated and why, who should be involved in the evaluation process, and expected outputs. Each ToR should be unique to the particular circumstances and the purposes of the evaluation. Since the ToR plays a critical role in establishing the quality criteria and use of the evaluation report, adequate time should be allocated to this exercise. Further guidance is available in Chapter 7 and a template is provided in Annex 3.

The outcome, project, thematic area or any other initiatives selected for evaluation along with the timing, purpose, duration and scope of the evaluation will dictate much of the substance of the ToR. However, because an evaluation cannot address all issues, developing the ToR involves strategic choices about the specific focus, parameters and outputs for the evaluation within available resources.

Organizing the relevant documentation

Once the scope of an evaluation has been defined, the evaluation manager, with help from the key stakeholders, starts to gather basic documentation that will be provided to the evaluation team. Preliminary deskwork may be carried out to gather information on activities and outputs of partners, previous UNDP-related assistance, and the current situation of the project, programme or outcome. Table 26 presents different sources of information that may be useful for an evaluation team.

Selecting the evaluators

The choice of the evaluators is important to the quality of evaluations. As discussed in Section 6.1, UNDP and evaluation stakeholders should, to the extent possible, engage independent evaluation institutions within the existing national monitoring and evaluation system, including national non-governmental institutions or evaluators to carry out the evaluation. A mapping of key players in the national evaluation system and an assessment of their capacity should be done prior to commissioning the work. This way necessary arrangements, such as working with experienced international evaluators or institutions and incorporating capacity development training as part of the exercise, can be made to address the capacity gaps while making sure that the end product will meet the agreed quality criteria.

UNDP selects evaluators through a competitive and transparent process in accordance with the organization's rules and regulations for procurement. Areas of expertise to be considered in the team composition include the following:

- Proven expertise and experience in conducting evaluations

- Technical knowledge and experience in UNDP thematic areas, with specifics depending on the focus of the evaluation, and cross-cutting issues such as gender, rights-based approach, and capacity development

Table 26. Sources of information for an evaluation team

Sources of Information	Description of Information
Country, regional and global programme results frameworks	These address the key outcomes that UNDP plans to achieve in a three- to five-year period. CPDs also provide background information and the UNDP perspective on development in a given country.
Monitoring (regular reporting, reviews) and evaluation reports	These include evaluation reports on related subjects commissioned by the UNDP Evaluation Office, programme units, government, or other development partners and stakeholders; quarterly progress reports; CPAP annual reports; field visit reports; and other outcome and key programme or project documentation. The ERC can be used to search for relevant evaluations carried out by other UNDP units on similar topics.
Data from official sources	Information on progress towards outcome achievement may be obtained from sources in the government, private sector, academia and national, regional and international research institutes, including those in the UN system. In many cases, nationally adopted DevInfo and the websites of national statistical authorities are good sources for national statistics.
Research papers	Topics related to the outcome being evaluated may have been addressed in research papers from the government, NGOs, international financial institutions and academia.
National, regional and global reports	Useful data can be found in various reports such as the National Human Development Report, national MDG report, and other reports published by national, regional and subregional organizations, international financial institutions and UN organizations.
Financial and management information (Atlas, balanced-score card, audit, ERBM platform, etc.)	A number of corporate tools provide financial and other management information that is relevant to evaluation. They include delivery, resource mobilization and human resource management.
Additional sources at the country level	
Reports of related regional and sub-regional projects and programmes	These reports indicate the extent to which these projects and programmes have complemented contributions by UNDP and its partners to progress towards the outcome.
Country office CPAP and Results Oriented Annual Report	The CPAP and Results Oriented Annual Report should, ideally, identify all of the projects, programmes, subprogrammes and soft assistance that contribute to each outcome. Also included is information on key outputs, the strategic partners, partnership strategy, how much progress has been reported in previous years, the quality of outcome indicators, the need for further work, and baseline information.
UNDAF annual reviews	These documents include baseline information on the country development situation, partnerships and joint activities of UNDP and other UN organizations.

- Knowledge of the national situation and context
- RBM expertise
- Familiarity with policy-making processes (design, adoption and implementation), if the evaluation is to touch upon policy advice and policy dialogue issues

External evaluation institutions, firms or individual evaluators may be national or international, or a combination of both. Annex 5 provides a comparison of advantages and disadvantages of hiring firms versus individuals as evaluators. It is advisable to have a team comprised of at least two evaluators. This will allow for the team members to compare notes, verify the accuracy of information collected and recorded, divide efforts to interview more people, and bounce ideas off of each other. In addition, **evaluation teams should be balanced, to the extent possible, in their gender and geographical composition.**

> **TIP** The Evaluation Office offers a roster of vetted evaluation experts on its intranet site (intra.undp.org/eo).

In addition to the competency of the evaluators and geographical and gender balance of the team, considerations should be made to safeguard the independence of the evaluation exercise. **Independence** comprises impartiality and being free from **conflict of interest**. Potential conflict of interest can be addressed at the time of selecting the evaluation team members, and impartiality can be ensured throughout the design, analysis and implementation of the evaluation. Conflict of interest in the selection of evaluators could be defined as a situation whereby because of a person's work history or possibilities for future contracts, the consultant will not be able to provide objective and impartial analysis of the evaluation subject (see Box 34).

It is good practice to share the curriculum vitae of the potential candidates with wider stakeholders and partners before engagement. This will help ensure that there is no potential conflict of interest or objection to the selection. Check references by talking to colleagues and partners who have worked with the candidates before to verify their competency as evaluators.

STEP 3: MANAGING THE CONDUCT OF THE EVALUATION

Briefing and supporting the evaluation team

It is often misunderstood that safeguarding the independence of an evaluation means not interfering with the evaluation teams. On the contrary, the success of the evaluation depends on the level of cooperation and support rendered by the commissioning unit to the evaluation team. Key roles of the commissioning unit and the task manager include the following:

- Brief the evaluators on the purpose and scope of the evaluation and explain expectations from UNDP and its stakeholders in terms of the required standards for the quality of the process and the evaluation products. Provide them with relevant evaluation policy guidelines including the quality standards for evaluation reports, UNDP evaluation policy, and UNEG norms and standards for evaluation in the UN system.[44] In particular, evaluators must understand the requirement to

---

44   UNEG, 'Norms for Evaluation in the UN System', 2005. Available at: http://www.unevaluation.org/unegnorms. UNEG, 'Standards for Evaluation in the UN System', 2005. Available at: http://www.unevaluation.org/unegstandards.

Box 34. Avoiding and mitigating conflict of interest in evaluation (examples)

Case A: Conflict of interest due to past engagement

As a general rule, UNDP commissioning units will not assign consultants to the evaluation of projects, programmes, sectors and themes, strategies, corporate processes or policies for which they have had prior involvement in design, implementation, decision making or financing. Following this principle, UNDP staff members—including advisers based in regional centres and Headquarters-units—civil servants or employees of non-government organizations that may be or have been directly or indirectly related to the programme or project should not take part in the evaluation team. If a former staff member is being considered, special screening of past involvement with the project(s) to be evaluated should be reviewed.

Case B: Conflict of interest due to potential future involvement

The programme units must ensure that the evaluators will not be rendering any service (related or unrelated to the subject of the evaluation) to the implementation agency of the project or programme to be evaluated in the immediate future. Preferably, there should be a 'cooling off' period of at least one year before the evaluator is engaged in the implementation of a programme or project that was the subject of the evaluation. For example, an evaluator of the UNDP electoral support project should refrain from working for the national electoral commission as a technical adviser for at least one year.

Case C: Conflict of interest due to involvement in multiple assignments

If a consultant applies for two related assignments, ask the consultant to rank his or her choice. UNDP programme units should consider whether conducting two assignments could create a conflict of interest and take necessary action to mitigate.

On the part of the evaluator, he or she must inform UNDP and stakeholders of any potential or actual conflict of interest. The evaluation report should address any potential or actual conflict of interest and indicate measures put in place to mitigate its negative consequences. If conflict of interest is uncovered or arises during the evaluation, the organization should determine whether the evaluator should be dismissed or the evaluation terminated.

Drawn from various sources including: UNEG, 'Norms for Evaluation in the UN System', 2005, available at: http://www.unevaluation.org/unegnorms; UNEG, 'Standards for Evaluation in the UN System', 2005, available at: http://www.unevaluation.org/unegstandards; International Fund for Agricultural Development (IFAD), 'Conflict of Interest of Consultants and Widening the Pool of Evaluation Specialists'; Asian Development Bank, 'Operations Evaluation Department (OED) Guidelines to Avoid Conflict of Interest in Independent Evaluations', April 2005, available at: http://www.adb.org/documents/guidelines/evaluation/independent-evaluation.pdf; and the World Bank, 'Consulting Service Manual 2006: A Comprehensive Guide to the Selection of Consultants', Washington DC, 2006, available at: http://siteresources.worldbank.org/INTPROCUREMENT/Resources/2006ConsultantManual.pdf.

follow ethical principles as expressed in the UNEG ethical guidelines for evaluators by signing the Code of Conduct for Evaluators in the UN system.[45]

- Ensure that all information is made available to the evaluators. If they encounter any difficulty in obtaining information that is critical for the conduct of evaluation, provide necessary support to the extent possible.

- If asked by the evaluators, provide a preliminary list and contact information of stakeholders whom they should meet. However, the evaluation consultants are ultimately responsible for identifying whom to meet and UNDP cannot interfere with their decision.

- Organize a forum to introduce the evaluation team to the partners and stakeholders to facilitate the initial contact. The evaluation team can also take this opportunity to receive inputs from the stakeholders in the formulation of the evaluation

---

45 UNEG, 'Code of Conduct', June 2008. Available at: http://www.uneval.org/search/index.jsp?q=code+of+conduct.

questions, seek clarifications in the ToR, and exchange ideas about the ways in which the evaluation will be carried out.

- Arrange interviews, meetings and field visits.

- Provide comments on and quality assure the work plan and the inception report (if existing) with elaborated evaluation methodology prepared by the evaluation team.

- Ensure security of consultants, stakeholders and accompanying UNDP staff, particularly in crisis situations. The evaluation team members should have passed relevant UN security exams and be aware of and compliant with related security protocols.

> **TIP** There is a delicate balance between providing adequate support for the evaluation and maintaining the independence of the exercise. While UNDP is expected to organize meetings and visits, UNDP or government staff working for the organization responsible for the project or programme should not participate in them, as interviewees and participants might not feel comfortable to speak freely in their presence.

Reviewing the inception report prepared by the evaluation team

Based on the ToR, initial meetings with the UNDP programme unit or evaluation manager, and the desk review, evaluators should develop an inception report. The description of what is being evaluated illustrates the evaluators' understanding of logic or theory of how the initiative is supposed to work, including strategies, activities, outputs and expected outcomes and their interrelationships. The inception report should include, *inter alia*:

- **Evaluation purpose and scope**—A clear statement of the objectives of the evaluation and the main aspects or elements of the initiative to be examined.

- **Evaluation criteria and questions**—The criteria and questions that the evaluation will use to assess performance and rationale.

- **Evaluation methodology**—A description of data collection methods and data sources to be employed, including the rationale for their selection (how they will inform the evaluation) and their limitations; data collection tools, instruments and protocols and discussion of reliability and validity for the evaluation; and the sampling plan.

- **Evaluation matrix**—This identifies the key evaluation questions and how they will be answered by the methods selected (see Annex 3).

- A revised **schedule of key milestones**, deliverables and responsibilities.

- Detailed **resource requirements** tied to evaluation activities and deliverables detailed in the work plan.

NOTE **Good practice**—The commissioning unit and key stakeholders should review and assure the quality of the inception report. The inception report provides an opportunity to clarify matters—such as resource requirements and deliverable schedules—at an early stage of the evaluation exercise and ensure that the commissioning party, stakeholders and the evaluators have a common understanding on how the evaluation will be conducted.

Reviewing the draft evaluation report

Once the first draft of the evaluation report is submitted, the evaluation task manager with key evaluation stakeholders should assure the quality of the report and provide comments. UNDP programme units may call for evaluation experts or the advisory panel to assess the technical rigour of the evaluation. The evaluation report should be logically structured; contain evidence-based findings, conclusions, lessons and recommendations; and be presented in a way that makes the information accessible and comprehensible. It should meet the criteria outlined in Box 35.

The evaluation report quality standards provided in Annex 7 can be used as a basis for assessing the quality of the report. If shortcomings exist and there are questions about the methodological rigour, UNDP programme units should ask the evaluators to improve the report.

Depending upon the complexity of the evaluation findings, the programme unit should consider organizing a stakeholder meeting at which the evaluators make a presentation to the partners and stakeholders. This helps ensure that there is a common understanding of the findings, facilitates feedback on the report draft, and fosters ownership and future use of the evaluation. When soliciting comments from stakeholders, care must be taken to safeguard the independence of judgements made in the evaluation. Evaluation is an independent exercise. Comments should be limited to issues regarding the applied methodology (see Chapter 7 on evaluation design for more guidance) and **factual errors** and **omissions**.

Box 35. Criteria for evaluation reports

A quality evaluation report should:
- Be well structured and complete
- Describe what is being evaluated and why
- Identify the questions of concern to users
- Explain the steps and the procedures used to answer those questions
- Present findings supported by credible evidence in response to the questions
- Acknowledge limitations
- Draw conclusions about findings based on of the evidence
- Propose concrete and usable recommendations derived from conclusions
- Be written with the report user and how they will use the evaluation in mind

Source: UNEG, 'Standards for Evaluation in the UN System', 2005. Available at: http://www.unevaluation.org/unegstandards.

At this point, the programme unit should also start discussing with key stakeholders the preparation of the management response, for example, who will be involved in the preparation; when, how and to what degree; and what issues should be highlighted.

STEP 4: USING THE EVALUATION—MANAGEMENT RESPONSE, KNOWLEDGE SHARING AND DISSEMINATION

Preparing the management response for decentralized evaluations

As one way of ensuring an effective use of evaluation, UNDP has institutionalized a management response system (a template is provided in Annex 6). Programme units are responsible for preparing a management response to key issues and recommendations raised in evaluations, and identifying key follow-up actions, responsible units for implementation, and estimated completion dates for these actions.

To foster learning and sharing of knowledge, the process of developing a management response should engage all key evaluation stakeholders to reflect on the key issues, findings and recommendations. In this process, follow-up actions and their associated responsible institutions and time frames are collectively identified and agreed upon. In preparing the response, UNDP, partners and other stakeholders should not only look at internal management issues such as the delivery and timing of inputs and outputs but also respond to issues raised with regard to UNDP contributions towards development results and focus on strategic issues.

> **NOTE** **Good practice**—Once the management response is finalized and endorsed by stakeholders, it is posted for public viewing in ERC for transparency and accountability reasons. The programme units are responsible for regularly updating the implementation status. Units exercising the oversight responsibility (for example, regional bureaux for country office evaluations) monitor the implementation of follow-up actions in ERC.

The preparation of a management response should not be seen as a one-time activity. Learning emanating from the management response process should be documented and reflected upon when designing a new project or programme or defining an outcome. There is often little incentive to prepare a management response to terminal evaluations when the project is operationally closed. However, the process of developing a management response to terminal project evaluations allows key stakeholders to reflect on the project results and generate lessons that are applicable beyond a particular project. It also supports UNDP accountability by being responsive to the evaluation findings and responsible for follow-up actions. For these reasons, the evaluation policy requires management responses to all evaluations regardless of the status of the initiative that was evaluated.

Knowledge sharing and dissemination

The evaluation process does not end when the evaluation report is complete. In fact, learning and active use of knowledge generated from the evaluation is the most important element of the evaluation exercise. Time and resources required for effective follow up and learning should be allocated at the outset of the programme and project design.

Reviewing evaluations prior to the new planning process

Lessons learned and knowledge generated from evaluations should be reviewed together with national stakeholders and partners to ensure they are incorporated in the design of new programmes and projects. This systematic application of knowledge from evaluations is a key element of MfDR. For more guidance on knowledge sharing and learning from evaluation, see Chapter 8.

6.3 KEY ELEMENTS OF THE JOINT EVALUATION PROCESS

Generally, the suggested steps in planning and conducting a joint evaluation are the same as for any other well-managed evaluation. However, there are a number of issues specific to joint evaluations that warrant greater attention.

DECIDING ON A JOINT EVALUATION—IS THERE A NEED?

It is important to assess whether the programme or project warrants a joint evaluation. To do so, ask the following questions:

- Is the focus of the programme on an outcome that reaches across sectors and agencies?
- Is the programme cofinanced by multiple partners?
- Is the topic a contentious issue, thus calling for a balanced approach?

In addition, a discussion surrounding the purpose of the programme evaluation may be necessary. For instance, if the programme evaluation is solely for accountability purposes, it may not warrant a full-blown joint evaluation. Time constraints for the production of the evaluation report can also be an issue. Joint evaluations tend to be lengthier in process and require greater coordination efforts. Other advantages and disadvantages should be discussed both internally and with stakeholders (see Box 29 for benefits and challenges of joint evaluations).

DETERMINING THE PARTNERS—WHO IS KEY?

Like other evaluations, joint evaluations rely on national ownership and should contribute to the development of the capacity of stakeholders whenever possible. They also enable the voice of all stakeholders to be heard and help partners work together to assess the contributions of a programme or project. However, it is essential to determine the partners at an early stage to ensure their involvement and ownership. The partners could be determined by focusing on where the finances come from, who the implementing partners are, or by researching which other agencies are conducting similar work and thus may be contributing to the overall development goal or outcome. It is also important to assess the potential contributions of partners at this stage. For example, if a partner has a lot of other activities or constraints, it may not be best for them to get involved. It is always important to discuss the objectivity that partners may or may not bring to the table to ensure that the evaluation is independent and free from strong biases.

CHOOSING THE MANAGEMENT STRUCTURE AND DIVISION OF LABOUR

Effective management structures and communication systems are essential for a joint evaluation to function effectively. The following suggestions are drawn from various sources in the evaluation field:[46]

■ Agreeing on the management structure—The recommended structure is two tiered with a steering group that oversees the process and a smaller management group to ensure implementation goes smoothly. The steering group will normally comprise a representative from each partner organization and government entity. The steering group will meet at specific times to approve the ToR and the evaluation team, ensure oversight of the evaluation, introduce balance in the final evaluation judgements, and take responsibility for the use of results. Depending on the scope of the joint evaluation, a management group composed of technical representatives from concerned organizations or government entities should be created. The management group generally appoints one agency or an individual as the evaluation manager to handle the task of recruiting and managing the evaluation team. It is up to the commissioners of the evaluation to determine what works best within their particular context.

Box 36. Example of a management arrangement for a joint UNDAF evaluation

In a typical UNDAF evaluation, heads of agencies and key government officials may participate in the steering group, which provides overall guidance and direction to the process. M&E officers and technical officers in the management group are responsible for jointly drafting the ToR, managing the selection of evaluators and interacting with the evaluators on a regular basis. The Resident Coordinator's office or another UN organization may be appointed as an evaluation manager, who is responsible for the day-to-day management of the evaluation process and coordination amongst participating agencies.

■ Agreeing on the division of labour within the management group—The senior management of the UNDP programme unit should agree on the decision-making arrangements and the division of labour with other partners at the onset of the evaluation process. This involves determining who among the management group will take the lead role in each of the subsequent steps in the evaluation. A conflict resolution process should be determined to deal with any problems that may arise.

AGREEING ON THE SCOPE OF WORK

In general, it is more effective for all of the partners in a joint evaluation to discuss and agree upon the scope of the evaluation. Practical issues that should be clarified include the scope of the evaluation, the issues to be covered and the time frame of the exercise.

---

46 OECD, 'DAC Guidance for Managing Joint Evaluations', Development Assistance Committee (DAC), Paris, France, 2006, available at: http://www.oecd.org/dataoecd/28/14/37484787.pdf; Feinstein O and G Ingram, 'Lessons Learned from World Bank Experiences in Joint Evaluation', Room Document submitted to the Evaluation Network, OECD, Paris, France, 2003, available at: http://www.oecd.org/dataoecd/secure/15/13/31736431.pdf; and OECD, 'Effective Practices in Conducting a Multi-donor Evaluation', OECD, Paris, France, 2000, available at: http://www.oecd.org/dataoecd/10/28/2667318.pdf.

However, this is not always possible given the range of motivations for undertaking an evaluation, such as identifying lessons learned, establishing an empirical basis for substantive reorientation or funding revision, satisfying political constituencies in donor countries, or fulfilling institutional requirements that are particular to large projects.

- Drafting the ToR—It is generally practical for one party to take the lead in drafting the ToR, which defines the scope of work. After a draft is produced, it should be discussed and agreed upon by the partner organizations. It is important to satisfy the interests of all parties concerned in the ToR to the extent possible. Consideration should be given to creating a common agenda reflecting priorities that balance ownership with what is feasible.

- Determining whose procedures will be used—Since different organizations take different approaches to evaluation, it is important to allow flexibility to adapt and additional time to accommodate delays due to such differences. There are two common approaches to managing this issue: to agree that the evaluation will be managed using the systems and procedures from one agency, or to split the evaluation into components and agree whose systems will be used to manage which components.

SELECTING THE FUNDING MODALITY

A number of funding modalities are available for joint evaluations. If UNDP is taking the lead, the preferred approach should be for partners' financial support to be pooled into a fund (akin to a trust fund) that is administered by one agency and covers all costs related to the exercise. The second option, where individual partner(s) finance certain components of the evaluation while UNDP covers others (akin to parallel financing), is less preferable, as it increases transaction and coordination costs.

Box 37. Negotiating funding modalities for joint evaluations

These funding modalities mentioned earlier must be negotiated at the time of project or programme formulation with governments, and necessary resources should be ear-marked for a joint evaluation in the budget. If other donors are providing financial contributions, such discussions should take place while developing a project or negotiating the cost-sharing agreement. In order to facilitate discussions between UNDP programme units and donors, UNDP has prepared a clause for evaluation in the standard third-party, cost-sharing agreements.[47]

SELECTING THE EVALUATORS

There are several ways to approach the selection of experts for a joint evaluation. One option is to task one of the partners with recruiting the evaluation team, in consultation with the other partners. Another option is for each of the partners to contribute their own experts. In some cases, the approach taken to the selection of experts may need to

---

47 UNDP, 'Standard Third-Party Cost-Sharing Agreement', Partnership Bureau, 2007. Available at: http://content.undp.org/go/groups/brsp/Non-Core/Formats/?g11n.enc=ISO-8859-1.

correspond to the funding modality. For example, if parallel financing is used, each partner might need to bring its own expert to the team. In cases where each party brings its own evaluators to the team, evaluators may have difficulty in reporting to one actor while serving as a member of a joint team. To resolve this issue, all of the institutions involved should agree on the identity of the team leader at the onset, or delegate a particular agency to recruit the team leader and make clear to evaluators that the independence of the team will be respected and expected.

AGREEING ON THE REPORT AND DISSEMINATION STRATEGIES

Different organizations follow different practices over who has the final say on what is included in the report. For a joint evaluation, it is generally easiest if partners agree that: they have the opportunity to correct factual errors in the report; where it is impossible to resolve differences on the findings and conclusions, dissenting views should be included in the report; and the conclusions and recommendations should be the responsibility of the evaluators. However, sometimes measures, such as allowing for separate evaluation products, may be beneficial for the partners who have certain accountability or reporting requirements.

MANAGEMENT RESPONSE, FOLLOW-UP AND IMPLEMENTING RECOMMENDATIONS

All managers must follow up on the findings and recommendations of each evaluation report in UNDP. However, this can be particularly challenging for joint evaluations, given that the internalization of the findings and implementation of the recommendations need to be done at the level of individual institutions and at the level of the partnership between them. Therefore, partners need to agree on what to do individually and collectively, and decide upon a follow-up mechanism that monitors the status of the changes being implemented. In line with the evaluation policy requirement, UNDP may select recommendations that are pertinent to UNDP and prepare a management response focusing on these recommendations.

ASSURING THE QUALITY OF EVALUATION DESIGN AND METHODOLOGY

This chapter describes key components of quality evaluation design and elements of quality evaluation reports to help UNDP managers, evaluation managers and partners carry out effective **quality assurance of the evaluation process and products**. It is intended to enhance knowledge about available methods and tools to ensure that key evaluation products—such as the ToR, evaluation design and reports—meet the quality criteria as defined by the governing norms, standards and policies. This chapter also aims to help external evaluators understand the quality standards that are expected of evaluations in UNDP.

While external evaluators are responsible for refining the methodology and carrying out the evaluation, overall design and methodology is largely determined by the information provided in the evaluation ToR. Therefore, those responsible for drafting the ToR can refer to this chapter for information on key elements of the design and the role of stakeholders, defining the context, the evaluation purpose, and focusing the evaluation before drafting and finalizing the ToR. Quality assurance considerations for the evaluation methodology (Section 7.5) are also covered in this chapter.

7.1 OVERVIEW

Developing a quality evaluation design involves a thorough understanding of what is being evaluated (**the initiative and its context**) and making decisions about the following key elements and how each will contribute to valid and useful evaluation results:

- The **purpose** of the evaluation
- The **focus** of the evaluation, that is, the **key questions** that the evaluation seeks to answer
- The **sources and methods** for obtaining information that is credible and defensible
- The procedures that will be used to **analyse and interpret data and report results**

- The **standards** that must be reached for the initiative to be considered successful

- The **evidence** that will be used to indicate how the initiative has performed and demonstrate its results (outputs and outcomes)

ROLE OF STAKEHOLDERS

Stakeholders play an important role in designing and carrying out a quality evaluation. Stakeholders include individuals and groups that have a vested interest in the initiative or the results of the evaluation. Their involvement at all stages of the evaluation—including focusing the evaluation, shaping the questions to be addressed, identifying credible sources of evidence, reviewing findings and assisting in their interpretation—increases the credibility, potential usefulness and sustainability of evaluation results. Typically, stakeholders can be divided into three major categories, which are not mutually exclusive:

- **Those involved in the implementation of the initiative**—for example, donors, collaborators, strategic partners, administrators, managers and staff

- **Those served or affected by the initiative**—for example, intended beneficiaries, relevant organizations and agencies, government officials, advocacy groups, skeptics, opponents and staff of the implementing or competing agencies

- **Primary users of the evaluation**—for example, the specific persons in a position to do or decide something regarding the initiative, such as donors, UNDP programmatic counterparts (programme or outcome board) and partners in joint evaluation

The level of involvement of stakeholders will vary among evaluations. When designing an evaluation, it is important for the commissioning programme unit to identify stakeholders early and draw upon their knowledge as the evaluation design is shaped, starting with their meaningful involvement in developing the ToR. This is particularly critical for joint evaluations, in which case partners involved in the evaluation should be involved in all phases of developing the evaluation design.

7.2   DEFINING THE CONTEXT

UNDP evaluations support the UNDP human development focus "to help people build a better life" by generating knowledge about what works, why and under what circumstances. Therefore, quality evaluations not only focus on the attainment of outputs and outcomes but also assess how initiatives adapt to the contexts in which they operate and how and why they contribute to outputs and outcomes.

Evaluations must be conceived and designed with a thorough understanding of the initiative and the context within which it operates. The UNDP commissioning unit and relevant stakeholders who are engaged in drafting of ToRs (see Annex 3) are responsible for articulating necessary information for evaluators to have a good understanding of the initiative, the evaluation context, focus and purpose of the evaluation, and key questions to be addressed in the evaluation.

To produce credible information that will be useful for decision makers, evaluations must be designed with a clear understanding of the initiative, how it operates, how it was intended to operate, why it operates the way it does and the results that it produces. It is not enough to know what worked and what did not work (that is, whether intended outcomes or outputs were achieved or not). To inform action,

Table 27. Key aspects of the initiative	
Key Aspect	**Questions to Ask**
Demand	What is the need or demand for the initiative? What problem or development opportunity is the initiative intended to address?
Beneficiaries	Who are the beneficiaries or targets of the initiative? Who are the individuals, groups or organizations, whether targeted or not, that benefit directly or indirectly from the development initiative?
Scope	What is the scope of the initiative in terms of geographic boundaries and number of intended beneficiaries?
Outputs and Outcomes	What changes (outcomes) or tangible products and services (outputs) are anticipated as a result of the initiative? What must the project, programme or strategy accomplish to be considered successful? How do the intended outcomes link to national priorities, UNDAF priorities and corporate Strategic Plan goals?
Activities	What activities, strategies or actions, both planned and unplanned, does the programme take to effect change?
Theory of Change or Results/ Outcome Map	What are the underlying rationales and assumptions or theory that defines the relationships or chain of results that lead initiative strategies to intended outcomes? What are the assumptions, factors or risks inherent in the design that may influence whether the initiative succeeds or fails?
Resources	What time, talent, technology, information and financial resources are allocated to the effort?
Stakeholders and Partnership Strategy	Who are the major actors and partners involved in the programme or project with a vested interest? What are their roles, participation and contributions—including financial resources, in-kind contributions, leadership and advocacy—including UN organizations and others? How was the partnership strategy devised? How does it operate?
Phase of Implementation	How mature is the project or programme, that is, at what stage or year is the implementation? Is the implementation within the planned course of the initiative? Is the programme mainly engaged in planning or implementation activities?
Modifications from Original Design	What, if any, changes in the plans and strategies of the initiative have occurred over time? What are the potential implications for the achievement of intended results?
Evaluability	Can the project or programme as it is defined be evaluated credibly? Are intended results (outputs, outcomes) adequately defined, appropriate and stated in measurable terms, and are the results verifiable? Are monitoring and evaluation systems that will provide valid and reliable data in place?
Cross-cutting Issues	To what extent are key cross-cutting issues and UN values intended to be mainstreamed and addressed in the design, implementation and results?

evaluations must provide credible information about why an initiative produced the results that it did and identify what factors contributed to the results (both positive and negative). Understanding exactly what was implemented and why provides the basis for understanding the relevance or meaning of project or programme results.

Therefore, evaluations should be built on a thorough understanding of the initiative that is being evaluated, including the expected results chain (inputs, outputs and intended outcomes), its implementation strategy, its coverage, and the key assumptions and risks underlying the Results Map or Theory of Change. The questions outlined in Table 27 should be understood by the evaluators in conducting the evaluation.

THE EVALUATION CONTEXT

The evaluation context concerns two interrelated sets of factors that have bearing on the accuracy, credibility and usefulness of evaluation results:[48]

- **Social, political, economic, demographic and institutional factors, both internal and external**, that have bearing on how and why the initiative produces the results (positive and negative) that it does and the sustainability of results.

- **Social, political, economic, demographic and institutional factors within the environment and time frame of the evaluation** that affect the accuracy, impartiality and credibility of the evaluation results.

Examining the internal and external factors within which a development initiative operates helps explain why the initiative has been implemented the way it has and why certain outputs or outcomes have been achieved and others have not. Assessing the

---

Box 38. Guiding questions for defining the context[49]

- What is the operating environment around the project or programme?
- How might factors such as history, geography, politics, social and economic conditions, secular trends and efforts of related or competing organizations affect implementation of the initiative strategy, its outputs or outcomes?
- How might the context within which the evaluation is being conducted (for example, cultural language, institutional setting, community perceptions, etc.) affect the evaluation?
- How does the project or programme collaborate and coordinate with other initiatives and those of other organizations?
- How is the programme funded? Is the funding adequate? Does the project or programme have finances secured for the future?
- What is the surrounding policy and political environment in which the project or programme operates? How might current and emerging policy alternatives influence initiative outputs and outcomes?

---

48 Evaluation results refer to the end product of the evaluation—the sum of information the evaluation generates for users, including findings, conclusions, recommendations and lessons.

49 Guiding questions within this chapter are illustrative, not exhaustive, of the possible questions that could be considered.

initiative context may also point to factors that impede the attainment of anticipated outputs or outcomes, or make it difficult to measure the attainment of intended outputs or outcomes or the contribution of outputs to outcomes. In addition, understanding the political, cultural and institutional setting of the evaluation can provide essential clues for how best to design and conduct the evaluation to ensure the impartiality, credibility and usefulness of evaluation results.

7.3   THE EVALUATION PURPOSE

All evaluations start with a purpose, which sets the direction. Without a clear and complete statement of purpose, an evaluation risks being aimless and lacking credibility and usefulness. Evaluations may fill a number of different needs. The statements of purpose should make clear the following:

- Why the evaluation is being conducted and at that particular point in time
- Who will use the information
- What information is needed
- How the information will be used

The purpose and timing of an evaluation should be determined at the time of developing an evaluation plan (see Chapter 3 for more information). The purpose statement can be further elaborated at the time a ToR for the evaluation is drafted to inform the evaluation design.

> **TIP** **Sample Purpose Statement**—"This project evaluation is being conducted at the request of the national government and UNDP to provide information about the status of project implementation to ensure accountability for the expenditures to date and the delivery of outputs and so that managers can make midcourse corrections as appropriate."

7.4   FOCUSING THE EVALUATION

EVALUATION SCOPE

The evaluation scope narrows the focus of the evaluation by setting the boundaries for what the evaluation will and will not cover in meeting the evaluation purpose. The scope specifies those aspects of the initiative and its context that are within the boundaries of the evaluation. The scope defines, for example:

- The unit of analysis to be covered by the evaluation, such as a system of related programmes, polices or strategies, a single programme involving a cluster of projects, a single project, or a subcomponent or process within a project
- The time period or phase(s) of the implementation that will be covered
- The funds actually expended at the time of the evaluation versus the total amount allocated

- The geographical coverage
- The target groups or beneficiaries to be included

The scope helps focus the selection of evaluation questions to those that fall within the defined boundaries.

EVALUATION OBJECTIVES AND CRITERIA

Evaluation objectives are statements about what the evaluation will do to fulfil the purpose of the evaluation. Evaluation objectives are based on careful consideration of: the types of decisions evaluation users will make; the issues they will need to consider in making those decisions; and what the evaluation will need to achieve in order to contribute to those decisions. A given evaluation may pursue one or a number of objectives. The important point is that the objectives derive directly from the purpose and serve to focus the evaluation on the decisions that need to be made.

> **TIP** **Possible project evaluation objectives**—"To assess the status of outputs; to assess how project outputs are being achieved; to assess the efficiency with which outputs are being achieved."

Evaluation criteria help focus evaluation objectives by defining the standards against which the initiative will be assessed. UNDP evaluations generally apply the following evaluation criteria to help focus evaluation objectives: relevance, effectiveness, efficiency, sustainability and impact of development efforts.[50]

Relevance concerns the extent to which a development initiative and its intended outputs or outcomes are consistent with national and local policies and priorities and the needs of intended beneficiaries. Relevance also considers the extent to which the initiative is responsive to UNDP corporate plan and human development priorities of empowerment and gender equality issues. Relevance concerns the congruency between the perception of what is needed as envisioned by the initiative planners and the reality of what is needed from the perspective of intended beneficiaries. It also incorporates the concept of responsiveness—that is, the extent to which UNDP was able to respond to changing and emerging development priorities and needs in a responsive manner.

An essential sub-category of relevance is the criteria of **appropriateness**, which concerns the cultural acceptance as well as feasibility of the activities or method of delivery of a development initiative. While relevance examines the importance of the initiative relative to the needs and priorities of intended beneficiaries, appropriateness examines whether the initiative as it is operationalized is acceptable and is feasible within the local context. For example, an initiative may be relevant in that it addresses a need that intended beneficiaries perceive to be important, but inappropriate because

---

50 OECD, 'DAC Criteria for Evaluating Development Assistance', Development Assistance Committee. Available at: http://www.oecd.org/document/22/0,2340,en_2649_34435_2086550_1_1_1_1,00.html.

the method of delivery is incongruent with the culture or not feasible given geographic or other contextual realities. In applying the criterion of relevance, evaluations should explore the extent to which the planning, design and implementation of initiatives takes into account the local context.

Effectiveness is a measure of the extent to which the initiative's intended results (outputs or outcomes) have been achieved or the extent to which progress toward outputs or outcomes has been achieved.

Evaluating effectiveness in project evaluations involves an assessment of cause and effect—that is, attributing observed changes to project activities and outputs—for example, the extent to which changes in the number of voters can be **attributed** to a voter education project. Assessing effectiveness in outcome evaluations will more likely examine UNDP contributions toward intended outcomes. For example, an outcome evaluation might explore the extent to which the observed outputs from a voter education project—along with other UNDP outputs and those of other partners, such as professionalizing the electoral administration—contributed towards achieving stated outcomes relating to inclusive participation measured by international observers and other reputable experts.

Assessing effectiveness involves three basic steps:

1. Measuring change in the observed output or outcome

2. Attributing observed changes or progress toward changes to the initiative (project evaluation) or determining UNDP contributions toward observed changes

3. Judging the value of the change (positive or negative)

Efficiency measures how economically resources or inputs (such as funds, expertise and time) are converted to results. An initiative is efficient when it uses resources appropriately and economically to produce the desired outputs. Efficiency is important in ensuring that resources have been used appropriately and in highlighting more effective uses of resources.

As the nature and primary purposes of project and outcome evaluations differ, the application of criterion will also differ. For example, in assessing efficiency, a project evaluation might explore the extent to which resources are being used to produce the intended outputs and how resources could be used more efficiently to achieve the intended results. An outcome evaluation may involve estimates of the total UNDP investment (all projects and soft assistance) toward a given development outcome. The application of this criterion, particularly in UNDP outcome evaluations, poses a challenge as the nature of UNDP initiatives (for example, soft assistance), does not always lend itself to conventional efficiency indicators. In such cases, some analysis of delivery rates, the reasons some initiatives are implemented more quickly than others, and overall management ratios at the programme level might be considered. It is also important to assess how the partnership strategy has influenced the efficiency of UNDP initiatives through cost-sharing measures and complementary activities.

Sustainability measures the extent to which benefits of initiatives continue after external development assistance has come to an end. Assessing sustainability involves evaluating the extent to which relevant social, economic, political, institutional and other conditions are present and, based on that assessment, making projections about the national capacity to maintain, manage and ensure the development results in the future.

For example, an assessment of sustainability might explore the extent to which:

- A sustainability strategy, including capacity development of key national stakeholders, has been developed or implemented.

- There are financial and economic mechanisms in place to ensure the ongoing flow of benefits once the assistance ends.

- Suitable organizational (public or private sector) arrangements have been made.

- Policy and regulatory frameworks are in place that will support continuation of benefits.

- The requisite institutional capacity (systems, structures, staff, expertise, etc.) exists.

Impact measures changes in human development and people's well-being that are brought about by development initiatives, directly or indirectly, intended or unintended. Many development organizations evaluate impact because it generates useful information for decision making and supports accountability for delivering results. At times, evaluating impact faces challenges: Confirming whether benefits to beneficiaries can be directly attributed to UNDP support can be difficult, especially when UNDP is one of many contributors. However, the impact of UNDP initiatives should be assessed whenever their direct benefits on people are discernible.

In general, applying the following most commonly applied criteria—**relevance, effectiveness, efficiency, sustainability** and **impact**—in combination will help to ensure that the evaluation covers the most critical areas of the initiative. However, not all criteria are applicable, or equally applicable, to every evaluation. Different criteria may need to be applied in unique cases. In determining which criteria to apply, consider the type of evaluation and the contributions of the information to the purpose relative to the cost (use of evaluation resources). For example, evaluations of humanitarian and conflict programming may additionally apply the criteria of connectedness, coherence, coverage and coordination.[51] Box 39 outlines guiding questions to help define evaluation criteria and associated evaluation questions.

Box 39. Guiding questions for defining evaluation criteria

- To what extent does the criterion inform the purpose of the evaluation?
- How much and what kinds of information do potential users need?
- Should there be equal focus on each of the criteria or will some information be more useful?
- Is this criterion a useful or appropriate measure for the particular evaluation?
- Which criterion will produce the most useful information given available resources?

---

51 For more detail see: Beck T, 'Evaluating Humanitarian Action Using OECD/DAC Criteria', 2006.

EVALUATION QUESTIONS

Evaluation questions, when answered, can give users of the evaluation the information they seek in order to make decisions, take action or add to the knowledge base. The evaluation questions refine the focus of the evaluation by making explicit the aspects of the initiative that will be considered when judging its performance.

Evaluation questions reflect the underlying chain of assumptions about how the initiative is expected to operate within its contexts pursuant to the intended outputs and outcomes. The questions chosen for an evaluation should follow from a thorough understanding of the initiative's operations, intentions and context and should be selected for their role in meeting the evaluation purpose, objectives and relevant evaluation criteria.

An indefinite number of questions could be asked for each evaluation criterion. Real world evaluations are limited in terms of time, budget and resources. Therefore, it is important to be strategic in determining what information is needed most and to prioritize evaluation questions. It is better to answer fewer questions robustly than to answer more superficially. A clear and concise set of the most relevant questions ensures that evaluations are focused, manageable, cost efficient and useful.

To ensure that the key questions selected for the evaluation are the most relevant and most likely to yield meaningful information for users, UNDP programme units must solicit input from and negotiate agreement among partners and other stakeholders, including the evaluation team. Commissioning offices should ensure that the evaluation matrix in the evaluation inception report makes clear the linkages among the evaluation criteria, the evaluation questions and the information needs of intended users (see Annex 3 for more details).

GENDER, EXCLUSION SENSITIVITY AND RIGHTS-BASED APPROACH

Consistent with UNDP development efforts, UNDP evaluations are guided by the principles of gender equality, the rights-based approach and human development.[52] Thus, as appropriate, UNDP evaluations assess the extent to which UNDP initiatives: have addressed the issues of social and gender inclusion, equality and empowerment; contributed to strengthening the application of these principles to various development efforts in a given country; and incorporated the UNDP commitment to rights-based approaches and gender mainstreaming in the initiative design.

Mainstreaming a gender perspective is the process of assessing the implications for women and men of any planned action, including legislation, policies or programmes,

---

52 UNDP, 'The Evaluation Policy of UNDP', Executive Board Document DP/2005/28, May 2006. Available at: http://www.undp.org/eo/documents/Evaluation-Policy.pdf.

in all areas and at all levels. It is a strategy for making gender-related concerns and experiences an integral dimension of the design, implementation, monitoring and evaluation of policies and programmes in all political, economic and societal spheres so that women and men benefit equally and inequality is not perpetuated. UNDP evaluations should assess the extent to which UNDP initiatives have considered mainstreaming a gender perspective in the design, implementation and outcome of the initiative and if both women and men can equally access the initiative's benefits to the degree they were intended. Similarly, evaluations should also address the extent to which UNDP has advocated for the principle of equality and inclusive development, and has contributed to empowering and addressing the needs of the disadvantaged and vulnerable populations in a given society.

The rights-based approach in development efforts entails the need to ensure that development strategies facilitate the claims of rights-holders and the corresponding obligations of duty-bearers. This approach also emphasizes the important need to address the immediate, underlying and structural causes for not realizing such rights. The concept of civic engagement, as a mechanism to claim rights, is an important aspect in the overall framework. When appropriate, evaluations should assess the extent to which the initiative has facilitated the capacity of rights-holders to claim their rights and duty-bearers to fulfill their obligations.

Evaluations should also address other cross-cutting issues, depending on the focus of the evaluation, such as the extent to which UNDP has incorporated and fostered South-South cooperation, knowledge management, volunteerism and UN coordination in its initiative.

7.5 EVALUATION METHODOLOGY

The evaluation design must detail a step-by-step plan of work that specifies the methods the evaluation will use to collect the information needed to address the evaluation criteria and answer the evaluation questions, analyse the data, interpret the findings and report the results.

Evaluation methods should be selected for their rigour in producing empirically based evidence to address the evaluation criteria and respond to the evaluation questions. The **evaluation inception report** should contain an **evaluation matrix** that displays for each of the evaluation criteria, the questions and subquestions that the evaluation will answer, and for each question, the data that will be collected to inform that question and the methods that will be used to collect that data (see Box 40). In addition, the inception report should make explicit the underlying theory or assumptions about how each data element will contribute to understanding the development results—attribution, contribution, process, implementation and so forth—and the rationale for data collection, analysis and reporting methodologies selected.

Box 40. Questions for evaluators

The commissioning office should, at a minimum, ensure that the evaluation methods detailed in the evaluators' inception report respond to each of the following questions:

- What evidence is needed to address the evaluation questions?
- What data collection method(s) will be used to address the evaluation criteria and questions? Why were these methods selected? Are allocated resources sufficient?
- Who will collect the data?
- What is the framework for sampling? What is the rationale for the framework?
- How will programme participants and other stakeholders be involved?
- What data management systems will be used? That is, what are the planned logistics, including the procedures, timing, and physical infrastructure that will be used for gathering and handling data?
- How will the information collected be analysed and the findings interpreted and reported?
- What methodological issues need to be considered to ensure quality?

DATA COLLECTION METHODS

The data to be collected and the methods for collecting the data will be determined by: the evidence needed to address the evaluation questions; the analyses that will be used to translate the data into meaningful findings in response to the evaluation questions; and judgements about what data are feasible to collect given constraints of time and resources. UNDP evaluations draw heavily on data (performance indicators) generated through monitoring during the programme or project implementation cycle. Performance indicators are a simple and reliable means to document changes in development conditions (outcomes), production, or delivery of products and services (outputs) connected to a development initiative (see Chapter 2).

Performance indicators are useful but have limitations. Indicators only indicate; they do not explain. Indicators will not likely address the full range of questions the evaluation seeks to address. For example, indicators provide a measure of what progress has been made. They do not explain why that progress was made or what factors contributed to the progress. UNDP evaluations generally make use of a mix of other data sources, collected through multiple methods, to give meaning to what performance indicators tell us about the initiative.

Primary data consists of information evaluators observe or collect directly from stakeholders about their first-hand experience with the initiative. These data generally consist of the reported or observed values, beliefs, attitudes, opinions, behaviours, motivations and knowledge of stakeholders, generally obtained through questionnaires, surveys, interviews, focus groups, key informants, expert panels, direct observation and case studies. These methods allow for more in-depth exploration and yield information that can facilitate deeper understanding of observed changes in outcomes and outputs (both intended and unintended) and the factors that contributed by filling out the operational context for outputs and outcomes.

Secondary data is primary data that was collected, compiled and published by someone else. Secondary data can take many forms but usually consists of documentary

Table 28. Summary of common data collection methods used in UNDP evaluations[53]

Method	Description	Advantages	Challenges
Monitoring and Evaluation Systems	Uses performance indicators to measure progress, particularly actual results against expected results.	Can be a reliable, cost-efficient, objective method to assess progress of outputs and outcomes.	Dependent upon viable monitoring and evaluation systems that have established baseline indicators and targets and have collected reliable data in relation to targets over time, as well as data relating to outcome indicators.
Extant Reports and Documents	Existing documentation, including quantitative and descriptive information about the initiative, its outputs and outcomes, such as documentation from capacity development activities, donor reports, and other evidence.	Cost efficient.	Documentary evidence can be difficult to code and analyse in response to questions. Difficult to verify reliability and validity of data.
Questionnaires	Provides a standardized approach to obtaining information on a wide range of topics from a large number or diversity of stakeholders (usually employing sampling techniques) to obtain information on their attitudes, beliefs, opinions, perceptions, level of satisfaction, etc. concerning the operations, inputs, outputs and contextual factors of a UNDP initiative.	Good for gathering descriptive data on a wide range of topics quickly at relatively low cost. Easy to analyse. Gives anonymity to respondents.	Self-reporting may lead to biased reporting. Data may provide a general picture but may lack depth. May not provide adequate information on context. Subject to sampling bias.
Interviews	Solicit person-to-person responses to predetermined questions designed to obtain in-depth information about a person's impressions or experiences, or to learn more about their answers to questionnaires or surveys.	Facilitates fuller coverage, range and depth of information of a topic.	Can be time consuming. Can be difficult to analyse. Can be costly. Potential for interviewer to bias client's responses.
On-Site Observation	Entails use of a detailed observation form to record accurate information on-site about how a programme operates (ongoing activities, processes, discussions, social interactions and observable results as directly observed during the course of an initiative).	Can see operations of a programme as they are occurring. Can adapt to events as they occur.	Can be difficult to categorize or interpret observed behaviours. Can be expensive. Subject to (site) selection bias.
Group Interviews	A small group (6 to 8 people) are interviewed together to explore in-depth stakeholder opinions, similar or divergent points of view, or judgements about a development initiative or policy, as well as information about their behaviours, understanding and perceptions of an initiative or to collect information around tangible and non-tangible changes resulting from an initiative.	Quick, reliable way to obtain common impressions from diverse stakeholders. Efficient way to obtain a high degree of range and depth of information in a short time.	Can be hard to analyse responses. Requires trained facilitator. May be difficult to schedule.

---

53 Methods described are illustrative and not exhaustive of the types of methods that have applicability for UNDP evaluation context.

Method	Description	Advantages	Challenges
Table 28 (cont-d). Summary of common data collection methods used in UNDP evaluations			
Key Informants	Qualitative in-depth interviews, often one-on-one, with a wide-range of stakeholders who have first-hand knowledge about the initiative operations and context. These community experts can provide particular knowledge and understanding of problems and recommend solutions.	Can provide insight on the nature of problems and give recommendations for solutions. Can provide different perspectives on a single issue or on several issues.	Subject to sampling bias. Must have some means to verify or corroborate information.
Expert Panels	A peer review, or reference group, composed of external experts to provide input on technical or other substance topics covered by the evaluation.	Adds credibility. Can serve as added (expert) source of information that can provide greater depth. Can verify or substantiate information and results in topic area.	Cost of consultancy and related expenses if any. Must ensure impartiality and that there are no conflicts of interest.
Case Studies	Involves comprehensive examination through cross comparison of cases to obtain in-depth information with the goal to fully understand the operational dynamics, activities, outputs, outcomes and interactions of a development project or programme.	Useful to fully explore factors that contribute to outputs and outcomes.	Requires considerable time and resources not usually available for commissioned evaluations. Can be difficult to analyse.

evidence that has direct relevance for the purposes of the evaluation. Sources of documentary evidence include: local, regional or national demographic data; nationally and internationally published reports; social, health and economic indicators; project or programme plans; monitoring reports; previous reviews, evaluations and other records; country strategic plans; and research reports that may have relevance for the evaluation. Documentary evidence is particularly useful when the project or programme lacks baseline indicators and targets for assessing progress toward outputs and outcome measures. Although not a preferred method, secondary data can be used to help recreate baseline data and targets. Secondary information complements and supplements data collected by primary methods but does not replace collecting data from primary sources.

Given the nature and context of UNDP evaluations at the decentralized level, including limitations of time and resources, evaluators are often likely to use a mix of methods, including performance indicators, supplemented relevant documentary evidence from secondary sources, and qualitative data collected by a variety of means.

Table 28 presents brief descriptions of data collection methods that are most commonly applied in evaluations in UNDP for both project and outcome evaluations.

Commissioning offices need to ensure that the methods and the instruments (questions, surveys, protocols, checklists) used to collect or record data are: consistent with quality standards of validity and reliability,[54] culturally sensitive and appropriate for the populations concerned, and valid and appropriate for the types of information sought and the evaluation questions being answered. In conflict-affected settings, factors such as security concerns, lack of infrastructure, limited access to people with information and sensitivities, and ethical considerations in terms of working with vulnerable people should be considered in determining appropriate data collection methods.

ISSUES OF DATA QUALITY

UNDP commissioning offices must ensure that the evaluation collects data that relates to evaluation purposes and employs data collection methodologies and procedures that are methodologically rigorous and defensible and produces empirically verified evidence that is valid, reliable and credible.

Reliability and validity are important aspects of quality in an evaluation. **Reliability** refers to consistency of measurement—for example, ensuring that a particular data collection instrument, such as a questionnaire, will elicit the same or similar response if administered under similar conditions. **Validity** refers to accuracy in measurement—for example, ensuring that a particular data collection instrument actually measures what it was intended to measure. It also refers to the extent to which inferences or conclusions drawn from data are reasonable and justifiable. **Credibility** concerns the extent to which the evaluation evidence and the results are perceived to be valid, reliable and impartial by the stakeholders, particularly the users of evaluation results. There are three broad strategies to improve reliability and validity that a good evaluation should address:

- Improve the quality of sampling

- Improve the quality of data gathering

- Use mixed methods of collecting data and building in strategies (for example, **triangulating** or multiple sources of data) to verify or cross-check data using several pieces of evidence rather than relying only on one

Improve sampling quality

UNDP evaluations often gather evidence from a sample of people or locations. If this sample is unrepresentative of a portion of the population, then wrong conclusions can be drawn about the population. For example, if a group interview only includes those from the city who can readily access the venue, the concerns and experiences of those in outlying areas may not be adequately documented. The sample must be selected on the basis of a rationale or purpose that is directly related to the evaluation purposes and is intended to ensure accuracy in the interpretation of findings and usefulness of evaluation results. Commissioning offices should ensure that the evaluation design makes clear the characteristics of the sample, how it will be selected, the rationale for

---

54 See discussion of validity and reliability in the Issues of Data Quality section of this chapter.

the selection, and the limitations of the sample for interpreting evaluation results. If a sample is not used, the rationale for not sampling and the implications for the evaluation should be discussed.

Ensure consistency of data gathering

Whether using questionnaires, interview schedules, observation protocols or other data gathering tools, the evaluation team should test the data collection tools and make sure they gather evidence that is both accurate and consistent. Some ways of addressing this would be:

- Train data collectors in using observation protocols to ensure they record observations in the same way as each other

- Check the meaning of key words used in questionnaires and interview schedules, especially if they have been translated, to make sure respondents understand exactly what is being asked

- Consider how the characteristics of interviewers (especially age, gender and whether they are known to the informants) might improve or reduce the accuracy of the information provided

'Triangulate' data to verify accuracy: Use multiple data sources

Good evaluation evidence is both consistent and accurate. Building in strategies to verify data will enhance the reliability and ensure valid results.

- Use a mix of methods to collect data rather than relying on one source or one piece of evidence. For example, triangulate the evidence from once source (such as the group interview) with other evidence about the experiences of those in rural areas. (This might be documentary evidence from reports or key informant interviews with people who are credible and well-informed about the situation.)

- Use experts to review and validate evidence.

The challenge for UNDP evaluations is to employ rigorous evaluation design methods that will produce useful information based on credible evidence that is defensible in the face of challenges to the accuracy of the evidence and the validity of the inferences made about the evidence.

ETHICAL CONSIDERATIONS

Evaluations should be designed and conducted to respect and protect the rights and welfare of people and the communities of which they are members, in accordance with the UN Universal Declaration of Human Rights[55] and other human rights conventions. Evaluators should respect the dignity and diversity of evaluation participants

---

55 United Nations, 'Universal Declaration of Human Rights'. Available at: http://www.un.org/en/documents/udhr/.

when planning, carrying out and reporting on evaluations, in part by using evaluation instruments appropriate to the cultural setting. Further, prospective evaluation participants should be treated as autonomous, be given the time and information to decide whether or not they wish to participate, and be able to make an independent decision without any pressure. Evaluation managers and evaluators should be aware of implications for doing evaluations in conflict zones. In particular, evaluators should know that the way they act, including explicit and implicit messages they transmit, may affect the situation and expose those with whom the evaluators interact to greater risks.[56] When evaluators need to interview vulnerable groups, evaluators should make sure interviewees are aware of the potential implications of their participation in the evaluation exercise and that they are given sufficient information to make a decision about their participation. All evaluators commissioned by UNDP programme units should agree and sign the Code of Conduct for Evaluators in the UN System.[57] For more information on ethics in evaluation, please refer to the 'UNEG Ethical Guidelines for Evaluation'.[58]

Box 41. Human rights and gender equality perspective in evaluation design

Evaluations in UNDP are guided by the principles of human rights and gender equality. This has implications for evaluation design and conduct, and requires shared understanding of these principles and explicit attention on the part of evaluators, evaluation managers and evaluation stakeholders. For example, in collecting data, evaluators need to ensure that women and disadvantaged groups are adequately represented. In order to make excluded or disadvantaged groups visible, data should be disaggregated by gender, age, disability, ethnicity, wealth and other relevant differences where possible.

Further, data should be analysed whenever possible through multiple lenses, including sex, socio-economic grouping, ethnicity and disability. Marginalized groups are often subject to multiple forms of discrimination, and it is important to understand how these different forms of discrimination intersect to deny rights holders their rights.

ANALYSIS AND SYNTHESIS OF DATA

Data collection involves administering questionnaires, conducting interviews, observing programme operations, and reviewing or entering data from existing data sources. Data analysis is a systematic process that involves organizing and classifying the information collected, tabulating it, summarizing it, and comparing the results with other appropriate information to extract useful information that responds to the evaluation questions and fulfils the purposes of the evaluation. It is the process of deciphering facts from a body of evidence by systematically coding and collating the data collected, ensuring its accuracy, conducting any statistical analyses, and translating the data into usable formats or units of analysis related to each evaluation question.

---

56 OECD Guidance on Conflict Prevention and Peacebuilding Activities, Working Draft for Application Period, 2008.

57 UNEG, 'Code of Conduct', June 2008. Available at: http://www.uneval.org/papersandpubs/documentdetail.jsp?doc_id=100.

58 UNEG, 'Ethical Guidelines for Evaluation', June 2008. Available at http://www.uneval.org/search/index.jsp?q=ethical+guidelines.

Data analysis seeks to detect patterns in evidence, either by isolating important findings (analysis) or by combining sources of information to reach a larger understanding (synthesis). Mixed method evaluations require the separate analysis of each element of evidence and a synthesis of all sources in order to examine patterns of agreement, convergence or complexity.

Analysis plan

Data analysis and synthesis must proceed from an analysis plan that should be built into the evaluation design and work plan detailed in the inception report. The analysis plan is an essential evaluation tool that maps how the information collected will be organized, classified, inter-related, compared and displayed relative to the evaluation questions, including what will be done to integrate multiple sources, especially those that provide data in narrative form, and any statistical methods that will be used to integrate or present the data (calculations, sums, percentages, cost analysis and so forth). Possible challenges and limitations of the data analysis should be described. The analysis plan should be written in conjunction with selecting data collection methods and instruments rather than afterward.

Interpreting the findings

Interpreting findings is the process of giving meaning to the evaluation findings derived from the analysis. It extracts from the summation and synthesis of information derived from facts, statements, opinions, and documents and turns findings from the data into judgements about development results (conclusions). On the basis of those conclusions, recommendations for future actions will be made. Interpretation is the effort of figuring out what the findings mean—making sense of the evidence gathered in an evaluation and its practical applications towards development effectiveness.

Drawing conclusions

A conclusion is a reasoned judgement based on a synthesis of empirical findings or factual statements corresponding to specific circumstances. Conclusions are not findings; they are interpretations that give meaning to the findings. Conclusions are considered valid and credible when they are directly linked to the evidence and can be justified on the basis of appropriate methods of analysis and synthesis to summarize findings. Conclusions should:

- Consider alternative ways to compare results (for example, compared with programme objectives, a comparison group, national norms, past performance or needs)

- Generate alternative explanations for findings and indicate why these explanations should be discounted

- Form the basis for recommending actions or decisions that are consistent with the conclusions

- Be limited to situations, time periods, persons, contexts and purposes for which the findings are applicable[59]

---

59 Based on Joint Committee on Standards for Educational Evaluation, 'Programme Evaluation Standards: How to Assess Evaluations of Educational Programmes', 1994, 2nd ed, Sage Publications, Thousand Oaks, CA.

Making recommendations

Recommendations are evidence-based proposals for action aimed at evaluation users. Recommendations should be based on conclusions. However, forming recommendations is a distinct element of evaluation that requires information beyond what is necessary to form conclusions. Developing recommendations involves weighing effective alternatives, policy, funding priorities and so forth within a broader context. It requires in-depth contextual knowledge, particularly about the organizational context within which policy and programmatic decisions will be made and the political, social and economic context in which the initiative will operate.

Recommendations should be formulated in a way that will facilitate the development of a management response (see Chapter 6 and Annex 6 on Management Response System). Recommendations must be realistic and reflect an understanding of the commissioning organization and potential constraints to follow up. Each recommendation should clearly identify its target group and stipulate the recommended action and rationale.

Lessons learned

The lessons learned from an evaluation comprise the new knowledge gained from the particular circumstance (initiative, context outcomes and even evaluation methods) that is applicable to and useful in other similar contexts. Frequently, lessons highlight strengths or weaknesses in preparation, design and implementation that affect performance, outcome and impact.

ENHANCING THE USE OF KNOWLEDGE FROM MONITORING AND EVALUATION

Benefits of using information from monitoring and evaluation are multiple. The value of a monitoring and evaluation exercise is determined by the degree to which the information is used by intended decision makers and a wider audience. This chapter is intended to help UNDP managers, programme and project staff, M&E specialists, and communications officers in UNDP and partner organizations effectively apply information from monitoring and evaluation in their daily work for accountability, improvements in performance, decision making and learning. It addresses examples of the use of evaluative evidence, available tools and means for effective knowledge and information sharing, and practical guidance to support publication and dissemination of evaluation information.

8.1 WHY USE MONITORING AND EVALUATION?

Each monitoring and evaluation activity has a purpose. UNDP places great importance on monitoring and evaluation because, when done and used correctly, they strengthen the basis for **managing for results**, foster **learning** and **knowledge generation** in the organization as well as the broader development and evaluation community, and support the public **accountability** of UNDP.

Knowledge gained from monitoring and evaluation is at the core of the UNDP organizational learning process. Monitoring and evaluation provide information and facts that, when accepted and internalized, become knowledge that promotes learning. UNDP uses and applies learning from monitoring and evaluation to improve the overall performance and quality of results of ongoing and future projects, programmes and strategies. The key role of knowledge generated from monitoring and evaluation is making RBM and MfDF work. For UNDP to be effective, learning must therefore be incorporated into the core function of a programme unit through an effective learning and information sharing system.

In addition, findings and lessons from monitoring and evaluation can be used for partnership building and advocacy. For example, if evaluations highlight achievements and good practices, they can be used to solicit support for UNDP work and share the vision and strategy for UNDP support for greater partnership. A systematic use of monitoring and evaluation not only enhances UNDP credibility as a public organization, but also promotes a culture of results-orientation and transparency within the organization and amongst its partners. Knowledge generated from monitoring and evaluation becomes a public good. As a leading knowledge-based organization, UNDP has a role in effectively sharing and dissemination such knowledge to contribute to the global efforts in MfDR.

8.2 LEARNING AND GENERATING KNOWLEDGE FROM MONITORING AND EVALUATION

ACCOUNTABILITY FOR LEARNING

The increasing focus of UNDP on MfDR and outcomes has shifted its emphasis from inputs, outputs and processes to development results at the outcome level. When the focus is on outcomes, which are influenced by multiple factors and are beyond the direct control of UNDP, the traditional view of assigning accountability to individuals for delivering outputs is no longer adequate. Accountability for outcomes encompasses RBM. Learning constructively from past mistakes and experiences is a critical part of MfDR and the UNDP accountability framework.

Monitoring and evaluation can only play a significant role in the accountability process if measures to enhance learning are put in place. Through regular exchange of information, reporting, knowledge products, learning sessions and the evaluation management response system, information from monitoring and evaluation can be fed back into the learning process and planning. UNDP needs to focus on learning from monitoring and evaluation to make a meaningful contribution to outcome achievement accountability and to encourage innovation for better results.

USING KNOWLEDGE IN PLANNING AND PROGRAMMING

One of the most direct ways of using knowledge gained from monitoring and evaluation is to inform ongoing and future planning and programming. Lessons from evaluations of programmes, projects and initiatives and management responses should be available when new outcomes are being formulated or projects or programmes are identified, designed and appraised. At the time of revising or developing new programmes, projects, policies, strategies and other initiatives, UNDP should call for a consultative meeting with key partners and stakeholders to review and share evaluative knowledge in a systematic and substantive manner.

Institutionalization of the learning process can be achieved in part by better incorporating learning into existing tools and processes. Knowledge from monitoring and evaluation should be incorporated in the following:

- Project revisions—Monitoring and evaluation should together answer a number of useful questions such as whether the project initiatives are relevant to development needs, the project implementation is on track (outputs are being delivered on time), the strategy and logic of the results chain are working, the partnership strategy is efficient, and the project is reaching its target beneficiaries as intended. In addition to answering these questions, evaluation provides information as to 'why' things are working or not working. Such information should be incorporated in the improvements of the project strategy and trigger adjustments in a timely manner. When budget or other revisions are made to the project document, the lessons associated with the purpose of such change should also be stated. Good documentation of lessons and their internalization in project revisions help UNDP and its partners manage for results and foster a culture of systematic learning.

- Replication and upscaling—Evaluation of pilot initiatives is a must before such initiatives are replicated or scaled up. Lessons on what has and has not worked should inform the replication process. Again, good documentation of lessons and their internalization in the replication and upscaling processes will help UNDP and its partners ensure that mistakes are not repeated.

Monitoring and evaluation lessons should be incorporated into the formulation of:

- New programme documents—Country, regional and global programmes are formulated taking into account results achieved and lessons learned from regular reporting tools, internal reviews, and relevant evaluations, including project and outcome evaluations and independent evaluations conducted by the Evaluation Office, such as the ADR, which looks at the UNDP contribution towards development results in a given country. The evaluations of the regional and global cooperation frameworks should also provide substantive inputs to the design of respective programmes. It is also helpful to consult reviews and evaluations conducted by UNDP partners and non-partners in a similar thematic or subject area to find out whether any lessons can be drawn from their experiences. It is good practice to document the sources of such evaluative information in a programme document as a future reference and for transparency purposes. Members of the Programme Appraisal Committee should ensure that there is clear evidence that relevant independent and decentralized evaluations are used in the formulation of new programme documents.

- Project documents or AWPs—Project documents should include reference to the findings of relevant reviews or evaluations in the situation analysis section. Members of the Project Appraisal Committee should ensure compliance with this requirement by requesting explicitly which evaluation findings and lessons have informed the project design.

CONTRIBUTION TO NATIONAL, REGIONAL AND GLOBAL KNOWLEDGE IN DEVELOPMENT AND EVALUATION

As a partner in development, UNDP should ensure that its evaluations contribute to a better understanding of development effectiveness in the development community

Box 42. Experience from the Nepal country office: Using evaluations in the CPD and project design

The Nepal country office has been making a concerted effort to learn from and use evaluations. Most recently, in preparation for the development of the new CPD (2008-2010), the office reviewed all outcome evaluations under the current programme, project evaluations from 2006 (approximately eight were conducted), and other reviews and assessments conducted between 2003 and the end of 2006. The office synthesized the main findings and recommendations—focusing on the recurring points, common lessons and most relevant issues for the development of the new programme—into a 40-page document that was used as a reference while preparing the CPD. The office has also referred to it and shared relevant sections summarizing lessons learned when discussing joint programming or collaboration possibilities with other UN organizations.

The country office uses evaluations, particularly project evaluations, when preparing successor projects or extensions. They have developed a checklist for approval of new projects and substantive revisions, which includes a section for the monitoring and evaluation team. In addition to checking the monitoring and evaluation sections of the narrative, the results frameworks, and other monitoring tools, if there has been a recent evaluation, the monitoring and evaluation unit in the office reviews the evaluation and the project document together to ensure that relevant recommendations have been incorporated in the new project or revision.

Source: UNDP Nepal—extract from contribution to the EvalNet discussion, June 2007.

beyond UNDP. Key findings, conclusions and recommendations from evaluations should be widely shared and made available to potential users, as dissemination to audiences beyond UNDP and its immediate stakeholders can increase the impact of evaluations in important ways. For this purpose, evaluation reports should be made available to a wider audience. However, users often find evaluation reports too long and not easily accessible. Therefore, lessons and knowledge from the evaluations can be 'packaged' in the form of a **knowledge product** to meet the needs of a wider audience.

In order to effectively target a broader audience, there should be a thorough analysis of who the potential users of evaluation knowledge and lessons are, what they do, what their information needs are, how their learning takes place, and what kinds of communication and knowledge products are most suitable to achieve the objective of sharing knowledge. The commissioning programme unit should designate an individual (for example, a communications officer or knowledge management officer) to lead the process and coordinate activities to ensure effective sharing and dissemination of evaluation reports, lessons, knowledge and knowledge products.[60]

There are numerous ways to share information from evaluations. Below are some examples:

- Upload evaluation reports and other knowledge products based on evaluations on the **organization's public websites**. Ensure that the reports and the knowledge products are written clearly and made available in the most commonly used local languages.

---

60 UNDP Communications Tool Kit (http://comtoolkit.undp.org/) provides guidance on how to do effective communication and outreach.

- Organize a **meeting with interested stakeholders** to discuss lessons from the evaluation(s).

- Incorporate evaluation findings and lessons learned in the organization's existing **publications, such as annual reports, newsletters or bulletins**.

- Present findings and lessons at the **annual stakeholders meeting,** such as CPAP review meetings and forums with media.

- Develop a **brochure for UNDP activities and accomplishments**.

- Develop a **brief with a concise summary** in a plain language and widely circulate. UNDP may include the development of a brief in the ToR of the evaluators. Alternatively, the evaluation manager or a UNDP communications officer may develop it in consultation with the evaluators.

- Publish an **article for an academic journal** based on the evaluation findings.

- Present a **paper at a conference** related to the evaluation subject area.

- **Invite local researchers and academics** to discuss the data collected for the evaluation or to discuss the evaluation methodology and methods applied in the evaluation. This effort can also be supported by the evaluators.

- Share findings, recommendations and lessons learned at **training sessions and workshops** for UNDP staff, government counterparts and other partners. Training should focus on areas such as how to improve the quality of UNDP programmes and projects and develop skills in methodological innovations.

- Share lessons through **knowledge networks within and beyond UNDP**. For BDP, feed lessons into practice notes and other knowledge products developed by the policy and practice bureaux and units in Headquarters.

It is critical to make information from evaluations user friendly, easily accessible and advantageous to the audience. The following section provides guidance on how to develop a useful knowledge product.

8.3 KNOWLEDGE PRODUCTS AND DISSEMINATION

Knowledge products can take many different forms depending on the audience and their information needs. For meaningful learning and knowledge sharing, knowledge products should be of high quality with a clearly identified audience and purpose. The characteristics of a good knowledge product, including a good publication, are listed in Box 43.

Keeping these characteristics in mind before the starting analysis or preparing a knowledge product will help organize the evidence in an orderly fashion.

PRACTICAL STEPS FOR DEVELOPING KNOWLEDGE PRODUCTS AND DISSEMINATION

The **dissemination** is as important as the development of knowledge products. Only an efficient system of dissemination will ensure that the target recipients receive the monitoring and evaluation feedback that is relevant to their specific needs. Some of the

Box 43. Characteristics of a good knowledge product

- Based on an assessment of needs and demand for the product among targeted users to ensure relevance, effectiveness, usefulness and value of the product
- Designed for a specific audience, taking into consideration functional needs and technical levels
- Relevant to decision-making needs
- Timely
- Written in clear and easily understandable language
- Data is presented in a clear manner
- Based on the evaluation information without any bias
- When appropriate, developed through a participatory process and validated through a quality assurance process with relevant stakeholders
- Easily accessible to the target audience through most effective and efficient means
- Consistency in presentation of products to enhance visibility and learning

Source: UNDP, 'Ensuring Quality Control and Policy Coherence: BDP Quality Assurance and Clearance Process', Bureau for Development Policy, May 2007. Available at: http://intra.undp.org/bdp/clearance_process.htm.

most commonly applied dissemination methods for monitoring and evaluation products include: printed reports, HTML or PDF copies of the products shared on the internal and external Internet sites and through e-mail messages and list-serves, and CD-ROMs. The media can be a powerful partner in disseminating findings, recommendations and lessons from evaluation. In many countries, the media has played a critical role in advocating for accountability and addressing sensitive issues.

The following are practical steps for developing knowledge products from monitoring and evaluation and disseminating them.

Step 1: Identify target audiences and their information needs

Some of the commonly identified key target audiences for evaluation reports and knowledge products are the following:

- UNDP colleagues in country offices and other units

- Government counterparts who may or may not be directly involved in the project under evaluation but can facilitate the policy changes recommended by the evaluation or otherwise aid in the country-level advocacy of UNDP

- Development partners, other UN organizations, NGOs, and academic and research institutions

- Other networks of evaluators (for example, a national evaluation association)

Those responsible for knowledge sharing and dissemination should assess the information needs of the various groups, including when the information is most needed and is likely to serve as an 'agent of change.' For example, government counterparts may find certain information from an evaluation particularly useful in making critical policy decisions. When planning for a monitoring and evaluation exercise, the commissioning unit should be aware when the 'window of opportunity' for decision making arises and make the information available in a manner that is appropriate for the technical and functional needs of the target audience.

Step 2: Collect stakeholder contact information

The success of every dissemination effort is highly dependent on the recipient contact information gathered during the monitoring and evaluation processes. For example, the evaluation team members meet with key stakeholders and national counterparts who, regardless of their degree of involvement in the evaluation topic, constitute a critical audience and should be informed about the knowledge generated from evaluation. The contact information of these individuals should be gathered by the evaluation team and shared with those responsible for disseminating and sharing the knowledge.

Step 3: Determine types of products that meet the audience's information needs

In addition to publishing information from regular monitoring reports[61] and evaluation reports, a mix of knowledge products can be developed to meet the information demand of different groups. A systematic assessment of the needs and demand for specific products among targeted audiences can be undertaken to ensure the relevance and value of the products. The following are some examples of communication means and products for evaluation:

- Evaluation executive summary—Evaluation reports should include a succinct, yet comprehensive and information-rich executive summary. This summary can be used as a stand-alone product to enhance the readership of the evaluation.

- Evaluation brief—This should be a three- to five-page non-technical summation of the executive summary to increase general interest without overwhelming the reader. The Evaluation Office's publication manual provides information on how to write evaluation briefs using non-technical language.

- Evaluation blurb—This is a one-paragraph description designed to increase the visibility of published content and announce the report publication on the webpage and via electronic announcements and list serves.

It is the responsibility of UNDP to ensure relevant and high quality knowledge products are produced in a timely manner. In order to safeguard the integrity and accuracy of the evaluation information, the commissioning units may consider including the task of producing these knowledge products in the ToRs of the evaluation team.

Step 4: Identify language requirements per product and audience

In order to optimize the impact of knowledge sharing and dissemination efforts, knowledge products should be translated into local languages whenever possible. If resources are limited, the commissioning unit may determine language requirements per knowledge product or per audience group. At a minimum, the evaluation brief

---

61 Circumstances may not allow UNDP and its partners to publish monitoring reports 'as is' due to their internal nature. In order to share information widely, UNDP may need to extract critical knowledge from such information and package it in a manner that can be disseminated. Regarding evaluation, UNDP evaluation policy requires all evaluation reports to be publicly made available.

should be translated into the most widely used local language. Additionally, the language used in the product should be appropriate for the technical levels of the targeted audience. It is best to avoid technical jargon and heavy acronym usage.

Step 5: Determine efficient forms and dissemination methods per evaluation knowledge product

Most evaluation reports and knowledge products can be shared as an electronic copy. In order to enhance the efficiency in terms of time and cost, the organization's public webpage and the e-mail list should be strategically used as means for dissemination (see Box 44). For example, the evaluation reports should be uploaded on the organization's internal and external webpage with a blurb that summarizes the key information in the report.

Box 44. Tools and networks to support evaluation knowledge sharing

Evaluation Resource Centre: The ERC, available at erc.undp.org, is a repository of evaluation reports and serves as the organization's primary tool for knowledge management in evaluation. To date, it contains more than 1,000 evaluation reports and 400 evaluation ToRs. Reports can be searched by region, country, evaluation type, year and other key words. It also provides a list of evaluation focal points across UNDP to foster information exchange and learning on evaluation.

Knowledge products by policy and practice bureaux in Headquarters (BDP, BCPR and Partnership Bureau): Policy and practice bureaux in UNDP Headquarters produce a number of knowledge-based products in UNDP core results areas and their respective focus areas. Lessons from evaluations provide useful inputs to their ongoing work on knowledge consolidation and sharing.

Knowledge networks and communities of practice: In UNDP, there are networks and communities of practice that are linked to the UNDP worldwide system of subregional resource facilities and regional centres. Evaluation managers or UNDP communications officers can share evaluation reports or other related knowledge products with colleagues throughout the organization by submitting it to a practice-area knowledge network, such as the Governance Network (dgp-net) or the Poverty Network (pr-net).

The Evaluation Network or 'EvalNet': This functions more directly than the corporate knowledge management system to support the design and development of information and knowledge products from monitoring and evaluation activities. This network remains largely driven by stakeholder participation. EvalNet is a group of UNDP staff, mainly from country offices, that participate in UNDP evaluations, develop RBM tools and methodologies, and organize evaluation capacity development activities. The objectives of the network are to enhance UNDP as a learning organization and to promote results-oriented monitoring and evaluation as part of the UNDP organizational culture.

Additionally, knowledge from monitoring and evaluation can be shared widely by incorporating them in existing reports and publications, such as the country office's annual report or other key reports, brochures and news bulletins.

Step 6: Monitor feedback and measure results of dissemination efforts

There should be a feedback and learning mechanism for the effectiveness of the dissemination strategy and quality of the particular knowledge product. For example,

UNDP may conduct a quick survey among the recipients of the knowledge products or develop a feature on its website where users can provide their feedback directly online.

In analysing the feedback, the following should be asked: "To what extent has the monitoring and evaluation information been used in programming and policy making within and beyond UNDP?"; "Has such information been made in a timely manner to effectively influence decision-making processes?"; "Have the products reached both direct and indirect audiences in an efficient manner and were they easily accessible?"; "Did the audience find the knowledge products useful?"; "If not, why not?"; and "What could be done better next time?"

Lessons from the experience should be reflected in the future evaluation knowledge sharing and dissemination efforts so that evaluations in UNDP will continue to be relevant and contribute to organizational learning and the enhancement of a global knowledge base in development.

Annex 1. References

Asian Development Bank, 'Operations Evaluation Department (OED) Guidelines to Avoid Conflict of Interest in Independent Evaluations', April 2005. Available at: http://www.adb.org/documents/guidelines/evaluation/independent-evaluation.pdf.

Beck T, 'Evaluating Humanitarian Action Using OECD/DAC Criteria', 2006.

Feinstein O and G Ingram, 'Lessons Learned from World Bank Experiences in Joint Evaluation', Room Document submitted to the Evaluation Network, OECD, Paris, France, 2003. Available at: http://www.oecd.org/dataoecd/secure/15/13/31736431.pdf.

Global Environment Facility, 'Monitoring and Evaluation Policy', February 2006. Available at: http://www.undp.org/gef/05/documents/me/GEF_ME_Policies_and_Precedures_06.pdf.

IFAD, 'Conflict of Interest of Consultants and Widening the Pool of Evaluation Specialists'.

Joint Committee on Standards for Educational Evaluation, 'Programme Evaluation Standards: How to Assess Evaluations of Educational Programmes', 1994, 2nd ed, Sage Publications, Thousand Oaks, CA.

'Managing for Development Results (MfDR) Initiative'. Available at: http://www.mfdr.org.

Managing for Development Results (MfDR), 'Second International Roundtable Marrakech 2004; Annex 1: Promoting a Harmonized Approach to Managing for Development Results: Core Principles'. Available at: http://www.mfdr.org/documents/2CorePrinciples05Feb04.pdf.

OCHA, 'Guidelines: Results-Oriented Planning & Monitoring', 2007, p. 11.

OECD, 'Criteria from Evaluating Development Assistance', Development Assistance Committee (DAC). Available at: http://www.oecd.org/document/22/0,2340,en_2649_34435_2086550_1_1_1_1,00.html.

OECD, 'DAC Guidance for Managing Joint Evaluations', Development Assistance Committee (DAC), Paris, France, 2006. Available at: http://www.oecd.org/dataoecd/28/14/37484787.pdf.

OECD, 'DAC Principles for Evaluation of Development Assistance', Development Assistance Committee (DAC), Paris, France, 1991. Available at: http://www.oecd.org/dataoecd/21/32/41029845.pdf.

OECD 'DAC Workshop on Joint Evaluations: Challenging the Conventional Wisdom the View from Developing Country Partners', Development Assistance Committee (DAC), Nairobi, Kenya, April 2005. Available at: http://www.oecd.org/dataoecd/20/44/34981186.pdf.

OECD, 'Effective Practices in Conducting a Multi-donor Evaluation', Paris, France, 2000. Available at: http://www.oecd.org/dataoecd/10/28/2667318.pdf.

OECD, 'Glossary of Key Terms in Evaluation and Results-Based Management', Development Assistance Committee (DAC), Paris, France, 2002. Available at: http://www.oecd.org/dataoecd/29/21/2754804.pdf.

OECD, 'Guidance on Conflict Prevention and Peacebuilding Activities: Working Draft for Application Period', 2008. Available at: https://www.oecd.org/secure/pdfDocument/0,2834,en_21571361_30097720_39774574_1_1_1_1,00.pdf.

United Nations, 'Resolution Adopted by the General Assembly: Triennial Comprehensive Policy Review of Operational Activities for Development of the United Nations System', A/RES/59/250, 59th Session Agenda Item 90 (b), December 2004.

UNDG, 'CCA/UNDAF Monitoring and Evaluation Guidelines', 2007. Available at: http://www.undg.org/index.cfm?P=259.

UNDG, 'CCA and UNDAF Guidelines', 2007. Available at: http://www.undg.org/?P=232.

UNDG, 'Human Rights Based Approach to Development'. Available at: http://www.undg.org/index.cfm?P=74.

UNDP, 'Assessment of Development Results (ADR) Guidelines', Evaluation Office, New York, NY, January 2009. Available at: http://intra.undp.org/eo/documents/ADR/ADR-Guide-2009.pdf

UNDP, 'Ensuring Quality Control and Policy Coherence: BDP Quality Assurance and Clearance Process', Bureau for Development Policy, May 2007. Available at: http://intra.undp.org/bdp/clearance_process.htm.

UNDP, 'The Evaluation Policy of UNDP', Executive Board Document DP/2005/28, May 2006. Available at: http://www.undp.org/eo/documents/Evaluation-Policy.pdf.

UNDP, 'The Evaluation of Results-Based Management at UNDP', Evaluation Office, New York, NY, December 2007.

UNDP, 'Guidelines for an Assessment of Development Results (ADR)', Evaluation Office, New York, NY, January 2007. Available at: http://intra.undp.org/eo/documents/ADR/framework/ADR_Guide.pdf.

UNDP, 'Knowing the What and the How, RBM in UNDP: Technical Note', undated. Available at: www.undp.org/eo/documents/methodology/rbm/RBM-technical-note.doc.

UNDP, 'Practice Note on Capacity Assessment', October 2008.

UNDP, 'Programme and Operations Policies and Procedures', 2008. Available at: http://content.undp.org/go/userguide.

UNDP, 'RBM in UNDP: Technical Note'.

UNDP, 'Supporting Capacity Development: The UNDP Approach'.

UNDP, 'Standard Third-Party Cost-Sharing Agreement', Partnership Bureau, 2007. Available at: http://content.undp.org/go/groups/brsp/Non-Core/Formats/?g11n.enc=ISO-8859-1.

UNDP, 'Supporting Capacity Development: The UNDP Approach'. Available at: http://www.capacity.undp.org/indexAction.cfm?module=Library&action=GetFile&DocumentAttachmentID=2141.

UNDP, 'UNDP Strategic Plan, 2008-2011: Accelerating Global Progress on Human Development', Executive Board document DP/2007/43, (pursuant DP/2007/32), reissued January 2008.

UNEG, 'Ethical Guidelines for Evaluation', July 2007. Available at: http://www.uneval.org/search/index.jsp?q=ethical+guidelines.

UNEG, 'Guidance on Integrating Human Rights and Gender Equality Perspectives in Evaluations in the UN System'.

UNEG, 'Norms for Evaluation in the UN System', 2005. Available at: http://www.unevaluation.org/unegnorms.

UNEG, 'The Role of Evaluation in Results-Based Management', August 2007. Available at: http://www.unevaluation.org/papersandpubs/documentdetail.jsp?doc_id=87.

UNEG, 'Role of Evaluation in RBM: Final Report', Annual General Meeting, April 2007. Available at: http://cfapp1-docs-public.undp.org/eo/evaldocs1/uneg_2006/eo_doc_722014901.pdf.

UNEG, 'Standards for Evaluation in the UN System', 2005. Available at: http://www.unevaluation.org/unegstandards.

UNEG, 'UNEG Training—What a UN Evaluator Needs to Know?', Module 1, 2008.

UNSSC, 'Draft Technical Brief: Outcomes', September 11.

World Bank, 'Consulting Service Manual 2006: A Comprehensive Guide to the Selection of Consultants', Washington DC, 2006. Available at: http://siteresources.worldbank.org/INTPROCUREMENT/Resources/2006ConsultantManual.pdf.

World Bank, 'Sourcebook for Evaluating Global and Regional Partnership Programs: Indicative Principles and Standards', Independent Evaluation Group and DAC Network. Available at: http://siteresources.worldbank.org/EXTGLOREGPARPRO/Resources/sourcebook.pdf.

Annex 2. Field Visit Report Format

The content of the field visit report varies depending on the purpose of the visit. At a minimum, any field visit report must contain an analysis of the progress towards results, the production of outputs, partnerships, key challenges and proposed actions. **This format may be changed to suit local needs.**

Date of visit: _____

Subject and venue of visit: _____
[Project number(s) and title(s), venue visited]

Purpose of the field visit:

Outcomes	Update on outcomes	Outputs	Update on outputs	Reasons if progress below target	Update on partnership strategies	Recommenda-tions and proposed action
	A brief analysis on any relevant changes pertain-ing to the outcome as stated in results matrix.	State output from project document or work plan.	Achievements of the project in outputs (marking if strategic) and soft assistance (if any).	If applicable.		Actions on any matter related to outcome, progress of outputs, and/or partnerships. Corrective measures. Responsibilities/time.

PROJECT PERFORMANCE—IMPLEMENTATION ISSUES

[If the person conducting the field visit observes problems that are generic and not related to any specific output, or that apply to all of them, he or she should address the 'top three' such challenges.]

List the main challenges experienced during implementation and propose a way forward.
_____
_____
_____

PROGRESS TOWARDS RESULTS

LESSONS LEARNED

Describe briefly key lessons learned during the project:
_____
_____
_____

Participants in the field visit:

Prepared by: _____
(Name, title and organization)

Annexes
List of persons met
Other annexes

Annex 3. Evaluation Terms of Reference Template and Quality Standards

The Terms of Reference (ToR) template is intended to help UNDP programme units create ToRs based on quality standards for evaluations consistent with the concepts and terms presented in this Handbook and the UNEG 'Standards for Evaluation in the UN System'.[62]

The ToR should also explicitly state a requirement for the evaluation to assess the extent of UNDP commitment to the human development approach and how effectively equality and gender mainstreaming have been incorporated in the design and execution of the project or programme to be evaluated.

In terms of evaluation methodology, the ToR should retain enough flexibility for the evaluation team to determine the best methods and tools for collecting and analysing data. For example, the ToR might suggest using questionnaires, field visits and interviews, but the evaluation team should be able to revise the approach in consultation with key stakeholders, particularly the intended users and those affected by evaluation results. (See Chapter 7 for more information on design issues.)

The ToR should, at a minimum, cover the elements described below:

1. BACKGROUND AND CONTEXT

The background section makes clear what is being evaluated and identifies the critical social, economic, political, geographic and demographic factors within which it operates that have a direct bearing on the evaluation. This description should be focused and concise (a maximum of one page) highlighting **only** those issues most pertinent to the evaluation. The key background and context descriptors that should be included are listed below:

- Description of the intervention (outcome, programme, project, group of projects, themes, soft assistance) that is being evaluated.

- The name of the intervention (e.g., project name), purpose and objectives, including when and how it was initiated, who it is intended to benefit and what outcomes or outputs it is intended to achieve, and the duration of the intervention and its implementation status within that time frame.

---

62 UNEG, 'Standards for Evaluation in the UN System', 2005. Available at: http://www.unevaluation.org/unegstandards.

- The scale and complexity of the intervention, including, for example, the number of components, if more than one, and the size and description of the population each component is intended to serve, both directly and indirectly.

- The geographic context and boundaries, such as the region, country, landscape and challenges where relevant.

- Total resources required for the intervention from all sources, including human resources and budgets comprising UNDP, donor and other contributions.

- Key partners involved in the intervention, including the implementing agencies and partners, other key stakeholders, and their interest concerns and the relevance for the evaluation.

- Observed changes since the beginning of implementation and contributing factors.

- How the subject fits into the partner government's strategies and priorities; international, regional or country development goals; strategies and frameworks; UNDP corporate goals and priorities; and UNDP global, regional or country programmes, as appropriate.

- Key features of the international, regional and national economy and economic policy that have relevance for the evaluation.

- Description of how this evaluation fits within the context of other ongoing and previous evaluations and the evaluation cycle.

More detailed background and context information (e.g., initial funding proposal, strategic plans, logic framework or theory of change, monitoring plans and indicators) should be included or referenced in annexes via links to the Internet or other means of communication.

2. EVALUATION PURPOSE

The purpose section of the ToR explains clearly why the evaluation is being conducted, who will use or act on the evaluation results and how they will use or act on the results. The purpose should include some background and justification for why the evaluation is needed at this time and how the evaluation fits within the programme unit's evaluation plan (see Chapter 3). A clear statement of purpose provides the foundation for a well designed evaluation.

3. EVALUATION SCOPE AND OBJECTIVES

This section defines the parameters and focus of the evaluation. The section answers the following questions:

- What aspects of the intervention are to be covered by the evaluation? This can include the time frame, implementation phase, geographic area, and target groups to be considered, and as applicable, which projects (outputs) are to be included.

- What are the primary issues of concern to users that the evaluation needs to address or objectives the evaluation must achieve?

Issues relate directly to the questions the evaluation must answer so that users will have the information they need for pending decisions or action. An issue may concern the relevance, efficiency, effectiveness, sustainability, and impact of the intervention. In addition, UNDP evaluations must address how the intervention sought to strengthen the application of the rights-based approach and mainstream gender in development efforts.

4. EVALUATION QUESTIONS

Evaluation questions define the information that the evaluation will generate. This section proposes the questions that, when answered, will give intended users of the evaluation the information they seek in order to make decisions, take action or add to knowledge. For example, outcome evaluation questions might include:

- Were stated outcomes or outputs achieved?
- What progress toward the outcomes has been made?
- What factors have contributed to achieving or not achieving intended outcomes?
- To what extent have UNDP outputs and assistance contributed to outcomes?
- Has the UNDP partnership strategy been appropriate and effective?
- What factors contributed to effectiveness or ineffectiveness?

Evaluation questions must be agreed upon among users and other stakeholders and accepted or refined in consultation with the evaluation team.

5. METHODOLOGY

The ToR may **suggest** an overall approach and method for conducting the evaluation, as well as data sources and tools that will likely yield the most reliable and valid answers to the evaluation questions within the limits of resources. However, final decisions about the specific design and methods for the evaluation should emerge from consultations among the programme unit, the evaluators, and key stakeholders about what is appropriate and feasible to meet the evaluation purpose and objectives and answer the evaluation questions, given limitations of budget, time and extant data.

For example, the ToR might describe in an annex:

- Whether and how the evaluation was considered in the intervention design.
- Details of the results framework and M&E framework, including outcome and output indicators and targets to measure performance and status of implementation, strengths and weaknesses of original M&E design, and the quality of data generated.
- Availability of relevant global, regional and national data.
- Lists and descriptions of key stakeholders (evaluation users, partner donors, staff of executing or other relevant agencies, subject beneficiaries, etc.) and their accessibility.

6. EVALUATION PRODUCTS (DELIVERABLES)

This section describes the key evaluation products the evaluation team will be accountable for producing. At the minimum, these products should include:

- **Evaluation inception report**—An inception report should be prepared by the evaluators before going into the full fledged data collection exercise. It should detail the evaluators' understanding of what is being evaluated and why, showing how each evaluation question will be answered by way of: proposed methods, proposed sources of data and data collection procedures. The inception report should include a proposed schedule of tasks, activities and deliverables, designating a team member with the lead responsibility for each task or product. The inception report provides the programme unit and the evaluators with an opportunity to verify that they share the same understanding about the evaluation and clarify any misunderstanding at the outset.

- **Draft evaluation report**—The programme unit and key stakeholders in the evaluation should review the draft evaluation report to ensure that the evaluation meets the required quality criteria (see Annex 7).

- **Final evaluation report.**

- **Evaluation brief and other knowledge products** or participation in knowledge sharing events, if relevant (see Chapter 8).

7. EVALUATION TEAM COMPOSITION AND REQUIRED COMPETENCIES

This section details the specific skills, competencies and characteristics needed in the evaluator or evaluation team specific to the evaluation and the expected structure and composition of the evaluation team, including roles and responsibilities of team members.

The section also should specify the type of evidence (resumes, work samples, references) that will be expected to support claims of knowledge, skills and experience. The ToR should explicitly demand evaluators' independence from any organizations that have been involved in designing, executing or advising any aspect of the intervention that is the subject of the evaluation.[63]

8. EVALUATION ETHICS

The ToR should include an explicit statement that evaluations in UNDP will be conducted in accordance with the principles outlined in the UNEG 'Ethical Guidelines for Evaluation'[64] and should describe critical issues evaluators must address

---

63 For this reason, UNDP staff members based in other country offices, the regional centres and Headquarters units should not be part of the evaluation team.

64 UNEG, 'Ethical Guidelines for Evaluation', June 2008. Available at http://www.uneval.org/search/index.jsp?q=ethical+guidelines.

in the design and implementation of the evaluation, including evaluation ethics and procedures to safeguard the rights and confidentiality of information providers, for example: measures to ensure compliance with legal codes governing areas such as provisions to collect and report data, particularly permissions needed to interview or obtain information about children and young people; provisions to store and maintain security of collected information; and protocols to ensure anonymity and confidentiality.

9. IMPLEMENTATION ARRANGEMENTS

This section describes the organization and management structure for the evaluation and defines the roles, key responsibilities and lines of authority of all parties involved in the evaluation process. Implementation arrangements are intended to clarify expectations, eliminate ambiguities, and facilitate an efficient and effective evaluation process.

The section should describe the specific roles and responsibilities of the evaluators, including those of the members of the team, the evaluation manager, the management of the commissioning programme unit and key stakeholders. The composition and expected roles and responsibilities of the Advisory Panel members or other quality assurance entities and their working arrangements should also be made explicit. In the case of a joint evaluation, the roles and responsibilities of participating agencies should be clarified. Issues to consider include: lines of authority; lines of and processes for approval; and logistical considerations, such as how office space, supplies, equipment, and materials will be provided; and processes and responsibility for approving deliverables.

10. TIME FRAME FOR THE EVALUATION PROCESS

This section lists and describes all tasks and deliverables for which evaluators or the evaluation team will be responsible and accountable, as well as those involving the commissioning office, indicating for each the due date or time-frame (e.g., work plan, agreements, briefings, draft report, final report), as well as who is responsible for its completion. At a minimum, the time breakdown for the following activities should be included:

- Desk review
- Briefings of evaluators
- Finalizing the evaluation design and methods and preparing the detailed inception report
- In-country evaluation mission (visits to the field, interviews, questionnaires)
- Preparing the draft report
- Stakeholder meeting and review of the draft report (for quality assurance)
- Incorporating comments and finalizing the evaluation report

In addition, the evaluators may be expected to support UNDP efforts in knowledge sharing and dissemination (see Chapter 8). Required formats for the inception reports, evaluation reports and other deliverables should be included in the annexes of the ToR for the evaluation being commissioned. This section should also state the number of working days to be given to each member of the evaluation team and the period during which they will be engaged in the evaluation process (e.g., 30 working days over a period of three months).

11. COST

This section should indicate total dollar amount and other resources available for the evaluation (consultant fees, travel, subsistence allowance, etc.) This is not a detailed budget but should provide information sufficient for evaluators to propose an evaluation design that is feasible within the limits of available time and resources. If the available amount is not sufficient to ensure the high quality of evaluation products, discussions can take place between the evaluators and the commissioning unit early on in the process.

12. ANNEXES

Annexes can be used to provide additional detail about evaluation background and requirements to facilitate the work of evaluators. Some examples include:

- **Intervention Results Framework and Theory of Change**—Provides more detailed information on the intervention being evaluated.

- **Key stakeholders and partners**—A list of key stakeholders and other individuals who should be consulted, together with an indication of their affiliation and relevance for the evaluation and their contact information. This annex can also suggest sites to be visited.

- **Documents to be consulted**—A list of important documents and webpages that the evaluators should read at the outset of the evaluation and before finalizing the evaluation design and the inception report. This should be limited to the critical information that the evaluation team needs. Data sources and documents may include:

  - Relevant national strategy documents
  - Strategic and other planning documents (e.g., programme and project documents)
  - Monitoring plans and indicators
  - Partnership arrangements (e.g., agreements of cooperation with governments or partners)
  - Previous evaluations and assessments
  - UNDP evaluation policy, UNEG norms and standards, and other policy documents
  - Required format for the inception report

- **Evaluation matrix** (suggested as a deliverable to be included in the inception report)—The evaluation matrix is a tool that evaluators create as a map and reference in planning and conducting an evaluation. It also serves as a useful tool for summarizing and visually presenting the evaluation design and methodology for discussions with stakeholders. It details evaluation questions that the evaluation will answer, data sources, data collection, analysis tools or methods appropriate for each data source, and the standard or measure by which each question will be evaluated (see Table A).

Table A. Sample evaluation matrix						
Relevant evaluation criteria	Key Questions	Specific Sub-Questions	Data Sources	Data collection Methods/Tools	Indicators/ Success Standard	Methods for Data Analysis

- **Schedule of tasks, milestones and deliverables**—Based on the time frame present in the ToR, the evaluators should present a detailed schedule.

- **Required format for the evaluation report**—The final report must include, but not necessarily be limited to, the elements outlined in the quality criteria for evaluation reports (see Annex 7).

- **Code of conduct**—UNDP programme units should request each member of the evaluation team to read carefully, understand and sign the 'Code of Conduct for Evaluators in the UN System', which may be made available as an attachment to the evaluation report.

Annex 4. Global, Regional and National Evaluation Networks

Increasingly, evaluation communities at national, regional and global levels are making important contributions to the evaluation field. Their participation and engagement have helped to build stronger ties with civil society, local and national counterparts, and the government. Such groups have increasingly taken part in UNDP-run conferences and workshops, providing a vital link between UNDP initiatives and local and national stakeholders, increasing demand for high-quality evaluative evidence and knowledge, disseminating useful knowledge products and services, and improving learning in evaluation practices. Expertise of the members of these networks can be drawn upon to **support the quality assurance of decentralized evaluations and serve as external experts**. Some examples of national, regional and international evaluation networks include the following:

NATIONAL NETWORKS

American Evaluation Society (AEA), www.eval.org

Associazione Italiana di Valutazione (AIV), www.valutazioneitaliana.it

Australian Evaluation Society (AES), www.aes.asn.au

Brazilian Evaluation Network, www.avaliabrasil.org.br

Burkina Faso Evaluation Network

Canadian Evaluation Society (CES), www.evaluationcanada.ca

Danish Evaluation Society, www.danskevalueringsselskab.dk

Finnish Evaluation Society, www.finnishevaluationsociety.net

German Evaluation Society, www.degeval.de

Israeli Association for Program Evaluation, www.iape.org.il/en_index.asp

Japan Evaluation Society (JES), www.idcj.or.jp/JES

Malaysian Evaluation Society (MES), www.mes.org.my

Niger Network of Monitoring and Evaluation (ReNSE), www.pnud.ne/rense/HOMEUK.HTML

Polish Evaluation Society, www.pte.org.pl/x.php/1,71/Strona-glowna.html

Spanish Evaluation Society, www.sociedadevaluacion.org/website

Sri Lanka Evaluation Association (SLEvA), www.nsf.ac.lk/sleva

Swiss Evaluation Society, www.seval.ch/en

UK Evaluation Society, www.evaluation.org.uk

Zambia Evaluation Association

REGIONAL NETWORKS

African Evaluation Association (AfrEA), www.afrea.org

European Evaluation Society (EES), www.europeanevaluation.org

Latin American Evaluation Network (PREVAL), www.preval.org

Latin America and the Caribbean Network of Monitoring, Evaluation and Systematization (RELAC)

INTERNATIONAL NETWORKS

Active Learning Network for Accountability and Performance in Humanitarian Action (ALNAP), www.alnap.org

International Development Evaluation Association (IDEAS), www.ideas-int.org

International Organization for Cooperation in Evaluation (IOCE), www.internationalevaluation.com

Annex 5. Selecting Evaluators: Individuals versus Firms

The following are some of the issues to be addressed in determining the size and composition of the evaluation team and advantages and disadvantages in hiring individuals[65] and firms.

- **The number of evaluators in the team depends on a number of factors.** Multi-faceted evaluations need to be undertaken by multi-disciplinary teams. The members selected must bring different types of expertise and experience to the team. The ideal team should represent a balanced mix of knowledge of evaluation methodology required for that particular evaluation, knowledge of the subject to be evaluated, knowledge of the context in which the evaluation is taking place or familiarity with comparable situations, and knowledge of cross-cutting issues in evaluation, such as gender.

- **What is the mix of internal and external perspective?** If possible, the evaluation team should include at least one national team member. Ideally, an evaluation team combines national members (who bring the local perspective and experience) and international members (who bring the external perspective).

- **Should we use a firm or individuals?** There are two ways to establish an evaluation team: one is to select individual consultants to form a team, another is to ask a firm to propose a team. Table B gives an overview of advantages and disadvantages for both options, which the committee should take into consideration.

---

65 The Evaluation Office maintains a roster of evaluation experts at intra.undp.org/eo.

Table B. Advantages and disadvantages of individuals versus firms

	Individuals	Firms
Advantages	■ Individuals may bring specialized expertise and many years of experience in particular subjects. ■ The variety of backgrounds of individual team members contributes to debate and discussion that can enrich the exercise. ■ May be less expensive. ■ May be more amenable to last-minute changes in the ToR or other arrangements. ■ Especially for nationals, the evaluation process may provide opportunity for capacity development and learning amongst individual experts.	■ Fees are agreed as a package that is unlikely to vary, unless there is a change in the ToR. ■ Members of the team are used to working together. ■ The firm assures the quality of the products. ■ A multidisciplinary approach is guaranteed. ■ Hiring procedures, although they can be longer than for an individual, are usually easier. ■ The firm develops the methodology or proposal for the evaluation. ■ In the event of sudden unavailability (e.g., illness) of an evaluator, the firm is responsible for providing a substitute.
Disadvantages	■ Identification of individual consultants is time-consuming and there are risks in selecting evaluation team members solely on the basis of claims made in their applications. ■ A team of professionals that have never worked together can have difficulty developing a sense of cohesiveness and coherence in their work, and internal conflicts can affect progress. ■ Changes in the schedule can result in additional costs in fees, per diem and travel arrangements. ■ Logistics to be provided by the commissioning unit.	■ Logistics to be provided by the firm ■ The fees may be higher, as the firm's overhead will be included. ■ If the firm has been overexposed to the topic or the organization, the credibility of the exercise can be compromised. ■ Team members tend to have similar approaches and perspectives, thereby losing some of the richness of different positions. ■ Bidding procedures can be lengthy and cumbersome. ■ Firms may have difficulty supplying a mixture of nationals and internationals.

Annex 6. Management Response Template

UNDP Management Response Template
[Name of the Evaluation] Date:

Prepared by: Position: Unit/Bureau:
Cleared by: Position: Unit/Bureau:
Input into and update in ERC: Position: Unit/Bureau:

Evaluation recommendation 1.				
Management response:				
Key action(s)	**Time frame**	**Responsible unit(s)**	**Tracking***	
			Comments	**Status**
1.1				
1.2				
1.3				
Evaluation recommendation 2.				
Management response:				
Key action(s)	**Time frame**	**Responsible unit(s)**	**Tracking***	
			Comments	**Status**
2.1				
2.2				
2.3				
Evaluation recommendation 3.				
Management response:				
Key action(s)	**Time frame**	**Responsible unit(s)**	**Tracking***	
			Comments	**Status**
3.1				
3.2				
3.3				

*Status of implementation is tracked electronically in the Evaluation Resource Centre database (ERC).

Annex 7. Evaluation Report Template and Quality Standards

This **evaluation report template** is intended to serve as a guide for preparing meaningful, useful and credible evaluation reports that meet quality standards. It does not prescribe a definitive section-by-section format that all evaluation reports should follow. Rather, it suggests the content that should be included in a quality evaluation report. The descriptions that follow are derived from the UNEG 'Standards for Evaluation in the UN System' and 'Ethical Standards for Evaluations'.[66]

The evaluation report should be complete and logically organized. It should be written clearly and understandable to the intended audience. In a country context, the report should be translated into local languages whenever possible (see Chapter 8 for more information). The report should also include the following:

Title and opening pages—Should provide the following basic information:

- Name of the evaluation intervention

- Time frame of the evaluation and date of the report

- Countries of the evaluation intervention

- Names and organizations of evaluators

- Name of the organization commissioning the evaluation

- Acknowledgements

Table of contents—Should always include boxes, figures, tables and annexes with page references.

List of acronyms and abbreviations

Executive summary—A stand-alone section of two to three pages that should:

- Briefly describe the intervention (the project(s), programme(s), policies or other interventions) that was evaluated.

- Explain the purpose and objectives of the evaluation, including the audience for the evaluation and the intended uses.

---

66 UNEG, 'Standards for Evaluation in the UN System', 2005, available at: http://www.unevaluation.org/unegstandards; and UNEG, 'Ethical Guidelines for Evaluation', June 2008, available at http://www.un-eval.org/search/index.jsp?q=ethical+guidelines.

- Describe key aspect of the evaluation approach and methods.

- Summarize principle findings, conclusions, and recommendations.

Introduction—Should:

- Explain why the evaluation was conducted (the purpose), why the intervention is being evaluated at this point in time, and why it addressed the questions it did.

- Identify the primary audience or users of the evaluation, what they wanted to learn from the evaluation and why, and how they are expected to use the evaluation results.

- Identify the intervention (the project(s) programme(s), policies or other interventions) that was evaluated—see upcoming section on intervention.

- Acquaint the reader with the structure and contents of the report and how the information contained in the report will meet the purposes of the evaluation and satisfy the information needs of the report's intended users.

Description of the intervention—Provides the basis for report users to understand the logic and assess the merits of the evaluation methodology and understand the applicability of the evaluation results. The description needs to provide sufficient detail for the report user to derive meaning from the evaluation. The description should:

- Describe **what is being evaluated, who seeks to benefit**, and the **problem or issue** it seeks to address.

- Explain the **expected results map or results framework**, **implementation strategies**, and the key **assumptions** underlying the strategy.

- Link the intervention to **national priorities**, UNDAF priorities, corporate multi-year funding frameworks or strategic plan goals, or other **programme or country specific plans and goals.**

- Identify the **phase** in the implementation of the intervention and any **significant changes** (e.g., plans, strategies, logical frameworks) that have occurred over time, and explain the implications of those changes for the evaluation.

- Identify and describe the **key partners** involved in the implementation and their roles.

- Describe the **scale of the intervention**, such as the number of components (e.g., phases of a project) and the size of the target population for each component.

- Indicate the **total resources**, including human resources and budgets.

- Describe the context of the **social, political, economic and institutional factors**, and the **geographical landscape** within which the intervention operates and explain the effects (challenges and opportunities) those factors present for its implementation and outcomes.

- Point out **design weaknesses** (e.g., intervention logic) or other **implementation constraints** (e.g., resource limitations).

Evaluation scope and objectives—The report should provide a clear explanation of the evaluation's scope, primary objectives and main questions.

- Evaluation scope—The report should define the parameters of the evaluation, for example, the time period, the segments of the target population included, the geographic area included, and which components, outputs or outcomes were and were not assessed.

- Evaluation objectives—The report should spell out the types of decisions evaluation users will make, the issues they will need to consider in making those decisions, and what the evaluation will need to achieve to contribute to those decisions.

- Evaluation criteria—The report should define the evaluation criteria or performance standards used.[67] The report should explain the rationale for selecting the particular criteria used in the evaluation.

- Evaluation questions—Evaluation questions define the information that the evaluation will generate. The report should detail the main evaluation questions addressed by the evaluation and explain how the answers to these questions address the information needs of users.

Evaluation approach and methods[68]—The evaluation report should describe in detail the selected methodological approaches, methods and analysis; the rationale for their selection; and how, within the constraints of time and money, the approaches and methods employed yielded data that helped answer the evaluation questions and achieved the evaluation purposes. The description should help the report users judge the merits of the methods used in the evaluation and the credibility of the findings, conclusions and recommendations. The description on methodology should include discussion of each of the following:

- Data sources—The sources of information (documents reviewed and stakeholders), the rationale for their selection and how the information obtained addressed the evaluation questions.

- Sample and sampling frame—If a sample was used: the sample size and characteristics; the sample selection criteria (e.g., single women, under 45); the process for selecting the sample (e.g., random, purposive); if applicable, how comparison and treatment groups were assigned; and the extent to which the sample is representative of the entire target population, including discussion of the limitations of the sample for generalizing results.

- Data collection procedures and instruments—Methods or procedures used to collect data, including discussion of data collection instruments (e.g., interview protocols), their appropriateness for the data source and evidence of their reliability and validity.

---

67 The evaluation criteria most commonly applied to UNDP evaluations are relevance, efficiency, effectiveness and sustainability.

68 All aspects of the described methodology need to receive full treatment in the report. Some of the more detailed technical information may be contained in annexes to the report. See Chapter 8 for more guidance on methodology.

- Performance standards[69]—The standard or measure that will be used to evaluate performance relative to the evaluation questions (e.g., national or regional indicators, rating scales).

- Stakeholder engagement—Stakeholders' engagement in the evaluation and how the level of involvement contributed to the credibility of the evaluation and the results.

- Ethical considerations—The measures taken to protect the rights and confidentiality of informants (see UNEG 'Ethical Guidelines for Evaluators' for more information).[70]

- Background information on evaluators—The composition of the evaluation team, the background and skills of team members and the appropriateness of the technical skill mix, gender balance and geographical representation for the evaluation.

- Major limitations of the methodology—Major limitations of the methodology should be identified and openly discussed as to their implications for evaluation, as well as steps taken to mitigate those limitations.

Data analysis—The report should describe the procedures used to analyse the data collected to answer the evaluation questions. It should detail the various steps and stages of analysis that were carried out, including the steps to confirm the accuracy of data and the results. The report also should discuss the appropriateness of the analysis to the evaluation questions. Potential weaknesses in the data analysis and gaps or limitations of the data should be discussed, including their possible influence on the way findings may be interpreted and conclusions drawn.

Findings and conclusions—The report should present the evaluation findings based on the analysis and conclusions drawn from the findings.

- Findings—Should be presented as statements of fact that are based on analysis of the data. They should be structured around the evaluation criteria and questions so that report users can readily make the connection between what was asked and what was found. Variances between planned and actual results should be explained, as well as factors affecting the achievement of intended results. Assumptions or risks in the project or programme design that subsequently affected implementation should be discussed.

- Conclusions—Should be comprehensive and balanced, and highlight the strengths, weaknesses and outcomes of the intervention. They should be well substantiated by the evidence and logically connected to evaluation findings. They should respond to key evaluation questions and provide insights into the identification of and/or solutions to important problems or issues pertinent to the decision making of intended users.

---

69 A summary matrix displaying for each of evaluation questions, the data sources, the data collection tools or methods for each data source and the standard or measure by which each question was evaluated is a good illustrative tool to simplify the logic of the methodology for the report reader.

70 UNEG, 'Ethical Guidelines for Evaluation', June 2008. Available at http://www.uneval.org/search/index.jsp?q=ethical+guidelines.

Recommendations—The report should provide practical, feasible recommendations directed to the intended users of the report about what actions to take or decisions to make. The recommendations should be specifically supported by the evidence and linked to the findings and conclusions around key questions addressed by the evaluation. They should address sustainability of the initiative and comment on the adequacy of the project exit strategy, if applicable.

Lessons learned—As appropriate, the report should include discussion of lessons learned from the evaluation, that is, new knowledge gained from the particular circumstance (intervention, context outcomes, even about evaluation methods) that are applicable to a similar context. Lessons should be concise and based on specific evidence presented in the report.

Report annexes—Suggested annexes should include the following to provide the report user with supplemental background and methodological details that enhance the credibility of the report:

- ToR for the evaluation
- Additional methodology-related documentation, such as the evaluation matrix and data collection instruments (questionnaires, interview guides, observation protocols, etc.) as appropriate
- List of individuals or groups interviewed or consulted and sites visited
- List of supporting documents reviewed
- Project or programme results map or results framework
- Summary tables of findings, such as tables displaying progress towards outputs, targets, and goals relative to established indicators
- Short biographies of the evaluators and justification of team composition
- Code of conduct signed by evaluators

Annex 8. Resources for Evaluation

A wealth of information is available within UNDP and the external community, containing key findings and lessons on the design, implementation and evaluation of technical cooperation programmes and projects in countries and regions around the world. Some of the most important sources for such information are listed below.

United Nations Evaluation Group (UNEG) website (www.unevaluation.org)— UNEG is a professional network for the units responsible for evaluation in the UN system. The goal of UNEG is to strengthen the objectivity, effectiveness and visibility of the evaluation function across the UN system and to advocate the importance of evaluation for learning, decision making and accountability. As of 2009, UNEG had 43 member agencies represented. The website details the UNEG current work programme and provides easy access to UNEG documents as well as links to other useful evaluation resources.

UNDP Evaluation Office internal (intra.undp.org/eo) and external websites (www.undp.org/eo)—The Evaluation Office produces a number of products to support learning from evaluation. Its website contains all evaluations conducted by the Evaluation Office, evaluation briefs and executive summaries, and the Annual Report on Evaluation, which presents key findings and lessons from independent evaluations. It also contains links to various references, norms, standards, guidelines on evaluation methodology and approaches, and other development partners' websites on evaluation.

Evaluation Resource Centre (ERC) website (erc.undp.org)—The ERC is the UNDP online evaluation information management centre. It is a publicly accessible database that contains evaluation reports, ToRs, and management responses for independent and decentralized evaluations of UNDP projects, programmes, outcomes and UNDAFs, among others. The database also includes evaluation plans and focal points for UNDP programme units, as well as a range of guidance and reference documents.

Index

criteria, 156, **168-170**, 171-173

decentralized, 17, **130-131**, 139-141, **147-159**

designing, 163-180

global programme, 124-125, 132, **135-136**

independence, 82, 89, 96, 128, 130, 140, 146, 149, **154-157**, 159, 162

independent, 16-17, 89, **130-131**, 133, 140, 146, 152, 183

initiating an, 147-149

managing/management structure of, 149-151, 160

mandatory, 87-88, 133-134, **142-143**

methodology, 156-157, **172-173**, 185

norms in, 9, **129-130**, 154, 163

objectives, 133, 156, **168-170**

policy, 129-130

purpose, 135, 137, 152, 154, 156, 159, 163, **167-171**, 175-176, 178-179

quality criteria, 147, 152, 163-172

real time, 138

regional programme, 124-125, 132, **135-136**

roles and responsibilities, 16-17, **139-141**, 145-146, 149-150

sampling, 176

scope, 92-93, 135-137, 151-152, 156, 160-161, **167-168**

standards, 16, **129-130**, 140-141, 150, 154, 157, 163-164, 168

timing, 83, 88-89, 128, **137**, 152, 167

types of, 130-139

uses of, 128-129, 181-189

See also: evaluation questions, impact evaluation, joint evaluation, meta evaluation, methodology, outcome evaluation, project evaluation, thematic evaluation, UNDAF evaluation

Evaluation manager, **149-151**, 152, 156, 160, 163, 178, 185, 188

Evaluation matrix, 150, **156**, 171-172

Evaluation Office, 4, 17, 88-89, 130-134, 136, 139-142, 153-154, 183, 187

Evaluation plan, 7-8, 16, 23, 29, **87**, 88-92, 139-143, 145, 147, 167

Evaluation policy (of the UNDP), 1, 127, **129-130**, 139, 142, 158

Evaluation questions, 156, 163-168, 170, **171,** 173, 178

Evaluation report (quality standards for), 157-158, 184, 186-188, Annex 7

Evaluation Resource Centre (ERC), 88, 140-141, 188

Evaluators

code of conduct, 155, 178

composition and competencies, 154, 177-178, Annex 5

conflict of interest, 154-156

selecting, 92-93, 130, **152-154**, 161-162, Annex 5

F

Field visits, 86, 90, 103-104, 110-112, **114-115**

G

Gender 14, **15**, 22, 30, 38, 110, 168, **171-172, 178**

analysis, 15, 30

in evaluation design, 91, 171-172, **178**

evaluation team composition, 154, 177

Government
  role in evaluation, 89, 93, 128-129, 135-139, 145-147, 160, 186
  role in monitoring, 101, 103, 105, 119, 124
  role in planning, 14, 21, 22, 24, 26, 28-29, 32, 57-58, 63, 76

H

Human rights based approach: *See: rights–based approach*

I

Impact, 51, 53-56, 58, 60-62, 73, 101, 136
  (as an evaluation criterion), 170
  evaluation, **136**
  indicators, **65**, 73
  statement, 54, **56**, 61
Importance/influence matrix, 20, 26, **28**, 37
Inception report (of an evaluation), 147, 150, **156-157**, 171-173, 179, Annex 3
Indicator(s), 29, **53-54**, 56, 58, 61-78, 83, 101, 107, 173-175
  impact, 65, 73
  levels, 65-69
  outcome, 58, 65-68
  output, 65, 67, 69
  performance, 61-62, 77-78, 173-175
  proxy, 64
  qualitative, 63
  quantitative, 63
  SMART, 63, 70
Input(s), 55, **60-61,** 102, 112, 134-135
Inspection, 9
Issues note, 20, **22-23**, 25

J

Joint evaluation, 89, 133, **138-139**, 146, 150, **159-162**, 164
Joint monitoring, 14, 95, 105-106, 114, **117**

K

Knowledge, **96**, 181-189
  network(s), 116, 185, 188
  product(s), 117, **185-186**
  sharing, 140-141, 147, 158-159, 185, **187-188**

L

Lessons learned, 17, 89, 93, 101, 105, 115-116, 121, 124, 133, 159, **180**, 183, 185
Logical framework, 42. *See also: results matrix*

M

Management response (to evaluation), 16, 128, 141-142, 146-147, **158-159, 162,** 180, 182, Annex 6

Managing for Development Results (MfDR), 5, 6, 14, 94, 159, 182

Mandatory requirements in evaluation, 133-134, **142-143**

Meta evaluation, 131

Millennium Development Goals (MDGs), 22, 56, 65, 111, 118, 119, 128, 136, 146, 153

Monitoring

    actions, 98-99, 102, 104, 107, 110, 116, 120-121, 123

    activities, 82-84, 94, 99, 102, 104, 106, 108, 113

    in crisis settings, 15, 90, **109-111**

    data/data collection, 83, 85-86, 90, 92-93, 95-96, 99, 107-112, 115-120, 123, 135

    framework, **83-84,** 88-92, 95, 99-101, 104-108, 116-117, 119-121, 125

    joint, 14, 91, 94-95, 105-106, 114, **117**

    methodology, 105-106

    national level, 94-98, 103-105, 117-122, 124

    operational context, **101-104,** 173

    outcome level, 101-104, 106, 108, 112, 115, **120-121**

    output level, 101-104, 106, 108, 112, 115

    policy (of UNDP), 101-102

    programme level, 104-108, 112, 115, **121-122,** 124

    project level, 102-103, 106, 108, 112, 115, **119-120**

    resources for, 90-92

    roles and responsibilities, 99, **104**

    scope, 108-109

    system, 99, 100, 103, 108, 118, 137

    timing, 105-106, 114

    tools, 99, 103, 104, 111-117, 177

    See also: annual work plan

Monitoring and evaluation framework, 16, **83-90**

N

National ownership, 6, 9, 14, 94, 103, 122, 149, 159

    of monitoring, evaluation and planning, 146

    see also ownership

National priorities, 13, 36, 73, 76, 82, 94, 109, 137

O

Outcome(s)

    country programme, 57, 67, 103

    evaluation, 4, 87-90, 121, 124, **131-133,** 134-135, 137, 142, 159, 175, 183

    formulation, 86-58

    model, 83, 88, 107, 148-149, 165

    project versus outcome evaluations, 134-135

    statement, 54, **56-58,** 61

    UNDAF, 57, 73, 75-76, 101, 103, 124, 137

    Unintended, 48, 51